Educational Digital Skills

ABOUT THE AUTHORS

PANNEER SELVAM is born in Salem - Valappady of Tamil Nadu. He started his career as school teacher in New Delhi in the year 1991. He joins as lecturer in DIET, perundurai of Erode in 2000. Bharathiyar University were gave the Philosophy in Doctorates in Language and Education. He is the seventh diploma holder from National University of Educational Planning and Administration (NUEPA), New Delhi in 2002. In 2005, the Tamil Nadu government was given the 'Excellence Award' for his unrivalled teaching activities and some organization also. He has published more than hundreds of Research Papers and books in the field of Education. At present he is working in the department of Education, Bharathidasan University, Tamil Nadu.

Mr. BABU THOMAS obtained his Master of Education and Master of Arts in Malayalam from Mahatma Gandhi University, Kottayam. He earned his Master of Science in Counsellingand Family Therapy (M.Sc-CFT) from IGNOU, New Delhi and in Applied Psychology from Bharathiar University, Coimbatore. He got his Post Graduate Diploma in Child, Adolescent and Family Counselling (PGD-CAFC) from Kerala University and Diploma in Training and Development (D-TD) from Indian Society for Training and Development (ISTD), New Delhi. He is a holder of UGC - NET (Education), SET, K-TET, Account Test & KER. He has 27 years of teaching experience in various reputed schools. At present working as a teacher in St. Ephrem's Higher Secondary School, Mannanam, Kottayam, Kerala. He received Air India – MalayalaManorama BOLT Award, All India AwardeeTeacher's Gurusreshta Award, MalankaraOrthodox Syrian Church Acharya Award. He is a Research Scholar in Education in Bharathidasan University, Tiruchirappalli, Tamil Nadu.

Educational Digital Skills

Dr. S.K. Panneer Selvam

Assistant Professor, Department of Education
Bharathidasan University, T.N.,India

Babu Thomas

St. Ephrem's Higher Secondary School
Mannanam, Kottayam
Kerala

AMIGA PRESS INC.

DELHI (INDIA)

AMIGA PRESS INC.
H.O.: 28-A, Indra Park,
Chander Nagar, Delhi-110051 (India)
Tel.: 011-22504028, +91-98736-57000
E-mail: amigapress@gmail.com
amigaeditorial@gmail.com
amigapub@gmail.com
info@amigapress.co.in
Website : www.amigapress.co.in

This edition is published by Amiga Press Inc.

ISBN: 978-93-84533-72-4

First Published 2020

Printed and bound in India by Replika Press Pvt. Ltd.

Contents

1.

Comparative Study of Effectiveness of Computer Assisted Instruction on Circulatory System for IX Standard Students

INTRODUCTION

This study investigated the compare effectiveness of computer-assisted instruction (CAI) and conventional teaching method in biology on senior high school students. A science class was selected in each of two randomly selected schools. The pre-test, post-test equivalent quasi experimental design was used. The students in the experimental group learned science concepts (circulatory system) through the CAI, whereas the students in the control group were taught the same concepts by the conventional approach. The conventional approach consisted of teaching, discussions and question and answer teaching methods. The students' pre-test and post-tests scores were subjected to Analysis of't' Test, ANOVA. The results indicated that students that were instructed by the experimental group performed better on the post-test than those instructed by the conventional approach. This may help teachers in organizing meaningful teaching learning experiences and adopt innovative methods and approaches in teaching. Computer assisted Instruction (CAI) is a supplementary instructional strategy ineffective teaching. In this paper, researcher elaborates use, utility and importance of CAI in teaching-Learning. To create new approaches technique and appropriate digital learning environment applying in education for present and future generation. Based on the research findings recommendations were made on the need to develop relevant CAI packages for teaching-Learning biology in secondary schools.

Education should be an individual activity to a much greater content. Not at all children should be forced to go through the same steps of learning at the same speed. The high achievers will move faster in their learning where as the under achievers will need more time. Children have their own ways of learning. Some children may learn better through the use of different learning materials them by merely listening to an inspirational talk by the teacher. The style of learning may also change according to age. They use their season in acquiring knowledge. An important feature of education is its use of physical and intellectual tools. Education must reflect the influence of technology. This new technology demands new interpretations of the instructional process and those changed with educating the next generation must engage in a continual cycle of education and revaluation in the light of technological influence at all levels.

Education Technology

Educational technology is not a simple combination of these two words. It is usually thought of even more than the sum of the following two interpretations.

1. Technology in Educatione the effectiveness of the educatioal l combination or seperately bjective - vis-a
2. Technology of Education

Technology in Education

This is based on the application of engineering principle for developing electro mechanical equipment like motion pictures, tape-recorders, teaching machines, computers, television etc. This approach of education a technology is a bye product of the 21th century. Davis (1971) thinks that the hardware approach is based on the application of physical science to the education and training system which mechanics the process of teaching gradually so that teachers would be able to deal with more students resulting in less cost and economy in finances. It is said that good teachers have always used visual ads to assist their teaching ancient great masters used illustrations and models to increase the interests of their students. Today educational technology is stressing modern audio – visual and computer equipment.

Technology of Education

It refers to the study of principles and theories, formulate to solve problems in the teaching, learning process. The main frame work of education technology is provided by Technology or Education. 'Technology in Education' provides the support to implement the broader instructional design. It primarily implies systematic approach to instructional design incorporating alternative methodologies, media and aids with reference to the objective vis-à-vis learning content. This accommodates the systems approach, programmed learning etc.

According to the encyclopedia of education (1971. vol-9 P.22) Educational Technology is the purposeful combination or separately of objects, techniques, devices, events and relationships to increase the effectiveness of the educational process.

Application of Education Technology

Educational Technology has gradually influenced and developed the teaching learning process. Since the world is moving towards Technological growth information and special place in education. The trend is to introduce technological principles in the classroom. Educational technology consists of all modern media, methods and materials, which can be used to maximizing the learning experience of student at various levels.

Historical Perspective of Individual Instruction

The classical conditioning of PAVLOV opened a new chapter in teaching and learning and the behaviour gave importance to reinforcement as a major condition for learning. Edward Thorn dike improved the reinforcement procedure with stimulus (reinforce) response reaction, SKINNER (1967) expanded this idea as operative conditioning which led to the invention of teaching machine. Both kin aesthetic and information feedback are identified to play crucial role in skill learning by GAGNE (1963) LUMSDANOE (1964) proposed a new definition to instructional technique which was later applied in programmed instruction. The five golden rules applied in this preparation of programmed learning material (PLM) and the need for defining the objectives in behavioural terms in the preparation of instructional software material are proposed as essential by DANIEL DAVIS (1965). The three phases that help the teacher to decide in the ongoing focus on pedagogy are; what to teach (objectives) whom to teach (entering behaviour) and how to flash the procedures which are similar to the CAI model. FLANDERS' (1964) recommendation for interactivity in learning are subjoined through various learning activities built in the CAI package.

Individualized Instruction

Individualized instruction is the one-to-one relationship between a student and what he learns (DUNN and DUNN 1977). Individualized instruction is one of the most active areas in the education innovations. This kind of instruction helps the learner to learn at his own pace. Modern class rooms are characterized by a high degree of heterogeneity. Individual differences are pronounced among learners in large classes and to cater to the needs of the learners in such classes individualized instruction bodies is required.

Through individualized instruction materials self learning can be enhanced. This land of self learning helps the learners to learn even more difficult contents and learning of higher categories. Through self learning the needs and levels of the learners are considerably satisfied. The individual differences are considered and hence individualized instruction certainly leads to mastery level of learning.

Individualized instruction may be provided for the following reasons (DUNN and DUNN 1977)

A gifted student, able to come with new consents or skills independently may work well ahead of his peers through the use of this method. He need not wait to learn until the teacher can work with him individually or the rest of his peers catch up with him.

An interested student may learn more about a given topic, consent or skill after most of his peers have mastered it, may spend as much time as needed reinforcing the knowledge at his desire and pace until he too is ready to move ahead.

An interested student may learn more about a given topic, consents or skill at the moment in time when he wants to, not when the teacher is able to get to the subject.

An average student who cares to something new in an interesting way may become sufficiently motivated to work on his own because of the nature of the varied multi sensory experience.

Individualized instruction materials should have certain characteristics. According to MORE (1968), an individualized instructional material should have the following features. It should as

1. Permit the learners to explore freely.
2. Inform the learner about the consequence of his action.
3. Be self – pacing that is the student can more at his own rate of learning.
4. Permit the learner to make full use of his capacity for discovering relations of various kinds.

GOLDSCHMID (1973) maintain that any form of individualized instruction should possess the following characters. It should

1. Emphasize learning
2. Ensure active students participation
3. Stress evaluation and feed back
4. Principle of individual pacing

There are different forms of individualized instruction. Some of them are

1. Learning Module
2. Multimedia Package
3. Programmed Learning Material (PLM)
4. Personalized system of instruction (PSI)
5. Audio Tutorial Instruction (ATI)
6. Learning Module

A learning module is a short unit of instruction dealing with a single unit of subject matter self contained with define objectives. Based on the specified instructional objectives, questions are given and the learner assesses his/her performance in the subject.

Multimedia Package

A multimedia package consists of a collection of soft ware's of several media dealing with a specific topic on subject area and forming an integrated whole. Based on the interest and aptitude of the students, the students can select the media through which they want to learn the subject.

Programmed Learning Material (PLM)

Skinner has pronounced Programmed Learning Material (PLM) based on the theory of operant conditioning PLM consists of planned sequence of learning activity for achieving mastery in terms of stimulus response reinforcement relationship.

Personalized System of Instruction (PSI)

The Personalized System of Instruction refers to training which is based on self pacing and master learning. In PSI, learners work in their own and they must achieve mastery of a series of written learning unit. They are assisted by teachers and professors. It is possible to apply PSI.

Audio Tutorial Instruction (ATI)

Here the instructor's remarks, directions and interpretations of learning assignments and resources are given through audio cassettes. The cassettes are prepared by the concerned subject experts keeping in mind the target for which the cassette is prepared. Even for distance education system, audio cassettes are being used for instruction.

Computer Assisted Instruction (CAI)

The most exciting innovation in educational technology is the Computer Assisted Instruction (CAI). Though it was not skill developed like other individualized instructional materials, the day is not far off when it will revolutionize the whole process of instruction. **Taneja (1999)**

A computer is programmed with linear or branching programmes. It acts like a super teaching machine catering to the needs of a number of students at the same time. The characteristic aspects of the CAI is its capacity to initiate flexible instructional with the student. In this respect it is superior to the teaching machine. The computer can do this in different ways. The computer is able to record and store all the responses of all the students. It can use the information in deciding what information is to be given to the student next. It can branch not just in terms of on answer but also in terms of a whole series of previous answers. It can also record the time taken to answer a question and the decree of correctness of the student's response. It uses the information in planning to determine which branch or format would be conductive to a learner for effective instruction.

Computer Assisted Instruction is not merely a sophisticated type of programmed instruction but a different kind of instruction but a different kind of instruction altogether. No doubt, data processing, data communication, consents of audio-visual and media theory, communication theory, system theory and learning theory are annelid in the preparation of the CAI material. In contrast to CAI, Computer Managed Instruction (CMI) analysis the relationship between various factors concerned with the learning of a pupil and suggests activities appropriate to individual students.

Different Forms of Computer Assisted Instruction

Computer Assisted Instruction can be take any one of the following modes depending on the purpose of the material, the five different modes of CAI are

- Drill and Practice
- Tutorial Mode
- Simulation Mode
- Discovery Mode
- Gaming Mode

Tutorial Mode

In this mode information is presented in small units followed by a question. The student's response is analyzed by the computer and an appropriate feedback is provided. This is similar to programmed instruction. As in programmed instruction, the information may be given in a linear fashion as in branched pathways. The greater the number of alternative paths, more adaptive the tutorial can be to individuals.

Drill and Practice Mode

The learner, provided with a number of graded examples on the concepts and principles learnt earlier. The idea is to develop proficiency and fluency through doing all the correct responses are reinforced and the incorrect responses are diagnosed and corrected. The compute continues the drill and the learners continue his practice until mastery is achieved by the learner.

Simulation Mode

In this mode, the learners are presented with scheduled down stimulated. Situations bearing correspondence with real situation. Simulations are made to avoid risk, save money and conserve time, simulation of an aero plane in flight, an experiment on titration, a nuclear reaction, collision of two bodies are good examples of the simulation models in science.

Discovery Mode

The individual approach to teaching and learning is as followed. The learner is encouraged to proceed through trial and error approach i.e., by solving a given problem, realizing where and how he/she went wrong, trying again and finally solving the complex problem.

Gaming Mode

In this mode, the learner is engaged in playing opposite. The computer or opposite another learner. The extent of learning depends upon the type of the game. Games on spelling names of places and general knowledge are some examples of the gaming mode.

Information Handling

One area where processing and information handling capacity of computer is profitably used in counseling and guiding the computer stores complete cumulative records and match them against employment needs and potentialities as required for personal and vocational guidance.

Merits of Computer Assisted Instruction

Computer Assisted Instruction has several advantages over other systems of instructions.

- Each student receives instruction at his own pace
- Each student receives immediate feedback for his response
- Each student responds continuously as he receives instruction

All units of learning are broke down into subunits and elements of learning in accordance with skinner's approach of teaching in small steps

Reinforcement of learning is achieved by personal message

Learning sessions are not manageable by designing the duration between half an hour to one hour

- Student can access the computer any place
- Students can learn in their own styles and ways
- Students can test their own learning at any point of time to an end

Lesson from the theories of learning are taken into account at stage instructional design

Teacher's time is saved from the routine job of giving activity and employed in innovative instruction design and student guidance

Objectives of the Study

- To understand about computer system and its working
- To understand the educational application of computer
- To develop scientific attitude among school students
- To provide a broad – based biological knowledge, stimulate a deep interest in the natural world
- To develop a CAI package for self instruction on the unit circulatory system in science for IX standard students

- To enable the pupils to utilize effectively the instructional material in learning biology
- To verify whether there is any difference in learning level between
- Boys and Girls
- Rural and Urban School
- Government, Government Aided and Unaided Schools
- Hypothesis

There is no significant difference between the pretest and posttest scores of government school pupils' following the Computer Assisted Instruction.

There is no significant difference between the pretest and posttest scores of Aided School Pupils' following the Computer Assisted Instruction.

There is no significant difference between the pretest and posttest scores of Unaided School Pupil following the Computer Assisted Instruction.

There is no significant difference between the pretest and posttest mean scores of the experimental group following Computer Assisted Instruction.

There is no significant difference in post test performance of Computer Assisted Instruction between the different types of school pupil.

There is no significant difference between the post test performance of Urban and Rural school pupil following Computer Assisted Instruction.

There is no significant difference between the post test performance of Boys and Girls following Computer Assisted Instruction.

Scope of the Study

The students can get more and adequate knowledge through self instruction material.

It helps the students to develop self study habits, since individual study can be brought out with the help of self instruction material.

The study is expected to help the students at all levels, since computer plays a vital role in all the aspects of life especially in the field of education.

The present study is experimental study to compose the effectiveness of CAI and on "Circulatory System" for IX standard students.

In future instruction materials will act as a source of the knowledge for the teacher and students.

It will help the teacher in the teaching learning process, as it can draw the attention of the students by teaching learning computer.

Studies Conducted on CAI in India

In India at present several efforts are being taken up to develop the software for CAI, for individual instruction several studies also have been conducted to identify the effectiveness of CAI and Handout over the achievement of the students. SHARMA and GEORGE (1979) developed a CAI package of mathematics. Their objectives were to study the effectiveness of the CAI for school children and the findings revealed that the CAI packages produced significant result over the achievement of the children. BADRINATH (1986) conducted a study on developing and validating CAI package for reflection of light at the VIII standard level. He found that experience in CAI program appeared to be an effective method than the conventional method.

NACHIMUTHU (1988) has studied the development of CAI program on "Leaves". He expressed in his thesis about the difficulties in programming a lesson. He also suggested that teaching will be more effective if the researcher himself programmed the lesson than using readymade diskettes. Because when the research programme, he can give all the points to be taught, as in conventional method and so the learners also will score marks up to the researchers' expectation.

PALANIAPPAN (1989) made a study on computers in education. He found that after introducing computers is schools for teaching, the attitude of teachers as well as students have changed. Many dull students scoreless through CAI, than the conventional method.

HEMALATHA (1989) studied on orientation of CAI. She concluded that the computers are commonly used in three main response sensitive strategies in CAI and suggested some levels of comparative involvement in decision making feature. They are drill and practice, tutorial and dialogue.

KARPAGA KUMARAVEL. R (1990) in his study on the effectiveness of computer assisted instruction video assisted instruction and conventional instruction in English language learning found that the achievement of video assisted instruction group in better than computer assisted instruction and conventional instructional group.

P. JEYAMANI (1991) pointed out that learning with computers offers a very powerful tool for educators and all efforts must be made to learners the potential of computers in education. This educational technology could therefore have a more on comparing role to play in the developing world. Thus the stimulation model of teaching through computer assisted instruction can readily be used for all types of teaching.

SARVANAN (1991) developed and validated a CAI package on X – rays for XI standard students. His findings revealed that the CAI packages were effective for individualized instruction.

PURUSHOTHAMAN and STELLA (1991) studied the effectiveness of CAI learning testing and guidance. The study reported that for low achievers self-testing and guidance through computer was found to be more effective.

BENEDICTO (1992) developed and validated a CAI packages on pollution for XI standard Biology students. The major findings of his study was learning the unit through CAI was faster for both slow and fast learners when compared with traditional teaching. He also reported the software developed ensures uniformity of achievement among Biology students.

MATHIVANAN (1994) attempted to develop and validate a CAI package on organisms an environment for IX standard pupils. His report revealed that the CAI package produced more significant effect on the achievement of the pupils of knowledge, comprehension, application and analysis level.

Dr. P. ANNARAJA and Smt. NIRMALA SUNDARARAJ (2005) made a study on power point presentation in teaching zoology pre post design was used in this that, they found that the power point presentation is effective in teaching zoology for higher secondary students.

JAYAKRUSHA CHOUDHARY (2005) conducted a study on effect of Computer Assisted Learning using method of enquiry in teaching physics in secondary school. Main objectives of this study was to test the efficiency of computer aided learning using method of inquiry in teaching physics at the secondary level on achievement and concept attainment. He found that CAI experimental method is to be more effective than conventional method of teaching.

G. SUBRAMANIAN (2006) pointed out major findings were computer assisted instruction significantly improves the performance of students, learning accountancy at higher secondary level. The combination of the colour, text, music and animation of the CAI package was well received by the students and the positive effect of same is perceptible from their achievement scores.

A computer factorial program on the laws and consents encountered in introductory physics courses among high school students was studied by EAUGHN AND KUHN (1979) these programmer were written with the weaker students in mind. But the researchers found that even stronger students used them presumably to check whether or not they really understood a particular phenomenon. This success was attributed to the fact that the programs were written so that each student's incorrect answer was dealt with in the novelty of using the computer encouraged students usage much more than the prospect of working from a study guide.

In another study, the efforts of CAI and reinforcement schedules on physics achievement towards physics of high school were measured by BANNET (1986). Seventy one high school students were taken as sample. The result of this study supported that students who received CAI would achieve significantly higher physics test scores. .

PASCUAL (1993) conducted a twofold study. He applied linguistics approach and empirical study designed to measure the degree of motivation in students learning English using CAI material and Non CAI material. He found that students belonging to CAI material showed more motivation than their counterparts.

SIEGLE (2000) the purpose of this study was to investigate whether exposure to multimedia and presentation software on laptop computers influenced student achievement in a secondary level anatomy and physiology science course. The study demonstrated that students learned more when they had access to laptop computers, were exposed to multimedia software, and created projects with presentation software.

VENDLINSKI et al (2002) conducted a quasi-experimental study with 134 first-year high school chemistry students using the Interactive Multimedia Exercises computer based learning and assessment tool to solve qualitative chemistry problems. Results of this study show a strong and significant correlation between computer aided measures of student understanding and the teacher's manual evaluation of student understanding using her own rubric.

SUSAN et al (2003) in his study examined 165 teachers' beliefs about student centered learning as they implemented Alien Rescue, a computer based programme for middle school science that was designed to create a Student Centered Learning Environment (SCLE) in the class room. Discusses the goal of student activity, the role of the teacher, assessment, and student interaction.

RABIA TABASSUM (2004) conducted a study on effect of Computer Assisted Instruction CAI on the Secondary School Students Achievement in Science. In his study analysis of data revealed that the class IX standard students taught through computer assisted instruction as supplementary strategy performed significantly better. The CAI was found equally effective for both male and female students.

WINTERS et al (2005) in this study 62 high school biology students, paired heterogeneously based on prior knowledge, learned about genetic using Gen Scope, a Computer Based Learning Environment. The results of this naturalistic study could potentially be used to inform educational practice by highlighting scaffolds that may foster self-regulated learning in a CBLE mediated science inquiry context.

HARSKAMP et al (2005) conducted a study on solving Physics Problems with the help of Computer Assisted Instruction" In this study the main goal of most Physics text books is to develop declarative and procedural knowledge exercises provide pupils with opportunities to apply this knowledge. The computer group taking part in the experiment did achieve higher results in solving problems.

CEPNI et al (2006) pointed out that the study on effects of Computer Assisted Instruction Material related to photosynthesis topic on student cognitive development misconceptions and attitudes. This study result showed that using CAIM in teaching photo synthesis topic was very effective for students to reach comprehension and application levels of cognitive domain.

MAHAMOOD FARHADIAN (2007) in his research, he studied the co-operative learning, Computer Assisted Instruction and combination of these two methods called Co-operative Computer Assisted Instruction (CCAI). In CCAI method with the use of computer and attractive software, there would be appropriate grounds in instruction and educational achievement of mathematics for students. This method was examined for small group of student in a workshop. He had investigated some hypotheses on reduce of the students negative beliefs about mathematics, the speed of learning mathematics and its independence from time scheduling. Findings of the study, the difference between pretest and posttest scores were meaningfully significant.

Methodology

Educational software development and validation is a major research and development activity in the field of education. The major area in educational software is occupied by the instructional software development. The nature and the impact of computer and learning were led to its acquiring more significance. In the latest concept of improvement in the instructional software produced and the role played by educational technologists in the consents and process of software development. The CAI package depends on the electronic device. Further there is need for the subject export, technical expert. Individualized instruction is the one-to-one relationship between learners and the subject to be learnt.

Selection of Area

The investigator has selected six schools in Udumalpet at Tiruppur District which come under the Tamil Nadu State Board of Education. The sample selected for study consists of boys and girls from rural and urban schools.

Selection of the Sample

Sample selection is an important aspect of the research study, violation of a proper sampling method may yield based information of research and therefore maximum care is necessary for solution of sample.

English medium students of standard were selected from different types study the investigator selected three hundred students. Hundred and fifty boys and hundred and fifty girls of ninth standard from two government schools, two governments aided schools and two unaided schools have been selected.

Considering the non-feasibility of formulating randomized groups in a school setting, it was decided to have purposive sampling as the method of sampling for this experiment. Hundred and fifty students of Class IX in each of the three type of schools were taken as CAI experimental group and hundred and fifty students of

Hundred and fifty students of Class IX in different types of rural schools and hundred and fifty students of Class IX in different types of urban schools were taken as the experimental group. The same schools are brought under the categories, group of different variables are follow. Purposive sampling procedure is applied for selecting the sampling and so that it is free from any prejudice. The following table presents the details of the samples selected for the study.

Sampling Technique Pupils orzied and e samples selected for the study. e from any pre-judice.

For the present study purposive sampling method is used. The purposive sampling is selected by some arbitrary method because it is known to be representative of the total population. It is appropriate in a study which lays special emphasis on the control of certain specific variables.

Design of the Study

The design selected for the study is the pretest and posttest of two groups.

1. Administrating a pretest measuring the dependent variable at initial stage for elimination of novelty factor.
2. Applying the treatment to the subject, to measure treatment effect.
3. Administering a posttest again for measuring the impact of the dependent variable.

Differences attributed to application of the experimental treatment are then determined by comparing pretest and posttest scores.

Development of Instructional Materials

The subject is to be converted into CAI package was "Circulatory System" in biology for IX standard students. The content frame work of the syllabus was adapted from the prescribed text by the Tamil Nadu State Board Text Book for IX standard. The teaching points were collected from the text books and other reference books mentioned and sequence according to the designed learning level of students in the local school. The content prescribed was corrected into a reading material in simple language according to their vocabulary level.

The teaching frames were structured on the learning materials following the norms and theories set for the preparation of CAI package. The teaching points were structured in small dosage called "Frame". Frames were arranged in proper sequence. In each frame information was presented with simple illustration or examples.

Objectives Starting Phase

Bloom's Taxonomy was used for objective formation specific behavioral objective was formulated as performance objectives on completion of learning the unit "Circulatory System" the student should be able to identify. Content analysis was done. Care was taken to link the content by appropriate sequencing strategy.

1. Define "Blood"
2. State the composition of blood
3. Name the types of blood
4. List the properties of blood
5. Distinguish RBC, WBC and Platelet
6. Describe the functions of blood and
7. Define "Blood Group"

Description of the Tool Used

a) Computer Assisted Instruction Package: The instructional soft ware package developed to help the learners through a prescribed form of self instruction the subject are to be converted into frame. In this study in biology CAI package was Circulatory System for IX standard students. This CAI package contains various stimuli such as showing pictures and animation. This CAI was an instructional effective material individualized.

b) Performa Sheet: The investigator herself has developed a Performa sheet to collect necessary information regarding the individuals back ground such as the name, age, sex, name and address of the school, locality, type of school, system of school,

c) Science Achievement Test In this present study the investigator was prepared the achievement test question paper based on the IX standard State Board Syllabus. The question has been given to IX students of the selected school situated in and around Coimbatore. In consists of 40 questions and each objective has been provided 4 multiple choice from which the individual is asked to mark the response which he/she feels to be right in their point of view.

d) Scoring Key: The answer scripts for the conducted achievement test were collected and scored based on the scoring key. The score the test it was decided to give one mark as weight age for each correct answer. Thus a maximum of 40 marks who give correct response for all the items.

JURY OPINION

The copies of achievement test were submitted to a group of five subject experts who are teachers in schools and colleges for their valuable suggestion. Based on their ideas, the structure of questions was modified, options of some questions were changed and the number of question was also increased. They were asked to examine whether the items fully covered the content of "Circulating System" presented for IX standard by Tamil Nadu Text-book society. Items which were choose or similar or deviant was dropped as recommended by experts. They items reflected the entire context. Thus the context validity of the test was established based on expert judgments. As a result the test tool for the final study was prepared with forty multiple choice questions.

Pilot Study

Pilot study is a vital factor is any research. The pilot study administered to 50 student of IX standard level.

Administration of Tool

The study was conducted and materials were distributed to the students after taking prior permission from the head master of the selected schools. The investigator personally visited each school and collected the data. The purpose and intention of the study were briefly explained. The subjects had been repeatedly assured that they could freely express their opinions without and reservation since the purpose was purely educational research. The co-operation extended by the respondents/students was encouraging remarkable.

Methods of Experimentation

Each sample was pre-tested with criteria referenced test to measure the entry level. Before the experiment or treatment the students were pre-tested using the test. The test was helpful in accessing subject knowledge of the students prior to treatment. The same test was administered again after treatment effects. The individual instruction analysis was carried by employing 't' test for difference between the CAI groups.

Data Collection

As presented pre test, post test was planned to achieve the objective of the study. The sample was selected for conducting the experiment. For conducting the experiment the investigator selected six Higher Secondary School, The investigator selected Higher Secondary School hence it would be easy to provide the treatment in the school to the sample.

Statistical Techniques Used in the Study

Appropriate statistical techniques were used which included the mean, standard deviation, t-test and ANOVA.

ANALYSIS AND INTERPRETATION OF THE DATA

Computation of Statistics

The first section deals with background information of the selected sample based on age, gender, type of school, educational status of parents, and socio-economic status of the family. In second section the scores of pre test and post test were calculated and the statistical techniques like mean, standard deviation, t-test and ANOVA were used for analyzing and interpreting.

Descriptive analysis for Background information of the selected sample

Differential Analysis

The collected data were consolidated, tabulated and analysed statistically by using the following tests.

1. Test of Significance ('t' Test and ANOVA)
2. Mean and Standard Deviation

(1) Test of significance: 't' Test and ANOVA

't' Test is used to find out the significant level of difference between two groups of population. The values are calculated with the help of the mean scores and standard deviation.

(2) Mean and Standard Deviation

Mean and standard deviation were done using the results of the study to make simple comparisons wherever necessary.

Analysis of 'T' Test Scores of Government Schools Pupil Following the Computer Assisted Instruction

Source	N	Mean	Standard Deviation	't' value
Pre test Score	50	14.300	3.2467	34.799 **
Post test Score	50	32.22	3.3030	

** Significant at 1% level.

There is no significant difference between the pretest and posttest scores of Government schools pupil following the Computer Assisted Instruction was rejected.

Analysis of 'T' Test Scores of Aided Schools Pupil Following the Computer Assisted Instruction

Source	N	Mean	Standard Deviation	't' value
Pre test Score	50	15.44	4.6342	22.206 **
Post test Score	50	29.76	4.3451	

** Significant at one percent level.

There is no significant difference between the pretest and posttest scores of Aided Schools Pupil following the Computer Assisted Instruction was rejected.

Analysis of 'T' Test Scores of Unaided Schools Pupil Following the Computer Assisted Instruction

Source	N	Mean	Standard Deviation	't' value
Pre test Score	50	13.16	3.6048	33.969 **
Post test Score	50	28.98	3.1975	

** Significant at 1% level.

There is no significant difference between the pretest and posttest scores of Unaided Schools Pupil following the Computer Assisted Instruction was rejected.

Significance of Difference between Pre and Post Tests Scores of Computer Assisted Instruction Group

Test	N	Mean	Standard Deviation	't' value
Pre test	150	14.30	3.9591	47.644 **
Post test	150	30.32	3.8831	

** Significant at 1% level.

There is no significant difference between the pretest and posttest mean scores of the experimental group following CAI was rejected.

Comparison of Posttest Performance of Computer Assisted Instruction Group between the Different Types of Schools

Type of the School	N	Mean	Standard Deviation	'F' value
Government School	50	32.22	3.3030	12.824 **
Aided School	50	29.76	4.6451	
Unaided School	50	30.32	3.1975	

** Significant at 1% level.

ANOVA test was applied and the calculated ANOVA value is 12.824, which is found to be significant at 0.01% level. There is no significant difference in posttest performance of Computer Assisted Instruction between the different types of schools pupil was rejected.

Comparison of the Post Test Performance of the Experimental Group Following the CAI with Reference to Locality

Area	N	Mean	Standard Deviation	**'t' value**
Urban	75	32.00	3.2715	5.862 **
Rural	75	28.64	3.7331	

** Significant at 1% level.

There is no significance difference between posttest performance of Urban and Rural Schools Pupil following the Computer Assisted Instruction was rejected.

Comparison of the Posttest Performance of the Experimental Group following the CAI with Reference to Gender

Gender	**N**	**Mean**	**Standard Deviation**	**'t' value**
Boys	75	29.6667	4.0415	2.084 **
Girls	75	30.9733	3.6279	

** Significant at 5% level.

There is no significance difference between the posttest performance of Boys and Girls following Computer Assisted Instruction was rejected.

Summary of the Study

The study is an attempt to find out, a comparative study of effectiveness of Computer Assisted Instruction and Handout Instruction on circulatory system for IX standard students.

A sample of 300 pupils studying in IX standard from six different schools in Udumalpet Taluk, Coimbatore District was selected. 150 formed of the 300 students experimental group following Computer Assisted Instruction. The experimental method was adopted in the study. Achievement test question paper was employed as a tool, at this time the treatment is administered on a small group of the target population. Pretest and post test are administered prior to starting and after the completion of the treatment respectively. The test scores were taken to assess the effectiveness of self learning through the Computer Assisted Instruction among students.

Findings of Study

1. The comparison of scores of pretest and post test of Government Schools Pupil following the Computer Assisted Instruction shows significant difference. The mean posttest scores is 32.22 for the Government Schools Pupil which is greater than pretest scores 14.30. This shows the Computer Assisted Instruction significantly influenced learning of pupil.

2. The mean posttest scores is 29.79 for the Aided Schools Pupil which is greater than pretest scores 15.44. This shows the CAI significantly influenced the learning of Aided Schools Pupil.

3. The mean posttest scores is 28.98 for unaided schools pupil which is higher than mean pretest scores 13.16. This shows the CAI significantly influenced the learning of unaided schools pupil.

4. The comparison of the scores of pretest and posttest of overall sample in target group following Computer Assisted instruction shows significant difference. This mean posttest scores is 30.32 for samples which is greater than the mean pretest scores 14.32. This shows CAI significantly influenced learning of all selected samples following CAI.

5. In this study it was found that same Government Schools has also showing better performance, while they received experimental treatment through CAI when compared to unaided schools and aided schools respectively in post test score.

6. The comparison of the posttest scores of urban and rural area in the CAI experimental group shows significant difference, the mean value of this CAI experimental group is 32.00 and 28.64 respectively.

7. Gender wise comparison in the CAI experimental group proved the significant. The calculated 't' value is 2.084. The mean scores of girls are 30.97, which is greater than the mean scores of boys 29.66 in the posttest performances.

Recommendation

Computer assisted instruction should be implemented in more number of the schools.

The Government should allot more funds to provide adequate number of computer materials for the schools.

It is recommended that Government may give concession for purchase of computer.

College students who are studying computer science may be asked to do projects in the development of necessary software for high school syllabus. This can solve the problem of non availability of software.

Special training shall be given to the teachers through in-service training programme to inculcate knowledge about different instructional strategies.

Educational institutions should have adequate instructional materials.

Training shall be given to the teachers to prepare and handle instrumental materials.

Instruction materials of learning provide scope for self instructional activities. Here the role of the teacher is limited and maximum activities are prescribed to the learners.

Teacher can improve their competence by attending in service training camps and also by writing research articles in the field of educational technology.

The students can learn effectively when they learn on their own. Self learning develops critical thinking in handling of study materials on one's own and enhances communication skills and self reliance.

The teachers must motivate the pupils to make more instructional package for self learning.

Suggestions for Further Research

A Research study would be incomplete if it doesn't provide necessary guidelines as well as potential research topics for further exploration. The following suggestions are made for further research in this area.

A similar study can be carried out in different types of school in different parts of Tamil Nadu.

In the present study researcher didn't take students from Tamil medium high schools students from such schools can be taken for further study.

Conclusion

The density of the country is destined in the classroom. Yes, it is true. The education has a wider meaning now-a-days. The education in the present trend does not mean the mere text book learning. It aims at giving complete life to the pupils. It is more important for the learners to know how to learn rather than what to learn.

From the results of the study, the investigator has ideas of Computer Assisted Instruction provided greater learning opportunities for children both theoretical and practical. Its use in bringing new kinds of experiences for children in school is really interesting and meaningful. The investigator therefore desires that the more number of educational institutions should come forward to make the learning best out of all available instruction materials for learning. So, this amount is just the beginning… not the end.

References

Aggarwal J.G (1995), Essential of Educational Technology; Teaching Leaning Innovations in Education New Delhi.

Bloom, Benjamin S (1956), Taxonomy of Educational Objective Hand books. The cognitive domain. Logmas Publication, New York.

Chauhan S.S (1983), Innovations in Teaching Learning Process, New Delhi.
Coulson S.E (1962), Programmed Learning and Computer based instruction.

David Hawkeridge (1990), New information in Technology and Education, Croomhelm.

David Layton (1992), Innovations in Science and Technology Education, Edition III, UNESCO.

Ellington, Henry (1985), producing teaching materials. A Hand book for Teachers and Trainers, London.

Forcier (2000) The Computer as a Productivity Tool in Education, Prentice Hall of India.Glass G.V (1970), Statistical method in Education and Psychology,

Prentice Hall, Englewood Cliffs.

S.P.Gupta (1985), Statistic methods Sultan Chand & Sons Pub. New Delhi. Pp930.

Henry, Ellington, Percival, Fred and Race, Phil (2003), Hand book of Educational Technology, New Delhi. Hemalatha Parasnis, An Orientation to Computer Instruction Experiments in Education. July 1989.

John Best. W (1963), Research in Education Prentice Hall of India Private Limited, New Delhi.

Jaganath Mohanty, Modern Trends in Educational (2003).

Kothari C.R (1993), Research Methodology Methods and Techniques.

Krishnamoorthy. R (1995) Computer Programming, JJ Publishers, Madurai.

Kulkarni S.S (1986), Introduction to Educational Technology, New Delhi. Oxford, IBH Pub. Co.,

Mangal S.K (2000), Reversed Edition Foundation of Education Technology.

Murthy S.K (1995), Educational Technology Parkash Brothers, Jallandhar.

Narayana L.M, A text book of Chordates, Saras Publication, Nagercoil.

Palaniappan, V.P (1990), Effectiveness of Computer Assisted Instruction in Learning Triangles, Media and Technology for Human Resource Development.

Pillay, Subramania G (1995), Readings in Educational Technology, Nirmal Publication, Madurai.

Rajaraman, V (1985), Fundamentals of Computer, New Delhi, Prentice Hall of India Pvt. Ltd.,

Rao B, Anand and Ravishankar. S (1989), Reading in Educational Technology. Himalaya Publishing House, Bombay.

Romesh Verma, Suresh Sharma (1998), Modern Trends in Teaching Technology, Anmol Publications Pvt. Ltd., New Delhi.

Sadha and Singh (1982) Methodology of Educational Research, Prentice Hall of India.

Sampath and Pannerselvam (1994), Introduction to Educational Technology, Sterling Publishers, New Delhi.

Satyanarayana (1985), Research Methodology, Methods and Techniques, Atlantic Pub.

Vachan Sing (2005), Practical Approach Educational Technology, Akansha Publishing House, New Delhi.

S.Venkataian (2000), Encylopedio of Contemporary Education Series Science Education, Anmol Pub.

M.S.Yadav (2000), Modern method of teaching sciences, Anmol Publisher, Delhi.

S.M.Zaidi (2004), Modern method of teaching Science, Anmol Publisher, New Delhi.

Journals

Kiboss, et al Journal of Educational Multimedia Hypermedia, Vol. 15/4, Pp.397-410, October 2006.

G.Subramanian, Journal of Educational Research & Extension, Vol.43/1, Pp.43, Jan-March 2006.

Cepni et al Computers and Education, Vol. 46/2 Pp 192-205, Feb 2006.

Harskamp, International Journal of Science Education, Vol.27/4, P.451-469, March 2005.

Roger (2005), Journal of Educational Computing Research, V/33/2, Pp.189-217.

Jayakrishna Choudhury, School Science, June 2005, Pp 99.

Sharon et al (2005), Journal of Computers In Mathematics and Science Teaching,V/24,No.2, Pp.149-156.

Ndirangu et al, Journal of Science, Education and Technology, V/13, No.2, Pp.207-213, June 2004.

Chang. C.Y, Journal of Computer Assisted Learning, Vol.20/1, Pp. 4-10, Feb 2004.

Susan (2003), Education Technology Research and Development, Vol.51/2, Pp. 57-76.

B.H. Helen Joy and L.SS. Manickam (2002), Perspectives in Education, Vol. 18/4, Pp 235.

❐

2.

Students Attitude towards Audio-Visual Aids Used by the Teachers

Introduction

Audio Visual aids or Graphic aids are the form of visuals that are represented on plane surface. The subject matter areas that are represented in Audio Visual aids or Graphic aids are in an abridged and easily understandable form. They convey meaning mainly through relatively conventionalized symbols that are nearer to reality perceptually than verbal symbols. They secure the attention of the pupils by their attractive format and simplicity of layout. They convey the expected message by combination of visual and pictorial message made meaningful by suitable captions. Pictures and words blended in harmony deliver the required information. The idea conveyed by any graphic aid should be a single concept. The layout and words should not be complicated so as to puzzle the viewer and make him lose interest in the same. The statement "one good visual which can secure and maintain attention and educate the viewer in the desired area is worth a thousand words" is quite correct. Graphics could be truly considered as the shorthand language of the idea presented. The criteria for good graphics are that they should be simple, bold, legible, brief and have adequate margins. Graphics are only two-dimensional and should be carefully planned to offset the limitation. An Audio Visual aids or a graphic aid by eliminating non–essentials and by using bold symbolic representations with attractive portrayal should be able to create interest and secure the attention of the pupils. Since the message to be conveyed pertains to a single concept and hence brief, the viewer will not get perplexed on being exposed to the visual but will try to read and understand what is implied (visual and words).Audio Visual aids or a graphic aids could easily be prepared by and teacher using simple materials that are easily available and stored for future use. Making graphics should form an integral part of the teacher's preparation for teaching. Almost any material involving illustrations is basically graphic in nature. There can be an infinite variety of graphic materials. It is difficult to give a rigid list of these materials. The present study aims to find out the students attitude towards audio-visual aids used by the teachers in Coimbatore district. A samples of 100 respondents selected randomly were studied. An interview schedule method of survey was used to find out the attitude towards audio-visual aids. Primary data were collected by using a structured interview scheduled. All the respondents were asked the same questions in the same fashion and they were informed the purpose of study. ANOVA, t-test and regression analysis were applied to test the hypotheses. The data collected through questionnaires have been tabulated. The findings and observations are the result and outcome of the interpretations made during the study of analysis.

Graphs, Diagram, Posters, Maps, Comics, Cartoons, Charts, Globes, Display Board, Peg Boards, Hook and loop board, felt board, magnetic board, marker board, chalk board, bulletin board, models, Epidiascope, slight projector, over head projector (OHP), fields trips, excursion, exhibition, museums, radio, Television, Tape recorder, Video Caste Record VCR and Computers. By using audio visual materials in accessible process, materials givens objects changes in time, speed and space could easily be brought to the class. Audio visual aids can helps to imaginative teachers to solve the communication problems. It also helps to extend human experience. Use of audio visual aids results in greater acquisition of knowledge of facts and ensures longer retention of the information gained. It can provide effective substitutes for direct contact of students with environment-social and physical. It also adds an expected change in attitude and behaviour of the students. It can provide integrated experiences varying from abstract to concrete. It helps in to secure and retain to attention as well as develop the communication skills. It could be used to motivate and stimulate interest of students to gain further knowledge. Lastly, In a conventional teaching method teacher is the centre of attention and the primary sources of information.

An attitude is a mental state of readiness exerting directive or dynamic influence upon individual's response to all objects and situations with which it is related. Therefore if we can have some judgement about the attitude of an individual towards a specific thing or activity then we can have a fair idea as to whether the individual can be persuaded to participate in a particular thing or activity and whether he shall adopt it with interest and sincerity or not.

The attitude is the degree of positive or negative effect associated with some psychological objects namely institution, ideal, symbol, phrase, slogan, job or idea towards which people can differ with respect to positive or negative effect (Thurstone, 1946). The attitude is a dispositional readiness to respond to certain situations, persons, objects in a consistent manner which has been learnt and has become one's typical mode of response (Free Mann, 1950). According to Guild (1950) attitude is a tendency of individual to favour or not to favour some type of situation. The attitude may be considered as motivational perceptual states, which direct perceptions and predispose a person to act in accordance with perceptions (Allport, 1955). The attitudes are learnt pre-dispositions to respond positively to certain objects, situations, institutions, concepts or other persons (Aiken, 1979).

Review of Literature

Glee Harrah Cady and **Pat Mc Gregor (2005)** describe that "Internet is a network of network and the internet mostly connects network of computers".

Barry (2006) studied the relationship between student's perceptions of their science class room learning environment and attitude to four different scores of scientific information experiments, books, promote positive attitude towards experiment as a source of information, while less favorable environment promoted more positive attitude to the more authoritarian sources of information.

Schafer (2007) compared third and fourth grade students using ESS units with students using laid low science serious on classification skills, science achievements and science attitudes. No achievement or classification skill different were noted but ESS students had more favorable attitudes.

Williams (2008), "Attitude of high school pupils towards general science and its relationship with achievement and its subjects". In her study it is found to examine if there are any differences among the different groups of students such as boys and girls. Rural school pupil and Urban school pupils in respect of their achievement in science, attitude towards science and attitude forwards science education.

Martis Anandi (2009) developed the test on scientific attitudes (TOSA), taking the point of view that attitudes must be inferred from the behavior of students. They developed a multiple – choice format test. The developed behavioral definitions of eight attitudes: (1) critical mindedness, (2) suspended judgment (3) Respect for evidence (4) Honesty, (5) Objectivity, (6) Willingness to change opinions, (7) Open – mindedness and (8) Questioning attitude. The behavioral definitions to these eight attitudes were used to develop items.

Mohanty Ajay Kumar (2010) investigated attitudes towards education, critical thinking ability and specific effective behavious of (1) Students who had studied, the BSCS environmental models "Investing your Environment" (IYE), (2) Those students using one of BSCS biological science version and (3) Those studying models of Biology. He found that the ability of students who had experienced BSCS Biological science was significantly increased but no other differences were found among the students on any of the other variables.

Objective

The present study attempts to investigate the attitude towards Audio-visual aids used by the teachers.

Methodology

Methodology is an important aspect of any research work. There are different methods followed at various stages of any investigation. The details of methods followed in this study such as selection of tools, sample frame, collection of data, and analysis of data are involved in this research paper. The study has been designed with the student's attitude towards Audio-visual aids used by the teacher's achievement. The major aim of the present study is to determine the student's Audio-visual aids used by the teacher.

Method of data collection

The investigator personally distributed the questionnaires to each member of the randomly selected sample. They were requested to answer the items in the booklet as per the instructions provided at the beginning of each questionnaire. Confidentiality of response was assured. The questionnaires were collected by the investigator from the employees. The responses were scored as per the scoring key of the respective questionnaire. Then the results were tabulated, analysed and discussed.

Sample

A sample is a finite number of observations (or) cases in a particular universe of which it is a pat (Good 1952). The investigator prepared a representative random sample of students studying VIII & IX standard in different schools at Coimbatore District. A sample of 100 students was finally selected.

Hypothesis

Students have favorable attitude towards use of Audio Visual Aids in Coimbatore district school.

Nature of the Tool

The inventory contained general instruction for the students and information about bio data. In addition to that the specific instruction ware given to on the first page of the inventory. Space for collecting personal data like students name type of school, locality of the school, class, gender, community, religion, group, medium of instruction, birth order of the child and parental literacy.

Data Processing

The collected data were analysed using appropriate statistical techniques. The descriptive statistics such as mean and S.D, t-ratio were computed. In order to study the functional dependencies to indicate the likelihood of causal relationships between the variables, inferential statistical techniques of ANOVA and Percentage analysis were computed.

Analysis and Interpretation

Table 1: Showing Mean, SD and t-test for respondent about students attitude towards audio visual aids used by the teachers on the basis of type of the school.

Types of the school	N	Mean	SD	t-value	LS
Government	62	70.48	6.50	2.78	0.01
Private	38	73.30	10.33		

Hypothesis 1: Students do not differ in their student's attitude towards audio visual aids used by the teachers on the basis of types of the school.

The calculated t-value (2.78), which is significant at 0.01 level, confirms that there is a significant difference in student audio visual aids on the basis of type of the school. Hence the stated hypothesis is rejected. So government students have high level of audio visual aids than private school students.

Table 2: Showing Mean, SD and t-test for respondent about students attitude towards audio visual aids used by the teachers on the basis of locality of the school.

Locality of the school	N	Mean	SD	t-value	LS
Urban	74	72.24	8.11	1.07	NS
Rural	26	71.14	9.19		

Hypothesis 2: Students do not differ in their student's attitude towards audio visual aids used by the teachers on the basis of locality of the school.

The calculated t-value (1.07), which is not significant at 0.05 level, confirms that there is no significant difference in their audio visual aids on the basis of locality of the school. Hence the stated hypothesis is accepted.

Table 3: Showing Mean, SD and t-test for respondent about students attitude towards audio visual aids used by the teachers on the basis of Gender.

Gender	N	Mean	SD	t-value	LS
Male	74	70.97	7.41	1.85	NS
Female	26	72.90	9.89		

Hypothesis 3: Students do not differ in their student's attitude towards audio visual aids used by the teachers on the basis of gender.

The calculated t-value (1.85), which is not significant at 0.05 level, confirms that there is no significant difference in their audio visual aids on the basis of gender. Hence the stated hypothesis is accepted.

Table 4: Showing Mean, SD and t-test for respondent about students attitude towards audio visual aids used by the teachers on the basis of group.

Group	N	Mean	SD	t-value	LS
Arts	56	69.19	5.37	5.58	0.01
Science	44	74.58	10.37		

Hypothesis 4: Students do not differ in their attitude towards audio visual aids used by the teachers on the basis of group.

The calculated t-value (5.58), which is significant at 0.01 level, confirms that there is a significant difference in student audio visual aids on the basis of group. Hence the stated hypothesis is rejected. So science students have high level of audio visual aids than art students.

Table 5: Showing Mean, SD and F-ratio for students attitude towards audio visual aids used by the teachers on the basis of medium of instruction.

Medium of instruction	N	Mean	SD	F-ratio	LS
Hindi	50	70.20	9.64	6.49	0.01
English	30	71.75	4.19		
Kannada	20	75.00	11.60		
Total	100	71.78	8.58		

Hypothesis 5: Students do not differ in their attitude towards audio visual aids used by the teachers on the basis of medium of instruction.

The calculated F-ratio (6.49), which is not significant at 0.05 level, confirms that there is a significant difference in students attitude of audio visual aids on the basis of medium of instruction. Hence the stated hypothesis is rejected.

Table 6: Regression for student demographic characters and their attitude towards audio visual aids used by the teachers

MODEL SUMMARY

Model	R	R Square	Adjusted R Square	Std. Error of the Estimate
1	.436[a]	.190	.159	7.87

a. Predictors: (Constant)

ANOVA[B]

Model	Sum of Squares	df	Mean Square	F	Sig.
Regression	.4189.756	11	380.887	6.155	.000[a]
Residual	17821.724	88	61.881		
Total	22011.480	99			

a. Predictors: (Constant) b. Dependent variable

COEFFICIENTSA

Model	Unstandardized Coefficients		Standardized Coefficients	t	Sig.
	B	Std. Error	Beta		
Name of the school	58.979	4.376		13.477	.000
Type of the school	2.387	1.116	.139	2.139	.033**
Locality of the school	-1.000	1.005	-.058	-.995	.320
Class	-.500	1.046	-.028	-.478	.633
Gender	1.989	1.052	.115	1.891	.060
Community	-1.365	.422	-.190	-3.233	.001**
Religion	.757	.627	.068	1.208	.228
Groups	5.255	.947	.306	5.548	.000**
Medium of instruction	2.183	.649	.191	3.365	.001**
Birth order of the child	-9.11	1.032	-.001	-.009	.993
Parental literacy (Father)	-.143	1.003	-.008	-.143	.887
Parental literacy (Mother)	-.585	.955	-.033	-.612	.541

a. Dependent Variable: Attitude towards Audi visual aids

** Significant at 0.01 level

According to the regression result it is known that the demographic variables are influenced nearly 19 per cent to measure their attitude towards audio visual aids. This is proved by the obtained r square value (0.19).

Further the calculated F-value (6.15) also significant at 0.01 level. It indicates that there is a significant influence between students demographic characters and their attitude towards audio visual aids.

Also from the obtained t- values the demographic variables such as type of school, community, group studied and medium of instructions the students studied are significant at 0.01 level. So it is concluded that there is a significant difference regarding attitude towards audio visual aids on the basis of these variables.

Conclusion

Audio Visual aids or graphic aids are the form of visuals that are represented on plane surface. The subject – matter areas that are represented in Audio Visual aids or graphic aids are in an abridged and easily understandable form. They convey meaning mainly through relatively conventionalized symbols that are nearer to reality perceptually than verbal symbols. They secure the attention of the pupils by their attractive format and simplicity of layout. They convey the expected message by combination of visual and pictorial message made meaningful by suitable captions. Pictures and words blended in harmony deliver the required information. The idea conveyed by any graphic aid should be a single concept. The layout and words should not be complicated so as to puzzle the viewer and make him lose interest in the same. The statement "one good visual which can secure and maintain attention and educate the viewer in the desired area is worth a thousand words" is quite correct. Graphics could be truly considered as the shorthand language of the idea presented. The criteria for good graphics are that they should be simple, bold, legible, brief and have adequate margins.

Findings of the study

Based on the results that students do not differ in their audio visual aids on the basis of types of the school

From the calculation that students do not differ in their audio visual aids on the basis of locality of the school

Based on the results that students do not differ in their audio visual aids on the basis of gender

Based on the results that students do not differ in their audio visual aids on the basis of group

From the analysis that students do not differ in their audio visual aids on the basis of medium of instruction

Discussion

Audio visual aids a process of inward journey to unravel the hidden potentialities of a being. It helps an individual to develop ones personality. A systematic approach of Audio visual aids helps an individual to see the all around development at physical, mental, intellectual and emotional level. The practice of use of audio visual aids makes an individual perfect. It removes the unwanted elements in the mind of the learner. It improves concentration and brings mental stability. Audio visual aids are an essential tool for students to achieve higher score in their studies as if improves concentration, memory and skills. The present study clearly indicates and recommends the students to use of audio visual aids as to develop positive attitude towards everything in their life which helps to excel themselves in their studies. The entire study concluded reveals that the use of audio visual aids has high achievement and expressed more favourable attitude.

Educational Implications

Audio-visual aids are very important and useful aids for teaching. As well as it creates high interest among the students to learn the subjects. So, the department of education shall take a steps to implement the latest audio-visual aids to all the school and colleges for teaching purpose.

For self-learning, these type of aids are very helpful to the students. Also students are very much interested in using latest technologies such as computers and internet. In internet lot of facilities are there to learn new information with visual appearance. From that students are also get more interest to use that.
In the case of teaching, in older days teachers follow interactive methods and oral demonstration. But these are not creating much interest. In order to create interest and attention audio-visual aids are highly useful. So, the concerned educational institution tries to provide these facilities. So that teachers and students get benefited.

Suggestions

The following suggestions are arrived from the research findings. Research found that use of audio visual aids will contribute more in students achievement. Also the result reveals that use of audio visual aids increases the memory power, concentration. Further it sharpens the intelligence. Apart from that it reduces misconception in learning. Further due to use of audio visual aids the sensory expression would be more exercised. So, the present research suggested that in all schools and colleges, the students advised to use of audio visual aids compulsory. The education department forms a rule for that and advises the educational institutions make a step to establish separate infrastructure for this one. Also the Government take a step to use audio visual aids effectively students in their academic. This will definitely help the students to be a good learner imbibing the concepts.

Conclusion

The present study attempted to identify the students attitude towards audio-visual aids used by the teachers. For that the researcher framed some objectives. On the basis of objectives, a questionnaire is framed. After framing the questionnaire, these are circulated to the selected samples. 100 samples were selected randomly. The responses were collected and coded using computerised. To test the hypotheses and characteristics of the data, some standard statistical tools were used. The statistical tools such as t-test, F-ratio and correlation were used. From the analysis the result concluded that the students have positive attitude towards audio-visual aids used by the teachers.

References

Glee Harrah Cady and Pat Mc Gregor (2005) "Internet is a network of network and the internet mostly connects network of computers". Journal of research in science teaching.

Barry (2006) "Relationship between students perceptions of their science class room learning environment and attitude", Journal of Educational Research.

Schafer (2007) vargo students science attitudes and self concept in science as a function of rose specific pupil/teacher interpersonal compatibility", San Francisco,

California, National association for research in science teaching.

Williams (2008), "Attitude of high school pupils towards general science and its relationship with achievement and its subjects". Journal Community and Guidance.

Martis Anandi (2009), in test on scientific attitudes (TOSA), taking the point of view that attitudes must be inferred from the behavior of students, Journal of All India Association for Educational Research, Vol.17, Nos. 1 & 2, March & June.

Mohanty Ajay Kumar (2010), Attitudes towards education, critical thinking ability and specific effective behavious, Journal of all India Association for Educational Research,Vol.14, Nos.3&4.

❒

3.

Learning Styles of Higher Secondary Students in Biological Science

Introduction

Learning style is a hypothetical contract that has been developed to explain the process of mediation between stimuli and response. Learning style as on integral concept that bridges the personality cognitive dimensions of the individuals. The learning styles are synonymous. He defines learning styles as the course of learning. Laycock (1978) describes learning styles as an individual characteristic way of responding to certain variable in the instructional environment. In simplest terms, a students learning style is the peculiar way with which he learns best. The present study aims to find out the learning styles of higher secondary students in biological science in Villupuram District. A samples of 100 respondents selected randomly were studied. A questionnaire method of survey was used to find out the learning styles of higher secondary students in biological science. The data were collected by using questionnaire as an instrument. Primary data were collected by conducting direct structured interview using questionnaire. All the respondents were asked the same questions in the same fashion and they were informed the purpose of study. Regression and correlation analysis were applied to test the hypotheses. The data collected through questionnaires have been tabulated. The findings and observations are the result and outcome of the interpretations made during the study of analysis. The result found that average learning styles of higher secondary students in biological science in Villupuram District.

The act or experience of one that learns. Knowledge or skill acquired by instruction or study. Modification of a behavioral tendency by experience (as exposure to conditioning). Adapted from How Learning Works by Ambrose et al.: an engagingly written, evidence-based text, well-illustrated by practical examples, and a book well worth your time, as a TA and as a student.

As teachers, our goal is to encourage learning in our classrooms. But what is learning, and what principles or factors affect how our students learn? In this section, we provide you with the very basics of what learning are, how and when it occurs, and how to structure your lessons to maximize student learning. There are three components to the definition of Learning:

"Learning is a process, not a product." Exam scores and term papers are measures of learning, but they are not the process of learning itself.

"Learning is a change in knowledge, beliefs, behaviors or attitudes." This change requires time, particularly when one is dealing with changes to core beliefs, behaviors, and attitudes. Don't interpret a lack of sea change in your students' beliefs or attitudes immediately following a lesson as a lack of learning on their part, but instead, consider that such a change will take time – perhaps a few weeks, perhaps until the end of the term, or even longer.

"Learning is not something done to students, but something that students themselves do." If you have ever carefully planned a lesson, only to find that your students just didn't "get it," consider that your lesson should be designed not just to impart knowledge but also to lead students through the process of their own learning.

Learning is the process by which one acquires, ingests, and stores or accepts information. Our experiences with learned information compose our bodies of knowledge. Learning is a process unique to each individual. Some learn quickly, scanning the information and mastering the concept or skill seemingly effortlessly. Others stumble while processing information, taking longer to grasp the concept or requiring numerous exposures over a sustained period of time. Some individuals store the information they've learned indefinitely, cementing it in their memories. Others find that the information they've learned slips away rapidly. Some learn best through text, others through practice, some through hearing. Learning styles are as unique and varied as our personalities. Learning is a lifelong endeavor. As long as one remains engaged in life, learning does not cease.

Until recently most people took learning styles for granted and left them to instinct. Realization that studying how learning should come before everything else is spreading in the world of education skill in this field can multiply efficiency. The use of higher level work skills can bring improvement in almost all fields. Improvement in athletic field and industrial productivity has been achieved in the way. Everyone is familiar with the difference in output of a self-taught typist who uses one finger of each hand and an expert who was taught the tough system. Other experiments has shown that the level of performance on such tasks as card sorting, pitch discrimination and puzzle solving is affected by the method employed and the limit to performance might be improved of better work was used.

These findings on effects of work methods on levels of performance led to the significant theoretical contribution to theories regarding the causes of individual difference in competence. It was long assumed that these differences were primarily due to two factors. (1) Learning and (2) Amount of training in a task. Dr. Seashare after studying may findings on effects of work method, concluded that method of work was a third variable in instruction. It is found that new levels in achievement are possible by improving the learning styles.

Both in common speech and educational literature the word "Read" is used to designate a wide variety of learned activities from the socially undesirable to the highly ethnical, form bodily skill, such as walking to mental activities such as learning of critical thinking and from specified abilities to generalized attitudes. The meaning of learning includes the ideal of facility in the performance of an act, combined with a persisting inclination towards the repetition of the act.

As Bagley has said "To teach a child to study effectively is to do that most valuable thing that could be done to help him adjust himself to any environment of modern civilized life into which they live. In 1917 strays and Newsworthy declared "Many teachers have taught subjects, but not how to study subjects, the latter is more important". H.R. Bhatia says, "unless opportunities for doing and respecting things are afforded to children it is futile to expect them to form habits". Sevmors and exhortations may help children to acquire normal vocabulary but not normal character. Percepta in the formation of learning unless children are afforded actual practice in those modes behaviour.

Review of Literature

Mary Lou Koran, John J. Koran (2006), conducted a study "Interaction of Learner aptitudes with question packing in learning from prose, he suggested that, in some cases, reduction in certain information Processing requirements may actually be an important prerequisite to affective utilization of other aptitudes (learning).

The over-all means used in the analysis are presented, both low and high aptitude students in "favourable" classrooms had higher achievements scores than the two groups in 'unfavourable' classroom. This contexts effect was present to some extent in both third and fourth grade class room aptitude, third grade students. It appears that being in a classroom with many high-aptitude students is beneficial for low-aptitude students and some high-aptitude students as well".

K.S Kahlon and Vinod Uppalo, (2007) studied on "women's aptitude and achievement in Relation to achievement motivation.

The Result of the present investigation fully supports the hypotheses on the basis of which the study had been undertaken.

There is significant, but imperfect relationship between aptitude (learning style) and academic achievement.

Discrepancy between aptitude (Learning style) and achievement bears no relationship with ability.

Discrepancy between aptitude (Learning Style) and achievement bears significant relationship with academic achievement.

Discrepancy between aptitude and achievement bears significant relationship with achievement motivation. That is, high achievement motivation goes with positive discrepancy where as low achievement motivation accounts for negative discrepancy"

Robert B. Burnes (2012) conducted a study on "The Relation of Aptitudes of Learning at different Points in the time during Instruction: The result of this study suggested that some aptitude-learning relations are not stable over time and that his instability is exhibited in different aptitudes being required at different points in time during instruction. These findings supported most of the Junior evidence examining aptitude correlates at different stages of learning and did not support the assumption made in ATI Research that aptitudes relate equally to learning for the during of treatment"

Moraddwaj Varma (2013) conducted a study on "Comparative achievement in science of Tharu Tribals and other at high school level. He found, that the achievement of Tharu tribals is lower than that of the non-tharus in all the three science subjects were significant at .01 level."

In **Jamur (2013)** made a study in Patna in relationship between study habits and achievement. His study showed a correlation of 0.51 between study habits and achievement of students and a correlation of 0.144 between study habits and intelligence.

Objectives

- To study the higher secondary learning styles in Biological science.
- To know the higher secondary different methods learning styles in Biological science.
- To find out the higher secondary factors learning styles in Biological science.

Methodology

The methodology adopted for the study is explained in detail. The sampling technique, size of the sample, variables of the study, description of the tool used and administration of tool are elaborated.

Sample

The sample selected for the present study is 100 higher secondary students in Villupuram district. Random sampling technique was used for the selection of sample.

Data Collection

Primary data, required for the present research work were collected by conducting direct interviews using questionnaire. All the respondents were given sufficient information about the Project work. These respondents were provided with the same questionnaires. They were also informed that they have to answer in the same fashion.

Tools used in the Study

SOLAT Tool of learning style D. Venketraman (1986) consists of 25 items. The learning style comprises 5 categories.

1. Verbal (1 to 5 items)
2. Content preference (6 to 10 items)
3. Class preference (11 to 15 items)
4. Learning preference (16 to 20 items)
5. Interest (20 to 25 items)

Scoring Procedure

The maximum score that a student obtains is 50 the minimum score that a student gain is 25.

Each item has two alternatives. If the student chooses the First alternative one mark is given. If the student chooses Second alternative the student it secures 2 marks. The first alternative of an item indicates the use of Right hemisphere of the brain and the second alternative of an item indicates the use of left hemisphere of the brain.

Tool validity and reliability

The main attributes needed to be considered regarding a good tool are validity and reliability.

Validity: A measuring instrument is said to be valid if it measures what it purpose to measure. Validity may be defined as the extent to which an instrument or a test does the job derived of it.

The kind of validity and the extent or degrees to which it should be established are the major consideration while establishing validity.

In the present study the researcher found out the content validity.

Content validity gives the logical evidence that the content of the items of a test is suitable for the purpose for which the test is designed and used. Content validity is established is 0.549.

Reliability

The efficiency of measuring the different items are called on aspect of reliability. Reliability determined test-retest method and it is found to be validity of the tool is (0.82).

Hypothesis

The level of learning styles among higher secondary students on the basis of their demographic variables.

The level of different method learning styles among higher secondary students on the basis of their demographic variables.

The level of factors learning styles among higher secondary students on the basis of their demographic variables.

Analysis and Interpretation

Table 1: Showing the Stepwise regression analysis predicting learning styles among higher secondary students and demographic variables

Sl.No	Step/Source	Unstandardized Coefficients Beta	Std. Error	Standardized Coefficients Beta	Step t	P
1.	Gender	1.342	0.343	1.245	5.432	0.01
2.	Locality	1.224	0.392	0.269	6.641	0.01
3.	Family Income	1.924	0.549	0.149	4.142	0.01
4.	Father Education	2.334	0.667	0.108	5.339	0.01

* P < 0.01

Four variables viz Gender, Locality, Family income and Father Education have significantly contributed for predicting the learning styles among higher secondary students. The Gender seems to be 5.432, Locality seems to be 6.641, Family income seems to be 4.142 and Father education seems to be 5.339. The predictive value of these variables separately is 0.01.

Table 2 : Showing the Stepwise regression analysis predicting different method learning styles and demographic variables

Sl. No	Step/Source	Unstandardized Coefficients Beta	Std. Error	Standardized Coefficients Beta	Step t	P
1.	Type of Family	1.133	0.505	0.434	2.246	0.01
2.	Religion	1.248	0.466	0.782	2.677	0.01
3.	Community	1.792	0.683	0.646	2.625	0.01
4.	Birth Place	2.338	0.670	0.954	3.490	0.01

* P < 0.01

Four variables viz Type of family, Religion, Community and Birth place have significantly contributed for predicting the method learning styles. The first variable Type of family seems to be 2.246, Religion seems to be 2.677, Community seems to be 2.625 and Birth place seems to be 3.490. The predictive value of these variables separately is 0.01.

Table 3: Showing the Stepwise regression analysis predicting factors learning styles among higher secondary students and demographic variables

Sl. No	Step/Source	Unstandardized Coefficients Beta	Std. Error	Standardized Coefficients Beta	Step t	P
1.	Gender	5.195	1.030	0.824	5.041	0.01
2.	Family Monthly Income	1.809	0.451	0.443	4.016	0.01

* P < 0.01

Two variables viz Gender and Family Monthly Income have significantly contributed for predicting the factors learning styles among higher secondary. The first variable Gender seems to be 5.195, when paired with the second variable Family monthly income is 1.809. The predictive value of these variables separately is 0.01.

Table 4: Showing the correlation between the learning styles of higher secondary students and demographic variables

Factors	Learning styles of higher secondary students
Gender	0.579*
Locality	0.782**
Family Income	0.591*
Father Education	0.572*
Type of Family	0.824**

* Significant at 0.01 level ** Significant at 0.05 level

Learning styles of higher secondary students is positively and significantly related to Gender (0.579), Locality (0.782), Family Income (0.591), Father Education (0.572) and Type of family (0.824). So the direct relationship between the Learning styles of higher secondary students and demographic variables.

Conclusion

The present study aims to find out the higher secondary students learning styles. The researcher framed objectives and hypotheses on the basis of the above context. The research was carried out in 100 samples based randomly. A questionnaire constructed by R was used to collect the relevant data. After collecting the data they were analyzed using statistical tools such as Regression and Correlation analysis. The result concluded that students have average level of learning styles at Higher Secondary level in Biological science in Villupuram District.

References

Hammet Gandhi, H. & Varma, M. (2008). Elucidating Mathematical problem solving through met cognition. Journal of Indian Education, 30(3).

Kaholan & Vinod uppal, (2007) Womens attitude and achievement in relation to achievement motivation, Journal of Education and Psychology, Vol. xxxviii, No 3: 198-201.

Live, Carl (2008) Formative Assessment Pre- Test to Identify College students' Prior Knowledge, Misconceptions and Learning Difficulties in Biology. International Journals of Science and Mathematics Vol.4.

LongDon, Bernard (2013) Genetics - Are there inherent learning difficulties?

Lovelace, M. K. (2005). Meta-Analysis of Experimental Research Based on the Dunn and Dunn Model. Journal of Educational Research, 98(3), 176-183.

Malini, Sujatha (2006) The Attitude of special and Normal School Teachers towards children with Disabilities.

Mary Lou Koran, John J. Koran (2006) Individual and teacher/class effects in aptitude treatment studies, American Educational Research Journal, Vol.17, No.3: 291-302.

Mary Lou Koran, John J. Koran (2006) Individual and teacher/class effects in aptitude treatment studies, American Educational Research Journal, Vol.17, No.3: 291-302.

Robert B. Burns, (2012) The relation of aptitude to learning at different points in the time during instruction, Journal of Educational Psychology, Vol. 72, No.6: 705-789.

❐

4.

Educational-Digital skill

Introduction

There is a tremendous revolution in science and technology. Information in communication technologies has a deep Cultural Revolution changing. There is a need to make a realistic assessment of what technology cannot do to reach a plateau of productivity when the technology consistently delivers to realistic goals.

The impact of science and technology among students:

Digital skill is a vast technique used by all people. Educational technology and mobile learning, multi- media learning are all digital skill. Science is a boon. Man has discovered many wonderful things from the treasure of developing every day. It has made our life easier, happier and more secure. Science and technology has conquered time and space. It has made very good communication and made the transport easier. With the help of science and technology, modern medicine and medical treatments, the doctors save the life of sick people from the jaws of death. Many organs are now transplanted. It is used in the field of agriculture. The impact of science and technology among students in the field is both good and bad.

Science laboratory, space centre ISRO are taken in the highest form. Television, telecommunication, type- recorder, films, LCD projectors, digital and white board, e- learning, e-teaching, teleconferencing, teaching machine cell phones such as all types of multimedia are boons to us. But the students are affected by this because of misusing. So they blamed science. We cannot blame science. It is a wonderful boon.

Digital skill in website

By the wrong use of face book, web site, web-camera, especially cell phones, net connection, lab top etc. Science and technology become down. But once for all where we use science and technology in proper, correct and perfect way it is a boon to us otherwise it is curse and demon to us.

A secondary Information and Communication Technology curriculum should contribute to the building up of teams of professionals with these new competencies. The use of Information and Communication Technology cuts across all aspects of economic and social life. Technological developments in Information and Communication Technology are very rapid. Technology quickly becomes obsolete requiring new skills and knowledge to be mastered frequently. Adaptation is only possible when based on a sound understanding of the principles and concepts of Information and Communication Technology.

Review of Literature

Lei, Jing (2010) studied on Quantity versus Quality: A New Approach to Examine the Relationship between Technology Use and Student Outcomes. It is found that that to examine the relationship between technology use and student outcomes, the quality of technology use--how, and what, technology is used--is a more significant factor than the quantity of technology use--how much technology is used. This argument was exemplified by an empirical study that used both angles to examine the association between technology use and student outcomes. When only the quantity of technology use was examined, no significant association was observed. However, when the quality of technology was examined by investigating the specific types of technology uses, a significant association was identified between technology use and all student outcomes. Furthermore, different types of technology use showed different influences on specific student outcomes. General technology uses were positively associated with student technology proficiency, while subject-specific technology uses were negatively associated with student technology proficiency. Social-communication technology uses were significantly positively associated with developmental outcomes such as self-esteem and positive attitude towards school. Entertainment/exploration technology use showed significant positive association with student learning habits. None of these technology uses had significant influence on student academic outcome.

Chen, Rong-Ji (2010) studied on Investigating Models for Preservice Teachers' Use of Technology to Support Student-Centered Learning. The study addressed two limitations of previous research on factors related to teachers' integration of technology in their teaching. It attempted to test a structural equation model (SEM) of the relationships among a set of variables influencing preservice teachers' use of technology specifically to support student-centered learning. A review of literature led to a path model that provided the design and analysis for the study, which involved 206 preservice teachers in the United States. The results show that the proposed model had a moderate fit to the observed data, and a more parsimonious model was found to have a better fit. In addition, preservice teachers' self-efficacy of teaching with technology had the strongest influence on technology use, which was mediated by their perceived value of teaching and learning with technology. School's contextual factors had moderate influence on technology use. Moreover, the effect of preservice teachers' training on student-centered technology use was mediated by both perceived value and self-efficacy of technology. The implications for teacher preparation include close collaboration between teacher education program and field experience, focusing on specific technology uses.

Eisenberg, Mike; Johnson, Doug; Berkowitz, Bob (2010) studied on Information, Communications, and Technology (ICT) Skills Curriculum Based on the Big6 Skills Approach to Information Problem-Solving. There is clear and widespread agreement among the public and educators that all students need to be proficient technology users. Technology literacy is among the attributes that appear in nearly every set of "21st Century Skills." However, while districts spend a great deal of money on technology, there seems to be only a vague notion of what technology literacy really means. Defining and describing technology skills is only a first step to assure all children become proficient information and technology users. Other critical elements will include a teacher-supported scope and sequence of skills, well designed projects, and effective assessments. Equally essential is fruitful collaboration among classroom teachers, teacher librarians, and technology teachers in order to present students with a unified and integrated approach to ensure that all children master the skills they will need to thrive in an information-rich future. This article presents the "Information, Communications, and Technology (ICT) Skills for Information Problem Solving" curriculum which defines technology capabilities and identifies associated skills based on the Big6 Skills Approach. The Curriculum describes levels of technology proficiency, and in so doing, promotes the skills and concepts basic to information and technology. In an information society, it is essential that students are technologically productive and able to solve information problems effectively and efficiently. This curriculum requires more than teaching computer skills, technology hardware, and software programs in an isolated approach. An effective technology curriculum must be integrated across content areas and grade levels to improve the learning process. Technology is successfully integrated when it seamlessly supports curricular goals. Students learn and refine their technology skills when they work on projects that require them to solve problems and make decisions.

Savage, Robert S.; Erten, Ozlem; Abrami, Philip; Hipps, Geoffrey; Comaskey, Erin; van Lierop, Dea (2010) studied on ABRACADABRA in the Hands of Teachers: The Effectiveness of a Web-Based Literacy Intervention in Grade 1 Language Arts Programs . Each teacher chose to use the program in qualitatively distinct ways that corresponded to the first three stages of Sandholtz, Ringstaff, and Dwyer's (1997) technology integration model, namely: "Entry," "Adoption" and "Adaptation." Growth in literacy between pre- and post-test revealed significant differences associated with technology integration style across all measures of literacy and related language skills. The largest and most-widespread effects were evident for the "Adaptation" group that linked technology content to wider learning themes in the classroom. In terms of overall growth in standardised literacy scores across all six such measures used, Adaptation proved to be 60% more effective than Adoption. Results suggest that explorations of exactly how teachers use technology have important implications for practice as well as for the interpretation of field-based studies of the effectiveness of educational technology.

Jun, Han; Zhuzhu, Wang (2010) studied on Capability Building in Educational Technology for Teachers in China. This paper gives a brief introduction to the project called Education Technology Capacity Building Plan for All Primary and Secondary Teachers now being implemented in China. Because information and communication technology skills training cannot match the demand of teachers' professional development, the Chinese Ministry of Education established the education technology standard for teachers and launched the project. This paper introduced the features of standard training and testing, and discusses the output and influence of the project.

McGarr, Oliver (2010) studied on Education for Sustainable Development in Technology Education in Irish Schools: A Curriculum Analysis. This paper explores the integration of Education for Sustainable Development (ESD) in technology education and the extent to which it is currently addressed in curriculum documents and state examinations in technology education at post-primary level in Ireland. This analysis is conducted amidst the backdrop of considerable change in technology education at post-primary level. The analysis of the provision of technology education found, that among the range of technology related subjects offered, the study of Technology and Society is only addressed in one in a comprehensive manner. The paper discusses the implications of this limited integration, examines the factors inhibiting greater integration of ESD and outlines opportunities for future development.

Waring, Scott M. (2010) studied on The Impact of a Technology Coordinator's Belief System upon Using Technology to Create a Community's History. As it has been shown that teachers of social studies content are less likely than teachers of other content areas to utilize technology in their classroom, this study focuses on one instructional technology coordinators' beliefs towards technology, instruction, and students and how these beliefs impacted how technology was utilized during a technology-enriched community history project with a group of fourth-grade students. It was determined that the instructional technology coordinators' beliefs included the following: (a) technology should serve as a tool and should be seamlessly integrated into the curriculum; (b) the teacher should construct meaningful experiences that allow students to become engaged in the learning process; however, before guiding student discovery, the teacher needs to explicitly teach basic technological skills; (c) and all students are able to learn and are capable of engaging in independent problem solving and critical thinking at some level. Her beliefs manifested themselves daily, particularly in the way that she approached instruction and integrated technology seamlessly into the curriculum. Through this study, it was found that the technology coordinator's beliefs toward technology, instruction, and her students directly impacted how technology was used in her classroom.

Jun, Han; Zhuzhu, Wang (2010) studied on Capability Building in Educational Technology for Teachers in China. This paper gives a brief introduction to the project called Education Technology Capacity Building Plan for All Primary and Secondary Teachers now being implemented in China. Because information and communication technology skills training cannot match the demand of teachers' professional development, the Chinese Ministry of Education established the education technology standard for teachers and launched the project. This paper introduced the features of standard training and testing, and discusses the output and influence of the project.

Ruzic-Dimitrijevic, Ljiljana; Dimitrijevic, Maja (2010) studied on Challenges IT Instructors Face in the Self-Education Process. We find that the earlier the instructors graduated, the smaller is the chance they studied the technologies similar to the ones they teach. We found that none of the surveyed instructors who graduated before 1979 teach a technology they studied. The analysis of the survey also supports the second hypothesis. The results show that 70% of the IT instructors have to change the course syllabus every 2-3 years due to the technology changes. We also found that the majority of the instructors primarily use textbooks and online tutorials to self teach new technologies, which supports the third hypothesis. By comparison, they take courses given by others and work on real life projects far less often. In contrast, most instructors agree that taking courses and working on projects would greatly help them in their self-education. Most instructors (16 out of 20) assert that the lack of time stops them from doing so, which according to the survey is found to be one of the major challenges they face in the process of self-education, supporting the fourth hypothesis. Considering the results of our research, as well as our own experience, we have identified a list of activities that make the process of self-education more efficient and/or effective for IT instructors. These activities include taking on-line tutorials, creating software programs using the environment/ language/tools covered in the courses, working on real life projects, taking organized courses, attending IT/CS conferences, seminars, and workshops, collecting experience from industry people, and using the help of advanced students. However, in order to create the time for IT instructors to apply the self-learning methods and stay on top of the new technologies, we conclude that it may be necessary that the university policy include the time for self-learning as a significant part of IT instructors' everyday duties, i.e., as a part of their "job description".

Larson, Lotta; Kuhn, Cyndi Danner; Collins, Royce Ann; Balthazor, Gerri; Ribble, Mike; Miller, Teresa Northern (2009) studied on Technology Instruction: Fixing the Disconnect. High school students spend much of their educational journeys immersed in "old" literacies of paper, pencil, and print books. But outside of the classroom, they are exposed to information and communication technologies--such as blogs, wikis, Internet browsers, multimedia, social networking sites, and a wide range of software--each of which demand new literacies. This disconnect is a serious problem for schools because it reflects a decline in school's relevancy to students' futures, and the gap between how schools teach and how students learn will only grow over time. The first step in updating a school's technology and instruction is to revisit and revise current vision statements by facilitating conversations with all stakeholders about expectations for student skills upon graduation. Vision setting must include the new literacies. Teachers and education leaders must model expectations and support visionary teaching and learning through technology. To make that happen, they need instructional technology specialists who not only have a strong knowledge of hardware, networks, and equipment maintenance but also understand the art of teaching and how to enhance and enrich the daily curriculum by integrating technology. To do this, instructional technology staff members and those creating the curriculum must engage in ongoing dialogue to ensure that computer language is translated into the language of teaching and is directly related to what teachers want to do in their classrooms. For schools to successfully integrate technology, leaders must encourage and support strong relationships between teachers and technology support staff members. Schools must also provide easy access to technology in classrooms so that teachers can effectively integrate technology into the curriculum. Limited resources and complicated check-out procedures often contribute to lack of use. In addition, frustrations over blocked sites or limited access to online resources prevent teachers from integrating technology. Leaders, teachers, and technology staff members need ongoing communication with one another to share needs, frustrations, and solutions. Schools must move ahead quickly. It may be understandable for teachers and leaders to be a bit behind in the use of technology, but it is no longer adequate or appropriate to hold students back. Students today will be leaders in a global society, and technology can connect them to that world in ways that were unimaginable 10 years ago. School leaders need to join students in their world--which includes all of the new literacies--so that everyone can function and contribute to the future.

Objectives

- To study the level of teachers attitude towards using new technology in teaching
- To find out whether there is any significant relationship between teachers attitude towards the use of new technology and their interest in teaching.

Methodology

The methodology adopted for the study is explained in detail. The sampling technique, size of the sample, variables of the study, description of the tool used and administration of tool are elaborated.

Sample

The study was conducted on 100 school teachers, Coimbatore district, Tamil Nadu.

Data Collection

Primary data, required for the present research work were collected by conducting direct interviews using questionnaire. All the respondents were given sufficient information about the study. These respondents were provided with the same questionnaires. They were also informed that they have to answer in the same fashion.

Analysis and Interpretation

Gender and attitude towards the use of new technology

Null Hypothesis No. 1

There is no significant difference between male and female teachers attitude towards the use of new technology.

Table 1: The Significance of the difference ('t' value) between mean scores of male and female teacher's attitude towards the use of new technology

Gender	N	Mean	SD	't' value	Level of Significance (0.05)
Male	50	100.30	11.81	4.89	Significant
Female	50	107.30	12.57		

It is evident from the table the calculated 't' value is 4.89 is significant at 0.05 level. Hence, the framed null hypothesis is rejected and research hypothesis is accepted. It is inferred that there is significant difference found between male and female teachers attitude towards the use of new technology.

Qualification and attitude towards the use of new technology

Null Hypothesis No. 2

There is no significant difference between undergraduate and post graduate teachers with respect to their attitude towards the use of new technology.

Table 2: The significance of the difference ('t' value) between undergraduate and post graduate teachers with respect to their attitude towards the use of new technology.

Qualification	N	Mean	SD	't' value	Level of Significance (0.05)
Under graduate	35	103.64	11.44	0.28	Not Significant
Post graduate	65	103.23	13.53		

It is evident from the table the calculated 't' value is 0.28 which is not significant at 0.05 level. Hence, the framed null hypothesis is accepted. It shows that there is no significant difference between undergraduate and post graduate teachers with respect to their attitude towards the use of new technology.

Locality of the School and attitude towards the use of new technology

Null Hypothesis No. 3

There is no significant difference between rural and urban school teachers attitude towards the use of new technology.

Table 3: The Significance of the difference ('t' value) between rural and urban school teachers attitude towards the use of new technology

Locality of the school	N	Mean	SD	't' value	Level of Significance (0.05)
Rural	65	103.42	11.23	0.06	Not Significant
Urban	35	103.33	14.15		

It is evident from the table the calculated 't' value is 0.06 which is not significant at 0.05 level. Hence, the framed null hypothesis is accepted. It shows that there is no significant difference between rural and urban school teachers attitude towards the use of new technology.

Type of School and attitude towards the use of new technology

Null Hypothesis No. 4

There is no significant difference between private and government school teachers attitude towards the use of new technology.

Table 4: The Significance of the difference ('t' value) between private and government school teachers attitude towards the use of new technology

Type of School	N	Mean	SD	't' value	Level of Significance (0.05)
Private	65	104.79	11.54	1.26	Not Significant
Government	35	102.78	13.01		

It is evident from the table the calculated 't' value is 1.26 which is not significant at 0.05 level. Hence, the framed null hypothesis is accepted. It shows that there is no significant difference between private and government school teachers attitude towards the use of new technology.

Level of teaching and attitude towards the use of new technology

Null Hypothesis No. 5

There is no significant difference between secondary and higher secondary school teachers attitude towards the use of new technology.

Table 5: The Significance of the difference ('t' test) between secondary and higher secondary school teachers attitude towards the use of new technology

Level of teaching	N	**Mean**	**SD**	**'t' value**	**Level of Significance** (0.05)
Secondary School	60	102.12	12.12	1.85	Not Significant
Higher secondary School	40	104.82	13.03		

It is evident from the table the calculated 't' value is 1.85 which is not significant at 0.05 level. Hence, the framed null hypothesis is accepted. It is inferred that there is no significant difference between secondary and higher secondary school teachers attitude towards the use of new technology.

Teaching Experience and attitude towards the use of new technology

Null Hypothesis No. 6

There is no significant difference among teachers who have different years of teaching experience with respect to their attitude towards the use of new technology.

Table 6: The Significance of the difference ('F' test) among school teachers with respect to their attitude towards the use of new technology

Teaching Experience	Sum of Squares	Mean Squares	df	'F' Value	**Level of Significance** (0.05)
Between Groups	2281.690	1140.845	2	7.48	Significant
Within Groups	45273.227	152.435	97		
Total	47554.917	-	99		

It is evident from the table the calculated 'F' value is 7.48 which is significant at 0.05 level. Hence, the framed null hypothesis is rejected and research hypothesis is accepted. It is inferred that there is significant difference among teachers who have different years of teaching experience with respect to their attitude towards the use of new technology.

Table 7: The Significance of the difference ('t' test) between teachers who have different years of teaching experience with respect to their attitude towards the use of new technology

Teaching experience	N	Mean	SD	**'t' value**	**Level of Significance** (0.05)
Below 10 years	49	109.33	11.05	3.06	Significant
10-20 years	20	103.03	12.80		
Above 20 years	31	101.67	12.47	4.16	Significant
Below 10 years	49	109.33	11.05		
10-20 years	20	103.03	12.80	0.81	Not Significant
Above 20 years	31	101.67	12.47		

From table, it is revealed that there is significant difference between teachers who have below 10 years of teaching experience and 10-20 years of teaching experience and teachers who have above 20 years of teaching experience and below 10 years of teaching experience. Whereas no significant difference is found between teachers who have above 20 years of teaching experience and 10-20 years of teaching experience.

Correlation Analysis

Correlation Analysis between teachers attitude towards the use of new technology and interest in teaching

One of the important objectives of the present investigation is to study the significant relationship between teacher's attitude towards the use of new technology and interest in teaching. For this purpose, the investigator applied the co-efficient of correlation ('r'). The computed values are given in the table. The investigator also framed a null hypothesis for testing the relationship between teacher's attitude towards the use of new technology and interest in teaching.

Null hypothesis No. 8

There is no significant relationship between teacher's attitude towards the use of new technology and interest in teaching.

Table 8: Co-efficient of Correlation between teacher's attitude towards the use of new technology and interest in teaching

Correlation	N	'r' value	Level of Significance at 0.05 level
Teacher's attitude towards the use of new technology and interest in teaching	100	0.56	Significant

It is evident from the table the computed correlation coefficient 'r' for entire sample is 0.56, which is significant at 0.05 level. Hence, the framed null hypothesis is rejected. It is inferred that there is significant relationship found between teacher's attitude towards the use of new technology and their interest in teaching.

Suggestions

The present study gives a clear-cut view about the present position of teachers attitude towards the use of new technology and their interest in teaching. Based on the important findings stated earlier the following recommendations are suggested.

Teachers must be provided with adequate opportunities to enhance their knowledge in new technologies and equipments. The government should provide more effective environment through schools for them to improve their skills in application of new technologies in teaching.

Periodical in-service training programmes should be organized to keep their interest and quest in teaching.

The finding of the present study reveals that the teachers have neutral attitude towards the use of new technology in teaching and low interest in teaching. This indicates that the Heads of the institutions must look into the varied problems that influence the interest of teachers and find amicable solutions to their difficulties.

More activities should be planned in the curriculum to bring forth different modes of creative expressions which will provide competition and generate interest of teachers in teaching.

Sincere work and involved performances of teachers must be recognized and honoured by the authorities. And application of innovative methods and technologies in instruction must be encouraged.

In addition with the above recommendation the government and all the other concerned authorities should realize the problems of experienced teachers and provide conductive environment of growth and mutual help of teachers should be ensured.

Conclusion

The present study is conducted on teachers attitude towards the use of new technologies in teaching and their interest in teaching. The findings of the present study revealed that the teachers have neutral attitude towards the use of new technology and low interest in teaching. Therefore, the authorities and government should find suitable measures to improve the interest of teachers in teaching and the application of innovative technologies in Teaching Learning Process.

References

Larson, Lotta; Kuhn, Cyndi Danner; Collins, Royce Ann; Balthazor, Gerri; Ribble, Mike; Miller, Teresa Northern (2009) Technology Instruction: Fixing the Disconnect. Principal Leadership, v10 n4 p54-58.

Chen, Rong-Ji (2010) Investigating Models for Preservice Teachers' Use of Technology to Support Student-Centered Learning. Computers & Education, v55 n1 p32-42.

Eisenberg, Mike; Johnson, Doug; Berkowitz, Bob (2010) Information, Communications, and Technology (ICT) Skills Curriculum Based on the Big6 Skills Approach to Information Problem-Solving. Library Media Connection, v28 n6 p24-27.

Jun, Han; Zhuzhu, Wang(2010) Capability Building in Educational Technology for Teachers in China British Journal of Educational Technology, v41 n4 p607-611.

Lei, Jing (2010) Quantity versus Quality: A New Approach to Examine the Relationship between Technology Use and Student Outcomes. 2010.

Lesisko, Lee J.; Wright, Robert J.; O'Hern, Brenda (2010) Technology

Integration: A Best Practice Perspective. Online Submission, Paper presented at the Annual Meeting of the Eastern Educational Research Association (Savannah, GA, Feb 10-13, 2010).

McGarr, Oliver (2010) Education for Sustainable Development in Technology Education in Irish Schools: A Curriculum Analysis. International Journal of Technology and Design Education, v20 n3 p317-332.

Ruzic-Dimitrijevic, Ljiljana; Dimitrijevic, Maja (2010) Challenges IT Instructors Face in the Self-Education Process. Journal of Information Technology Education, v9 pIIP-35-IIP-48.

Savage, Robert S.; Erten, Ozlem; Abrami, Philip; Hipps, Geoffrey; Comaskey, Erin; van Lierop, Dea (2010) ABRACADABRA in the Hands of Teachers: The Effectiveness of a Web-Based Literacy Intervention in Grade 1 Language Arts Programs . Computers & Education, v55 n2 p911-922.

Shapley, Kelly; Sheehan, Daniel; Maloney, Catherine; Caranikas-Walker, Fanny (2010) Effects of Technology Immersion on Teachers' Growth in Technology Competency, Ideology, and Practices. Journal of Educational Computing Research, v42 n1 p1-33.

❐

5.

An Assessment of Edu Digital Skills of Teachers in Namakkal District

Introduction

Teacher is an ideal personality whose knowledge and skill play a major role in the development of the nation to the global standard education in general and tapping the potentialities of students to the maximum extent in particular. Teachers are expected to learn forever to withstand the innovations in teaching and updating the knowledge and widen the clarity of the conceptual framework of the subject of specialization too. Unless and until the teachers prepared to meet the requirements and challenges, the dream and purpose of education will not be fulfilled. Nowadays the system of education has assumed the character which involves more students' participation and student centric which is highly enabled through the application of various educational technologies. Edu - digital skills is considered prerequisite for all teachers teaching for nursery to doctorate scholars. 21st century school curriculum has been enriched to meet the demands of world requirements of quality. Communication, collaboration, critical thinking, problem solving, creativity, invention, information and technology literacy and self direction will facilitate the achievement of aims and objectives of education. Teachers of 21st century are expected to equip themselves with modern technology application in teaching and learning process. A paradigm shift has happened to meet the demands of gen y and z learners which require innovative, explorative and interesting approach in teaching and learning. The curriculum will need withstand the futuristic vision for the global scenario. At this juncture the teachers of today should be enthusiastic to update their knowledge and skills forever in order to keep young to the youngest generation whom they meet and it may also be emphasized greatly as the professional ethics. This study has been attempted to assess the knowledge and skills of teachers in the field of information and communication technology which a teacher necessarily possess in the digital world.

Teacher is an ideal personality whose knowledge and skill play a major role in the development of the nation to the global standard education in general and tapping the potentialities of students to the maximum extent in particular. Teachers are expected to learn forever to withstand the innovations in teaching and updating the knowledge and widen the clarity of the conceptual framework of the subject of specialization too. Unless and until the teachers prepared to meet the requirements and challenges, the dream and purpose of education will not be fulfilled. Nowadays the system of education has assumed the character which involves more students' participation and student centric which is highly enabled through the application of various educational technologies. Edu - digital skills is considered prerequisite for all teachers teaching for nursery to doctorate scholars. 21st century school curriculum has been enriched to meet the demands of world requirements of quality. Communication, collaboration, critical thinking, problem solving, creativity, invention, information and technology literacy and self direction will facilitate the achievement of aims and objectives of education. Teachers of 21st century are expected to equip themselves with modern technology application in teaching and learning process. A paradigm shift has happened to meet the demands of gen y and z learners which require innovative, explorative and interesting approach in teaching and learning. The curriculum will need withstand the futuristic vision for the global scenario. At this juncture the teachers of today should be enthusiastic to update their knowledge and skills forever in order to keep young to the youngest generation whom they meet and it may also be emphasized greatly as the professional ethics. This study has been attempted to assess the knowledge and skills of teachers in the field of information and communication technology which a teacher necessarily possess in the digital world.

Educational Digital Skills

It is mentioned that in order to thrive in a digital economy, students will need digital age proficiencies. It is important for the educational system to make parallel changes in order to fulfill its mission in society, namely the preparation of students for the world beyond the classroom. Therefore, the educational system must understand and embrace the following 21st century skills within the context of rigorous academic standards.

The 21st Century Literacy Summit (2002) contends that "the explosive growth of technology in every aspect of society offers us a unique opportunity to engage our citizens in economic and civic life" The report further states that to take advantage of this opportunity, we must continually acquire and develop new knowledge and skills. Summit participants noted "Information and communication technologies are raising the bar on the competencies needed to succeed in the 21st century, and they are compelling us to revisit many of our assumptions and beliefs" The sheer magnitude of human knowledge, world to technology necessitates a shift in our children's education - from plateaus of knowing to continuous cycles of learning. Therefore, policymakers and educators alike must define 21st century skills, highlighting the relationship of those skills to conventional academic standards. As they do so, they must also recognize the need for multiple assessments to measure these skills within the context of academic standards, evaluating their application to today's technological and global society.

Technological Literacy

Demonstrate a sound conceptual understanding of the nature of technology systems and view themselves as proficient users of these systems. Understand and model positive, ethical use of technology in both social and personal contexts. Use a variety of technology tools in effective ways to increase creative productivity. Use communication tools to reach out to the world beyond the classroom and communicate ideas in powerful ways. Use technology effectively to access, evaluate, process and synthesize information from a variety of sources. Use technology to identify and solve complex problems in real-world contexts have been considered as Technological Literacy

Information Literacy

Before Accessing Information one should determine what is known and what is needed for problem solving, identify different sources of information, including text, people, video, audio, and databases and prioritize sources based on credibility and relevance. When Accessing Information one need identify and retrieve relevant information from sources and use technology to enhance searching. Revise information-gathering strategies that prove to be in effective when understands how information retrieved does or does not address original problem, evaluate information in terms of credibility and know what are the social, economic, political, legal, and ethical issues that may impact it to facilitate to use technology for evaluation. After Information is extracted, using retrieved information to accomplish a specific purpose, present information clearly and persuasively by using a range of technology tools and media and evaluate the processes and products of these activities have here been considered essential to assure one to be Literate in information.

Global Awareness

Global awareness is knowledge about the connectedness of the nations of the world historically, politically, economically, technologically, socially, linguistically, and ecologically and understand that these interconnections of positive benefits and negative consequences too. The ability to recognize, analyzes, and evaluates major trends in global relations and the interconnections of these trends with both their local and national communities. Participate in the global society by staying current with international news and by participating in the democratic process.

Objectives of the Study

To find the level of Edu-digital skill among school teachers and find whether there is significant different exist among them in relation to their personal variables such as sex, Age, Educational Qualification, Area of Residence, Management of the Institution, Subject of Specialization and the Location of the School.

Research Question

What is the level of educational digital Skills of School Teachers? Is there any Significant Difference Exists among them with respect to their Personal Variables?

Research Methodology

A Normative Descriptive Method of study has been attempted to assess the level of Educational Digital Skills among the School Teachers in Namakkal District.

Population, Sample and Sampling Technique of the Study

All teachers who teach in school education are the population of the study and the sample of the study has been chosen from teachers work in Namakkal district only and the sample was taken by stratified random sampling technique which consists of 250.

Tools and Technique of Data Collection

A tool consisted of 24 items related to some basic skills necessary for adopting computer enabled teaching technology, using internet connection which will benefit students to gain knowledge, understand the concept better, improve the critical thinking, problem solving ability, creativity and to enhance their communication skill and appropriate application of the knowledge gained for the betterment of himself and to the society. The scope of this study extent all teachers who teach in the classroom from kindergarten to plus two levels. The questionnaire has dimensions of using the computer for retrieving useful information via internet, knowledge about various search engines, and preparation of effective PowerPoint materials, video clippings, software package application, audio recording, connecting to virtual classroom and the facilities to publish the students works in internet. Knowledge and the application of MS word, Excel format, mobile for teaching and learning purpose and the ability to set ready LCD, mike and arrange show in the smart classroom and the application of social media in education have also been taken for assessing.

Scoring Procedure & Statistical Tools Used

Questionnaire used in the study has five point scale of the level of skill of the respondents in relation to their digital skill hence it has five options of known very well, known, moderately known, known little and Unknown which scored as 5, 4,3,2 and 1 respectively.

SPSS package has been used to analyze the data and the percentage analysis and the differential analysis have been used to describe and infer the details pertaining to the research question formulated for the study.

Table -1: An Analysis of Edu Digital Skills among Teachers in Namakkal District

Items	Very well Known		Well Known		Moderately Known		Known Little		Unknown		Total
	F	%	F	%	F	%	F	%	F	%	
Information Retrieval	41	16.4	59	23.6	62	24.8	75	30	13	5.2	250
Power point preparation	52	20.8	67	26.8	53	21.2	60	24	18	7.2	250
Efficient use of Windows operating system	35	14	48	19.2	75	30	81	32.4	11	4.4	250
Connecting to the Online Teaching of World Classroom	15	6	20	8	39	15.6	116	46.4	60	24	250
Skill in make it work well of LCD mike screen view	15	6	26	10.4	77	30.8	114	45.6	18	7.2	250
Knowledge about E learning material preparation	21	8.4	15	6	27	10.8	129	51.6	58	23.2	250
Account in social networking sites like Face-book, twitter	22	8.8	36	14.4	74	29.6	12	4.8	106	42.4	250
Using of videos and computer games in teaching	19	7.6	29	11.6	55	22	85	34	62	24.8	250
Application of Virtual classrooms and chat rooms in teaching and learning	13	5.2	18	7.2	17	6.8	56	22.4	146	58.4	250
Application of documentary film in deliverance of the instructional objectives	51	20.4	60	24	41	16.4	31	12.4	67	26.8	250

Items	Very well Known		Well Known		Moderately Known		Known Little		Unknown		Total
Using of web-Camera in virtual interaction	16	6.4	41	16.4	27	10.8	71	28.4	95	38	250
Application of white Board in teaching	25	10	16	6.4	19	7.6	43	17.2	147	58.8	250
Safety and security issues in using webmail	17	6.8	39	15.6	90	36	70	28	44	17.6	250
Security Challenges in instant messaging	15	6	35	14	78	31.2	98	39.2	24	9.6	250
Application of iPod and tables in teaching	11	4.4	23	9.2	67	26.8	80	32	69	27.6	250
Application of Video conferencing for teaching and learning	32	12.8	24	9.6	71	28.4	90	36	33	13.2	250
Application of YouTube	49	19.6	86	34.4	55	22	62	24.8	38	15.2	250
Application of Flicker & Picasa	19	7.6	25	10	62	24.8	104	41.6	40	16	250
Application of mobile phone for transferring data of video	21	8.4	27	10.8	80	32	90	36	32	12.8	250
Application of mobile phone for transferring data of voice	22	8.8	33	13.2	76	30.4	81	32.4	38	15.2	250
Application of mobile phone for transferring data of text	187	74.8	46	18.4	3	1.2	9	3.6	5	2	250

Items	Very well Known		Well Known		Moderately Known		Known Little		Unknown		Total
Assessment of students performance through online	25	10	52	20.8	58	23.2	105	42	10	4	250
Application of learning Management System - LMS	11	4.4	21	8.4	37	14.8	57	22.8	15	6	250
Application of Video-recording	17	6.8	26	10.4	51	20.4	78	31.2	78	31.2	250

Majority of teachers have necessary in Skill and knowledge in the application of MS office, Mobile technology in teaching and learning, information retrieval system from online resource centre but the majority teachers have moderate and least knowledge about e-content preparation, application of social media, and security issues in web mails, various learning management system and efficient use of ICT in teaching

Table -2: Significance of Difference in Edu-Digital Skill of Teachers

Demographic Variables	P Value	.Level of Sig
Sex	0.153	NS
Area of Residence	0.104	NS
Location of the School	0.214	NS
Teaching Experience	0.098	NS
Educational Qualification	0.521	NS
Management of the School	*0.021	S
Subject of Specialization	**0.001	S

There is no significant difference exist among the respondents in their Educational digital skill in relation to their personal variables of Sex, Area of Residence, Location of the School, Teaching Experience and their educational qualification. But the statistical report of analysis shows that there is significant difference exist among the sample in relation to their management of the school and their subject of specialization.

Educational Implications

Teacher Education curriculum should emphasize the ICT enabled education in B.Ed program

Workshops need to be conducted for B.Ed program in the practical application of ICT and training program can be organized for E- content preparation

Orientation and Refresher courses for the teachers in schools should be conducted frequently to enable teachers to facilitate them in the efficient use of ICT in teaching and learning environment

Collaborative Approach should be made in integrating ICT in education

Conclusion

Teachers are the forerunner of all developments and growth of the nation and the world; they play a significant role in bringing desirable outcome in the world with their adaptability and their ever learning behavior of updating knowledge and skills in any field. No technology can replace the teacher in any period of time but the teacher needs possess skills in the application of technology which facilitate desirable educational outcome in the field of education.

References

Felix.A & Jahitha Begum (2011) "An Awareness of E-resources related to ICT and Education among M.Ed Students and M.Phil Scholars" ICT in teaching and learning, APH Publishing Corporation, New Delhi, p.169

Nagarajan .K (2009) "Educational Innovations and Management" Ram Publishers, Chennai. Pp.135-185.

Natchimuthu.K (2012), "Need of E-Content Development in Education Today" APH Publication Corporation, New Delhi. P.76.

Rangarajan. P & Senthilnathan.S (2012) "Teacher Educators Attitude towards E Learning" Edutracks, Vol.No.12 No.1 pp. 21-32.

www.educatorstechnology.com/2012/06/33-digital-skills-every-21st-century.htm

http://www.educatorstechnology.com/2013/07/the-8-digital-skills-students-need-for.html

❐

6.

Hyper Diversed Teacher and Digital Skills

Introduction

Social media have risen to prominence in recent years, beginning first with sites like Classmates in the mid-1990s, followed by Friendsterin 2003. The most significant growth of social media has occurred since 2004 when Facebook.com was introduced. Today there are over 550 million Facebook users alone, along with millions more using sites such as Twitter, MySpace, Plaxo, LinkedIn and others. While early adopters of these sites were digital natives (i.e., those born and/or raised in the internet era), all age groups are now embracing these sites. Teacher Educators and Student teachers always find it easier to use the already made teaching aids for teaching practice for preparation of lessons and in their theory learning and submission of assignments .in such situation the modern technology i.e. internet is challenging them to be more innovative, explorative and modern in their teaching and learning experiences . Teaching faculty is challenged by the digital world to be in pursuit of skills development. At present there is a gap between campus pedagogy and social media usage among students and faculty. Teaching community need to be skilled digitally. This paper works to examine that chasm, and to draw some conclusions as to why it may be time to incorporate this technology into our classrooms. The researcher used the self constructed tool HYPER ADOPTION SCALE (HAS) to achieve this motive. The samples were 100 teacher educators and 200 student teachers. In methodology the statistical used were MEAN, Standard Deviation and't' test. The findings show that the level of hyper diversification among the samples is high, and there is no significant difference among the samples based on the variables Locality, Residence, Status(teacher educators/student teachers) and Educational qualification(UG/PG). However there exists a significant difference in term of Browsing habit. The educational implications suggest ways to diversify the teaching community and empower them digitally.

Social media have risen to prominence in recent years, beginning first with sites like Classmates in the mid-1990s, followed by Friendsterin 2003. The most significant growth of social media has occurred since 2004 when Facebook.com was introduced. Today there are over 550 million Facebook users alone, along with millions more using sites such as Twitter, MySpace, Plaxo, LinkedIn and others. While early adopters of these sites were digital natives (i.e., those born and/or raised in the internet era), all age groups are now embracing these sites. At present there is a gap between campus pedagogy and social media usage among students and faculty. Teaching community need to be skilled digitally. This paper works to examine that chasm, and to draw some conclusions as to why it may be time to incorporate this technology into our classrooms.

Need For the Study

Social media sites such as Face book and Twitter have come to dominate internet usage in recent years. Face book alone has over 550 million users as of fall 2010, while Twitter claims over 100 million users. While academia was fairly quick to adopt online education models in the 1990s, it has thus far not yet embraced social media portals as a way to deliver course content and engage students. This may be due to uncertainties regarding student perceptions about social media, its purposes, and its applications. Teacher Educators and Student teachers always find it easier to use the already made teaching aids for teaching practice for preparation of lessons and in their theory learning and submission of assignments .in such situation the modern technology i.e. internet is challenging them to be more innovative , explorative and modern in their teaching and learning experiences . Teaching faculty is challenged by the digital world to be in pursuit of skills development. Hence the need for the study.

Background of the Study

The researcher is involved in the educational institution which is in the forefront to promote quality of pedagogy. The experience of the researcher has often been frustrating with lack of digital climate .Since the Tamil Nadu Teachers Education University has created a platform for such pondering this study found its way out to reach out to the professional mob to leverage the educational system through virtualization of the academia. The HD (Hyper Diversified) Classroom is the need of the hour. Just as the digital divide vanished over time (males once dominated all computer and internet usage), it is possible that similar usage divides will also disappear. Online college courses, for example, have broad-based appeal, and even traditional campus-based courses often have high computer usage expectations. Given that social media are now part of the cultural fabric, it is necessary to explore if and how social media might find their place in academia. Therefore the researcher undertook this study.

Sample for the Study

300 Samples Comprising Teacher Educators and Student Teachers (100 teacher Educators and 200 Student Teachers)

Objectives of the Study

1. To construct a tool to find out the level of hyper diversification among teacher educators and student teachers
2. To realize the importance of hyper diversification and developing digital skills among teacher educators and student teachers.
3. To find out whether any difference exists among teacher educators and student teachers in their hyper diversification and digital skills in terms of the following variables:
   - Locality
   - Residence
   - Status(teacher/student)
   - Educational qualification(UG/PG)
   - Browsing habit
   - Hypotheses of the Study

The level of hyper diversification among teacher educators and student teachers is high.

There is a significant difference among teacher educators and student teachers in their hyper diversification and digital skills in terms of the following variables:

- Locality
- Residence
- Status(teacher/student)
- Educational qualification(UG/PG)
- Browsing habit

Methodology

In order to carry out the study the researcher used the following statistical

Standard Deviation

Standard deviation was calculated by the following formula

Where = Mean

X = Individual score

N = Total Number of the scores

Test of significant difference ('t' test)

Since the groups were large independent samples, the 't' test was applied through the statistical package by using the following formula:

Where M_1 - denotes mean of group 1

M_2 - denotes mean of group 2

σ_1 - denotes standard deviation of group 1

σ_2 - denotes standard deviation of group 2

N_1 - denotes total number of respondents in group 1

N_2 - denotes total number of respondents in group 2

Hypothesis 1

The level of hyper diversification and digital skills among teacher educators and student teachers is high.

Table 1 showing the analysis of hyper diversification and digital skills among teacher Educators and student teachers.

Entire Sample	N	Mean	S.D
Hyper Diversification	300	109.1	2.79
Digital Skills	300	24.21	3.40

The above table 1 shows that the mean and standard deviation on hyper diversification of the entire sample of teacher educators and student teachers' scores are 109.1 and 2.79 respectively. As 109.1 is higher than the mid-value of 64.1 (maximum score 129), it is concluded that the teacher educators and student teachers have a high level of hyper diversification. The mean and standard deviation on digital skills of the entire sample of teacher educators and student teachers' scores are 24.21 and 3.40 respectively. As 24.21 is higher than the mid-value of15 (maximum score 30), it is concluded that the teacher educators and student teachers have a high level of hyper diversification and digital skills.

Hypothesis 2(a): There is a significant difference among teacher educators and student Teachers in their hyper diversification and digital skills in terms of Locality.

The details of the results of the't' test in the level of hyper diversification and digital skills among teacher educators and student teachers based on Locality is given in table no.2.

Table- 2 Difference in the level of hyper diversification and digital skills based on Locality

Variables	Sub variables	N	Mean	SD	't' value	Level of Significance	Result
Locality	Urban	160	21.31	3.12	**1.13**	**0.05**	**NS**
	Rural	140	23.52	2.86			

It is evident from table no.2 that the calculated't' value 1.13 is less than the table value 1.96 at 0.05 level. This shows that there is no significant difference among teacher educators and student teachers in their hyper diversification and digital skills in terms of Locality.

Hence, there is no significant difference between the samples (teacher educators and student teachers) that live in Urban and Rural areas in their hyper diversification and digital skills.

Hypothesis 2(b): There is a significant difference among teacher educators and student teachers in their hyper diversification and digital skills in terms of Residence.

The details of the results of the 't' test in the level of hyper diversification and digital skills among teacher educators and student teachers based on Residence is given in table no.3.

Table- 3 Difference in the level of hyper diversification and digital skills based on Residence

Variables	Sub variables	N	Mean	SD	' t' value	Level of Significance	Result
Residence	Hostel	130	22.42	3.40	**1.049**	**0.05**	**NS**
	Home	170	25.63	4.60			

It is evident from table no.3 that the calculated 't' value 1.049 is less than the table value 1.96 at 0.05 levels. This shows that there is no significant difference among teacher educators and student teachers in their hyper diversification and digital skills in terms of Residence.

Hence, there is no significant difference between the samples (teacher educators and student teachers) who reside at hostel and at home in their hyper diversification and digital skills.

Hypothesis (2C): There is a significant difference among teacher educators and student teachers in their hyper diversification and digital skills in terms of Status (teacher educator/student teacher).

The details of the results of the 't' test in the level of hyper diversification and digital skills among teacher educators and student teachers based on Status((teacher educator/student teacher) is given in table no.4.

Table- 4 Difference in the level of hyper diversification and digital skills based on Status (teacher educator/student teacher)

Variables	**Sub variables**	**N**	**Mean**	**SD**	**t' value '**	**Level of Significance**	**Result**
STATUS	Teacher Educators	100	20.24	3.983	**1.61**	**0.05**	**NS**
	Student Teachers	200	22.57	3.793			

It is evident from table no.4 that the calculated 't' value 1.61 is less than the table value 1.96 at 0.05 levels. This shows that there is no significant difference among teacher educators and student teachers in their hyper diversification and digital skills in terms of Status.

Hence, there is no significant difference between the samples (teacher educators and student teachers) in Status in their hyper diversification and digital skills.

Hypothesis 2(d): There is a significant difference among teacher educators and student teachers in their hyper diversification and digital skills in terms of Educational Qualification (UG/PG).

The details of the results of the 't' test in the level of hyper diversification and digital skills among teacher educators and student teachers based on Educational Qualification(UG/PG) Is given in table no.5.

Table – 5 Difference in the level of hyper diversification and digital skills based on Educational Qualification(UG/PG)

Variables	Sub Variables	N	Mean	SD	' t' value	Level of Significance	Result
Educational Qualification	UG	100	22.35	3.902	**1.21**	**0.05**	**NS**
	PG	200	21.50	3.340			

It is evident from table no.5 that the calculated 't' value 1.21 is less than the table value 1.96 at 0.05 levels. This shows that there is no significant difference among teacher educators and student teachers in their hyper diversification and digital skills in terms of Educational Qualification(UG/PG).

Hence, there is no significant difference among teacher educators and student teachers in their hyper diversification and digital skills in terms of Educational Qualification (UG/PG).

Hypothesis 2(e): There is a significant difference among teacher educators and student teachers in their hyper diversification and digital skills in terms of Browsing habit. The details of the results of the 't' test in the level of hyper diversification and digital skills among teacher educators and student teachers based on browsing habit is given in table no.6

Table – 6 Difference in the level of hyper diversification and digital skills based on Browsing Habit

Variable	Sub variables	N	Mean	SD	' t' value	Level of Significance	Result
Browsing Habit	Frequently	120	17.73	3.679	**5.820**	**0.05**	S
	Rarely	180	19.28	3.431			

It is evident from table no.6 that the calculated 't' value 5.820 is higher than the table value 1.96 at 0.05 levels. This shows that there is a significant difference among teacher educators and student teachers in their hyper diversification and digital skills in terms of Browsing habit.

Hence, there is a significant difference among teacher educators and student teachers in their hyper diversification and digital skills in terms of Browsing habit.

Hypotheses Verification

The level of hyper diversification among teacher educators and student teachers is high-**Accepted**

There is a significant difference among teacher educators and student teachers in their hyper diversification and digital skills in terms of of Locality - **Rejected**

There is a significant difference among teacher educators and student teachers in their hyper diversification and digital skills in terms of Residence - **Rejected**

There is a significant difference among teacher educators and student teachers in their hyper diversification and digital skills in terms of Status(teacher/student) - **Rejected**

There is a significant difference among teacher educators and student teachers in their hyper diversification and digital skills in terms of educational qualification(UG/PG) - **Rejected**

There is a significant difference among teacher educators and student teachers in their hyper diversification and digital skills in terms of Browsing habit - **Accepted**

Educational Implications

The result of the study leads to encourage Teacher Educators Student teachers to be hyper diversified and digitally skilled .

The usage of virtual world can be enhanced in colleges to develop skills and build capacity as part of professional life.

Therefore Teacher Educators and Student Teachers can:

- create and edit digital audios
- use Social bookmarking to share resources with and between learners
- use blogs and wikis to create online platforms for students
- Exploit digital images for classroom use
- Use video content to engage students
- Use infographics to visually stimulate students
- Use Social networking sites to connect with colleagues and grow professionally
- Create and deliver asynchronous presentations and training sessions
- Compile a digital e-portfolio for their own development
- Have a knowledge about online security
- be able to detect plagiarized works in students assignments
- Create screen capture videos and tutorials
- Curate web content for classroom learning
- Use and provide students with task management tools to organize their work and plan their learning
- Use polling software to create a real-time survey in class
- Understand issues related to copyright and fair use of online materials
- Exploit computer games for pedagogical purposes

- Use digital assessment tools to create quizzes
- Use of collaborative tools for text construction and editing
- Find and evaluate authentic web based content
- Identify online resources that are safe for students browsing
- Use digital tools for time management purposes
- Learn about the different ways to use YouTube in your classroom
- Use note taking tools to share interesting content with your students
- Annotate web pages and highlight parts of text to share with your class
- Use of online graphic organizers and printables
- Use of online sticky notes to capture interesting idea
- Use of screen casting tools to create and share tutorials
- Exploit group text messaging tools for collaborative project work
- Conduct an effective search query with the minimum time possible
- Conduct A Research Paper Using Digital Tools
- Use file sharing tools to share docs and files with students online
- Reduce Infrastructure Costs Through Consolidation
- Virtualize the Most Demanding Workloads
- Virtualize for High Availability
- Improve Security and Reliability with Microkernelized Hypervisor
- Protect Important Data Using Live Backup
- Minimize Downtime with Quick Migration
- Delegate Virtual Machine Management
- Reduce Support Time with Integrated Management
- Save Time and Money with a More Flexible Test Environment
- Take Advantage of Broad Compatibility
- Reduce Support Time with Integrated Management
- Save Time and Money with a More Flexible Test Environment
- Take Advantage of Broad Compatibility
- Exploit Facebook,Youtube,Flickr and Social networking Sites(SNS) for sharing edu-information
- Use Smart phones, i phones, tablets as educational resources.

Accomplish content delivery and student engagement by creating and maintaining a Fan Page, at no cost to anyone involved, and completely away from the limitations of course management systems such as Black board, Angel and WebCT.

Bibliography

Baird, D., Fisher, M. (2005). Neomillennial user experience strategies: Utilizing social networking media to support "always on" learning styles. Journal of Educational Technology Systems. 34 (1) 5 - 32.

Bimber, B. (2000). Measuring the gender gap on the Internet. Social Sciences Quarterly, 81 (3):25-32.

Broos, A. (2005). Gender and information and communication technologies (ICT) anxiety: Male self-assurance and female hesitation. Cyber psychology & Behavior8(1):21-31.

Dennis, A.R., Kinney, S.T., & Hung, Y.T.C. (1999) Gender differences in the effects of media richness.Small Group Research . 30 (4): 405-437.

Dillon, D. (2001). E-books: The University of Texas Experience. Library Hi Tech. 19 (4) 350-62.

Gefen, D. & Straub, D. W. (1997) Gender differences in the perception and use of email: an extension to the technology acceptance model. MIS Quarterly 4: 389-400.

Horowitz, R. & Mohum, A. (1998). His and Hers: Gender Consumption & Technology. University of Virginia Press.

Jackson L.A., Ervin, K.S., Gardner, P.D. & Schmitt,N. (2001). Gender and the internet: women communicating and men searching.

Lenhart, M. (2010). Teens and Social Media, An Overview. Pew Internet and American Life Project.

Summerfield, M., Mandel, C., Kantor, P. (1999). Online books at Columbia: Early findings on use, satisfaction, and effect. Technology and Scholarly Communication. Berkley; University of California Press 282-308.

Wilska, A. (2003). Mobile use as part of young people's consumption styles.

❐

7.

Effectiveness of Computer Based Multimedia Learning Material

Introduction

Performance and behavioural outcome of the student is important aspects in school education here performance refers knowledge uplifted from the course of study. Behaviour outcome refers to social behaviour like responsible co-operation. Now a day complete is using in the entire field for the various purpose. In our education computer is used for giving instruction, administration and research. CAT, programmed instruction, PSI all is innovations in educational field to improve the performance. So the researcher has as her rightly chosen the study of the relevant effectiveness of computer based multimedia learning material on performance and behaviour outcome of high school students. The present study to find out the relevant effectiveness of computer based multimedia learning material on performance and behaviour outcome in Tindivanam Town. A samples of 100 respondents selected randomly were studied. A questionnaire method of survey was used to find out the effectiveness of computer based multimedia learning material on performance and behaviour outcome. The data were collected by using questionnaire as an instrument. Primary data were collected by conducting direct structured interview using questionnaire. All the respondents were asked the same questions in the same fashion and they were informed the purpose of study. T-test, One Way ANOVA and Correlation analysis was applied to test the hypotheses. The findings and observations are the result and outcome of the interpretations made during the study of analysis. The result found that there is a significant difference between traditional method and computer method of teaching.

Multimedia refers to any computer-mediated software or interactive application that integrates text, color, graphical images, animation, audio sound, and full motion video in a single application. Multimedia learning systems consist of animation and narration, which offer a potential venue for improving student understanding. Multimedia programme is an integral part of the educational technology. As a technique, it offers a high potential in application at different stages of education for the purpose of enhancing the teaching and learning processes, as is evident from the experience of developed countries.

The integration of multimedia technology into the communication environment has the potential to transform the students from passive recipients of information to active participants in a media-rich learning process. The introduction of multimedia or any other computer-based information technology is not intended to substitute a presenter. This new technology is intended to provide the presenter with a powerful tool that can greatly enhance communication by delivering a multisensory experience. With interactive multimedia technology, a teacher can communicate with the students by means of a presentation that becomes more than message-it becomes an active, exciting experience in a multisensory environment to create a multisensory experience. Multimedia reaches users in many different ways, enabling them to retain more knowledge and increase their understanding.

There are 4 steps in learning like attention, rehearsal, encoding and retrieval. A well designed multimedia application demands the simultaneous attention of several senses through dual encoding or the process of appealing to more than one sense simultaneously. Dual encoding facilitates and enhances the rehearsal process. Multimedia helps retrieval by associating sound, text and images with the concept being presented. Using text, images, animation and sound simultaneously greatly improves the students' retention of the knowledge and directs the students' attention to classroom (Louis, 2001).

Multimedia consists of the combination of video and movie clips and sound, text and graphic files all controlled by a piece of software and a computer which is equipped with a sound card, a video card, a CD-ROM drive and speakers or headphone. Sometimes, there is also a videodisk player, which is controlled by the software.

Computer based multimedia delivers information in a variety of ways but achieves its greatest effectiveness through interaction. In the first case, music and informative knowledge combine to convey the message. In the second case, technology provides a more effective presentation wherein information, images and sounds are technically and aesthetically integrated, focusing on a single specific purpose. The ability of students to work independently and to receive instruction suited to their needs and learning styles is inherently attractive.

Review of Literature

Dalacosta et al. (2009) developed and studied the effectiveness of Multimedia **application with animated cartoons in teaching science in elementary education.** The results of the study provide evidence that the use of animated cartoons significantly increases the young students' knowledge and understanding of specific science concepts, which are normally difficult to comprehend and often cause misconceptions to them.

Jian Hu et al. (2009) investigated the effects of introducing a software program, named the Dental 3D Multimedia System (D3DM), into the education of a group of junior dental students in their preclinical practice. One group received their training program in the traditional way, unassisted by 3D technology. The second group received their training program in the traditional manner, but also used the D3DM to supplement their education. The results showed that the D3DM-assisted group achieved higher scores and also indicated that the usage of 3D multimedia PC software had a positive impact on several aspects of subjects' performance.

Kanmani and Radha (2009) studied the Effectiveness of CAI package in basic electronics teaching. There was a significant difference between the control and the experimental group students in attainment of knowledge level, understanding level, and application level objective in the gain scores. Hence, the experimental group students were better than the control group students in attainment of knowledge level, understanding level, and application level objective in the gain scores. It was inferred from the finding that the experimental treatment is effective to the students.

Korakakis et al. (2009) made a study on the **"3D visualization types in multimedia applications for science learning for 8th grade students in Greece".** The aim of the study was to determine whether the use of specific types of visualization (3D illustration, 3D animation, and interactive 3D animation) combined with narration and text, contributes to the learning process in science courses. The results indicated that multimedia applications with interactive 3D animations as well as with 3D animations do in fact increase the interest of students and make the material more appealing to them.

She, Hsiao-Ching and Chen, Yi-Zen (2009) examined how middle school students constructed their understanding of the mitosis and meiosis processes at a molecular level through multimedia learning materials presented in different interaction and sensory modality modes. The dependent variables included subjects' pre-test, post-test, and retention-test scores, showing their understanding of mitosis and meiosis process at molecular level. The results of the study showed that the group which used multimedia learning material has a greater amount of visual attention and consistent with their long term retained learning than the group which did not use the same. This study adds empirical evidence of a direct correlation between the length of eye fixation behavior and the depth of learning. Moreover, it provides insight into the multimedia effect on students' cognitive process through the use of eye fixation behavior evidence.

Anboucarassy (2010) studied the effectiveness of Multimedia in Teaching Biological Science to IX Standard students. The results of the study revealed that experiment group performed better than the control group due to the exposure of multimedia based learning. Thus multimedia helps the students to sustain their interest and also their retention power compared to the traditional method of teaching. The constant use of multimedia will make students understand more and achieve more in their academic achievement. Hence it was concluded that the multimedia approach is considered to be one of the best techniques for biology teaching at IX standard level.

Ponraj and Sivakumar (2010) studied the effectiveness of Computer-Assisted Instruction in Teaching Zoology in Relation to Learners' Personality. The major findings of the study indicated that achievement scores of experimental group students were higher than the control group students after the treatment.

Yusuf, Mudasiru and Afolabi, Adedeji (2010) investigated the effects of computer assisted instruction (CAI) on secondary school students' performance in biology. The findings of the study showed that the performance of students exposed to CAI either individually or cooperatively were better than their counterparts exposed to the conventional classroom instruction. Based on the research findings recommendations were made on the need to develop relevant CAI packages for teaching biology in Nigerian secondary schools.

Objectives

- To measure behaviour and performance of high school student.
- To assess effectiveness in performance of high school student
- To assess effective in behaviuoral outcome of the high school student.
- To assess effectiveness in traditional and multimedia method of teaching.
- To find out relevant effectiveness of computer based multimedia learning material on performance and behaviour outcome.

Hypothesis of the Study

High school students do not differ in their average level of relevant effectiveness of computer based on multimedia learning material on performance and behaviour outcome in traditional method and multimedia teaching of entire samples.

Respondents do not differ in their relevant effectiveness of computer based multimedia learning material on performance and behaviour outcome in pre test on the basis of groups.

Respondents do not differ in their relevant effectiveness of computer based multimedia learning material on performance and behaviour outcome in pre test on the basis of type of school.

Respondents do not differ in their relevant effectiveness of computer based multimedia learning material on performance and behaviour outcome in pre test on the basis of parent's education.

Respondents do not differ in their relevant effectiveness of computer based multimedia learning material on performance and behaviour outcome in pre test on the basis of parent's income.

Respondents do not differ in their relevant effectiveness of computer based multimedia learning material on performance and behaviour outcome in post test on the basis of type of school.

Respondents do not differ in their relevant effectiveness of computer based multimedia learning material on performance and behaviour outcome in post test on the basis of parent's education.

Respondents do not differ in their relevant effectiveness of computer based multimedia learning material on performance and behaviour outcome in post test on the basis of parent's income.

Methodology

The methodology adopted for the study is explained in detail. The sampling technique, size of the sample, variables of the study, description of the tool used and administration of tool are elaborated.

Sampling Technique

The random sampling techniques used in the present study. The survey should cover all the aspects of the subject selected of the study others are inferred from a study of a sample group carefully selected to be representative of the total population. At time, the survey describes a limited population which is the only group under consideration. It involves a clearly defined problem and defined objectives. It requires expert and imaginative planning. Careful analysis and interpretation of the data gathered and logical and skillful reporting of the findings. There are different findings such as social surveys, market surveys. The survey method is applied to the analysis of existing social conditions including educational conditions and to the analysis of public opinion. So in this present study, the investigator has used stratified disposition random sampling method.

Sample

Samples of 100 high school students selected randomly were studied in Tindivanam Town. Out of these high schools as many as 5 higher secondary schools have been chosen by appropriate method. All the available high school students studying in each of this selected high school were chosen as sample. Stratified disposition random sampling technique has been used in the selection of the sample.

Data Collection

Primary data, required for the present research work were collected by conducting direct interviews using questionnaire. All the respondents were given sufficient information about the study. These respondents were provided with the same questionnaires. They were also informed that they have to answer in the same fashion.

Tools used for the study

Development of effectiveness of multimedia programme and Scale by the investigator. The scale for measuring the high school student's effectiveness of multimedia towards science in the study. This scale has as many as 25 statements of which 3 point scale method.

Analysis and Interpretation

Table 1: Showing the Mean, Standard deviation of relevant effectiveness of computer based multimedia learning material on performance and behaviour outcome in pre and post test of entire samples

Groups	N	Mean	SD	r value
Pre test	100	14.79	2.69	0.346**
Post test	100	19.30	2.86	

Hypothesis: High school students do not differ in their average level of relevant effectiveness of computer based on multimedia learning material on performance and behaviour outcome in traditional method and multimedia teaching of entire samples.

The mean and standard deviation of relevant effectiveness of computer based multimedia learning material on performance and behaviour outcome scores of entire samples are 14.79 and 2.69 in pre test and 19.30 and 2.86 in post test. The mean score of all categories are lay in between ($M \pm 1\sigma$) value. So it is concluded that average level of relevant effectiveness of computer based multimedia learning material on performance and behaviour outcome of entire samples.

Table 2: Showing the Mean, Standard deviation and t-test for relevant effectiveness of computer based multimedia learning material on performance and behaviour outcome on the basis of groups

Groups	Sample size	Mean	Standard Deviation	t-value	Level of Significance
Pre test	100	14.79	2.69	12.86	0.01 (Significant)
Post test	100	19.30	2.86		

Hypothesis: Respondents do not differ in their relevant effectiveness of computer based multimedia learning material on performance and behaviour outcome in pre test on the basis of groups.

The calculated t-value (12.86), which is significant at 0.01 level, confirms that there is a significant difference between relevant effectiveness of computer based multimedia learning material on performance and behaviour outcome on the basis of groups. So the null hypothesis is rejected and alternate hypothesis is accepted. Therefore it is concluded that pre test and post test groups differ in their effectiveness of computer based multimedia learning material on performance and behaviour outcome.

Table 3: Showing mean, standard deviation and t-value for traditional method among the high school student on the basis of type of school

Sl. No	Type of school	Sample size	Mean	Standard Deviation	t-value	Level of Significance
1	Government	75	14.73	2.71	0.37	0.716 (Not Significant)
2	Aided	25	14.96	2.67		

Hypothesis: Respondents do not differ in their relevant effectiveness of computer based multimedia learning material on performance and behaviour outcome in pre test on the basis of type of school.

The calculated t-value (0.37), which is not significant, confirms that there is a no significant difference between relevant effectiveness of computer based multimedia learning material on performance and behaviour outcome in pre test on the basis of type of school. So the null hypothesis is accepted and alternate hypothesis is rejected. Therefore it is concluded that government and aided school groups do not differ in their pre test score.

Table 4: Showing mean, standard deviation and t-value for traditional method among the high school student on the basis of parents education

Sl. No	Parents education	Sample size	Mean	Standard Deviation	F-value	Level of Significance
1	School	86	14.82	2.75	0.58	0.560 (Not Significant)
2	Under graduate	8	14.13	2.03		
3	Post graduate	6	14.21	2.44		
	Total	100	14.79	2.69		

Hypothesis: Respondents do not differ in their relevant effectiveness of computer based multimedia learning material on performance and behaviour outcome in pre test on the basis of parents education.

The calculated F-value (0.58), which is not significant, confirms that there is a no significant difference between relevant effectiveness of computer based multimedia learning material on performance and behaviour outcome in pre test on the basis of parents education. So the null hypothesis is accepted and alternate hypothesis is rejected. Therefore it is concluded that different parents education students groups do not differ in their pre test score.

Table 5: Showing mean, standard deviation and t-value for traditional method among the high school student on the basis of parents income

Sl. No	Parents income	Sample size	Mean	Standard Deviation	F-value	Level of Significance
1	Below Rs.50,000	70	14.51	2.53	1.56	0.215 (Not Significant)
2	Rs.50,000 – 2,00,000	24	15.50	3.09		
3	Above Rs.2,00,000	6	16.00	2.65		
	Total	100	14.79	2.69		

Hypothesis: Respondents do not differ in their relevant effectiveness of computer based multimedia learning material on performance and behaviour outcome in pre test on the basis of parents income.

The calculated F-value (1.56), which is not significant, confirms that there is a no significant difference between relevant effectiveness of computer based multimedia learning material on performance and behaviour outcome in pre test on the basis of parents income. So the null hypothesis is accepted and alternate hypothesis is rejected. Therefore it is concluded that different parents income students groups do not differ in their pre test score.

Table 6: Showing mean, standard deviation and t-value for multimedia method among the high school student on the basis of type of school

Sl.No	Type of school	Sample size	Mean	Standard Deviation	t-value	Level of Significance
1	Govt.	75	18.75	2.91	4.33	0.01 (Significant)
2	Aided	25	20.96	1.93		

Hypothesis: Respondents do not differ in their relevant effectiveness of computer based multimedia learning material on performance and behaviour outcome in post test on the basis of type of school.

The calculated t-value (4.33), which is significant at 0.01 level, confirms that there is a significant difference between relevant effectiveness of computer based multimedia learning material on performance and behaviour outcome in post test on the basis of type of school. So the null hypothesis is rejected and alternate hypothesis is accepted. Therefore it is concluded that aided school students (20.96) scored higher mean value than government school students (18.75).

Table 7: Showing mean, standard deviation and t-value for multimedia method among the high school student on the basis of parents education

Sl. No	Parents education	Sample size	Mean	Standard Deviation	F-value	Level of Significance
1	School	86	19.34	2.87	3.19	0.01 (Significant)
2	Under graduate	8	16.75	3.01		
3	Post graduate	6	20.12	2.63		
	Total	100	19.30	2.86		

Hypothesis: Respondents do not differ in their relevant effectiveness of computer based multimedia learning material on performance and behaviour outcome in post test on the basis of parents education.

The calculated F-value (3.19), which is significant at 0.01 level, confirms that there is a significant difference between relevant effectiveness of computer based multimedia learning material on performance and behaviour outcome in post test on the basis of parents education. So the null hypothesis is rejected and alternate hypothesis is accepted. Therefore it is concluded that different parents education students groups differ in their post test score.

Table 8: Showing mean, standard deviation and t-value for multimedia method among the high school student on the basis of parents income

Sl. No.	Parents income	Sample size	Mean	Standard Deviation	F-value	Level of Significance
1	Below Rs.50,000	70	19.11	2.64	3.29	0.01 (Significant)
2	Rs.50,000 – 2,00,000	24	20.04	3.24		
3	Above Rs.2,00,000	6	16.00	4.58		
	Total	100	19.30	2.86		

Hypothesis: Respondents do not differ in their relevant effectiveness of computer based multimedia learning material on performance and behaviour outcome in post test on the basis of parents income.

The calculated F-value (3.29), which is significant at 0.01 level, confirms that there is a significant difference between relevant effectiveness of computer based multimedia learning material on performance and behaviour outcome in post test on the basis of parents income. So the null hypothesis is rejected and alternate hypothesis is accepted. Therefore it is concluded that different parents income students groups differ in their post test score.

Findings

High school students differ in their average level of relevant effectiveness of computer based on multimedia learning material on performance and behaviour outcome in traditional method and multimedia teaching of entire samples.

Respondents differ in their relevant effectiveness of computer based multimedia learning material on performance and behaviour outcome in pre test on the basis of groups.

Respondents do not differ in their relevant effectiveness of computer based multimedia learning material on performance and behaviour outcome in pre test on the basis of type of school.

Respondents do not differ in their relevant effectiveness of computer based multimedia learning material on performance and behaviour outcome in pre test on the basis of parents education.

Respondents do not differ in their relevant effectiveness of computer based multimedia learning material on performance and behaviour outcome in pre test on the basis of parents income.

Respondents differ in their relevant effectiveness of computer based multimedia learning material on performance and behaviour outcome in post test on the basis of type of school.

Respondents differ in their relevant effectiveness of computer based multimedia learning material on performance and behaviour outcome in post test on the basis of parents education.

Respondents differ in their relevant effectiveness of computer based multimedia learning material on performance and behaviour outcome in post test on the basis of parents income.

Conclusion

In the present study, the researcher arrive the following conclusion based on the findings. In the present study, science students have relevant effectiveness of computer based multimedia learning material on performance and behaviour outcome of high school students in Tindivanam Town when compared with other students. The researcher framed objectives and hypotheses on the basis of the above context. 100 samples were selected randomly. A standard questionnaire was used to collect the relevant data. After collecting the data they were analyzed using statistical tools such as t-test and ANOVA in the both groups (pre and post test). The result concluded that the all the science students of average level of relevant effectiveness of computer based multimedia learning material on performance and behaviour outcome.

References

Anboucarassy, B. (2010). Effectiveness of Multimedia in Teaching Biological Science to IX Standard students. EDUTRACKS, 9(5): 37-38.

Annaraja, P., & Jenitha Rani, J. R. (2003). Development of Visual Basic based CAI package in Commerce and its effectiveness on Achievement in Commerce. Research and Reflections on Education.

Balasubramanian, N., & Jayaraman (2001). Relative Effectiveness among Different Modes of Computer Based Instruction. Experiments in Education, 29(2): 9-13.

Chang, Chun-Yen (2002). The impact of different forms of multimedia CAI on students' science achievement. Innovations in Education and Teaching International, 39 (4): 280-88. Retrieved March 20, 2010

Dalacosta, K., Kamariotaki-Paparrigopoulou, M., Palyvos, J.A., & Spyrellis, N. (2009). Multimedia application with animated cartoons for teaching science in elementary education. Computers & Education, 52(4): 741-748. Retrieved March 20, 2010

Dawson, M. E., Skinner, S., & Zeitlin, A. (2003). Rules of Engagement: Proceed with Caution when Integrating Multimedia learning Tools into Existing Course Formats. Electronic Journal of Science Education, 7(4). Retrieved March 21, 2010

Diseko, R. & Van Der Westhuizen, D. (2006). The Design and Development of a multimedia Tutorial for facilitation constructivist Learning among Nursing Science students: A Design experiment. Proceedings of World Conference on Educational Multimedia, Hypermedia and Telecommunications 2006, pp. 493-499. Retrieved March 20, 2010

Garnett, P., Hackling, M., & Oliver, R. (1997). An Interactive Multimedia Package Designed to Improve Beginning Students' Understanding of Chemical Equations. UniServe Science News, Vol. 8, pp. 18-21. Retrieved March 21, 2010

Jian Hu, Hao Yu, Jun Shao, Zhiyong Li, Jiawei Wang & Yining Wang (2009). Effects of dental 3D multimedia system on the performance of junior dental students in preclinical practice: a report from China. Advances in Health Sciences Education, 14(1): 123 – 133. Retrieved March 20, 2010

Junaidu, Sahalu (2008). Effectiveness of multimedia in learning & teaching data structures online. Turkish Online Journal of Distance Education-TOJDE, 9(4), Article 7. Retrieved March 21, 2010

Kadhiravan, S., & Suresh, V. (2001). Effect of Computer-assisted Instruction on Self-regulated Learning. Perspective in Education, 18(3): 161-169.

Kanmani, M., & Radha, M. (2009). "Effectiveness of CAI package in basic electronics teaching", Journal of All India Association for Educational Research, 21(1): 47-50.

Korakakis, G., Pavlatou, E.A., Palyvos, J. A., & Spyrellis N. (2009). 3D visualization types in multimedia applications for science learning: A case study for 8th grade students in Greece. Computers & Education, 52(2): 390-401. Retrieved March 21, 2010

Liao, Yuen-kuang & Chen, Yu-wen (2007). The Effect of Computer Simulation Instruction on Student Learning: A Meta-analysis of Studies in Taiwan. Journal of Information Technology and Applications, 2(2): 69-79. Retrieved March 21, 2010

O'Day, Danton H. (2007). The value of Animations in Biology Teaching: A Study of Long – Term Memory Retention. Journal of CBE - Life Science Education, 6(3): 217-223. Retrieved March 20, 2010

O'Day, Danton H. (2007). The value of Animations in Biology Teaching: A Study of Long – Term Memory Retention. Journal of CBE - Life Science Education, 6(3): 217-223. Retrieved March 20, 2010

Ozmen, Haluk (2008). The influence of Computer-Assisted Instruction on students' conceptual understanding of chemical Bonding and Attitude toward chemistry: A case for Turkey. Computers and Education, 51(1): 423-438. Retrieved March 21, 2010

Ponraj, P., & Nellaiyapen, N. O. (2008). CAI in teaching Zoology. Research and Reflections on Education, 6(2): 18-21.

Ponraj, P., & Sivakumar, R. (2010). Computer-Assisted Instruction in Zoology in Relation to Learners' Personality. EDUTRACKS, 9(6): 34-37.

Prinz, A., Bolz, M., & Findl, O. (2005). Advantage of three dimensional animated teaching over traditional surgical videos for teaching ophthalmic surgery: a randomised study. British Journal of Ophthalmology, 89(11): 1495-1499. Retrieved March 21, 2010

Pryor, Caroline R., & Bitter, Gary G. (2008). Using multimedia to teach in-service teachers: Impacts on learning, application, and retention. Computers in Human Behavior, 24 (6): 2668-2681. Retrieved March 20, 2010

Rotbain, Y., Marbach-Ad, G., & Stavy, R. (2008). Using a computer animation to teach high school molecular biology. Journal of Science Education and Technology, 17(1): 49-58. Retrieved March 21, 2010

Segers, E., & Verhoeven, L. (2002). Multimedia support of early literacy learning. Computers and Education, 39(3): 207-221. Retrieved March 20, 2010

She, Hsiao-Ching & Chen, Yi-Zen (2009). The impact of multimedia effect on science learning: Evidence from eye movements. Computers & Education, 53(4): 1297-1307. Retrieved March 20, 2010

Thilaka Suresh (2000). Instructional strategy change on the achievement in biotechnology and attitude towards science among higher secondary school students. Journal of All India Association for Educational Research, 12(3 & 7): 14-19.

Venkataraman, S. (2008). Relative effectiveness among selected modes of CAI in physics in relation to learner's personality. Unpublished Doctoral Dissertation, Annamalai University. Chidambaram.

Vernadakis, N., Zetou, E., Tsitskari, E., Giannousi, M., & Kioumourtzoglou, E. (2008). Student attitude and learning outcomes of multimedia computer-assisted versus traditional instruction in basketball. Education and Information

Technologies, 13(3): 167-183.

Victor, Adeosun Olufemi (2008). Relative effects of three Multi-Media Instructional Packages on Nigerian student's achievement in Social Studies. Pakistan Journal of Social Sciences, 5 (5): 415 – 420. Retrieved March 20, 2010

Yusuf, Mudasiru O., & Afolabi, Adedeji O. (2010). Effects of Computer AssistedIinstruction (CAI) on Secondary School students' performance in biology. TOJET: The Turkish Online Journal of Educational Technology, 9(1): 62-69. Retrieved March 21, 2010.

❐

8.

Effectiveness of Blended Learning Programme in Teaching Biology at Higher Secondary School Students

Introduction

The technology is an integral part in the lives of young people who are direct beneficiaries of the educational process. This was often made argument for the need to develop learning methods that use modern technology in the formative and educational. By such methods students are responsible for their own learning, on which they themselves have control and manage it according to their interests and needs. The specialists' researches reveal that the methods which combine the traditional education with the modern technologies (*blended learning*) have increased the effectiveness. Blended Learning is a strategy which integrates the teaching learning process with different learning environments like face-to-face, online, social networking etc. Its rapid growth has been facilitated by the Internet and other emerging technologies like cloud computing, social networking etc. This paper provides a view about the effectiveness of blended learning programme in teaching biology at higher secondary school students

The recent research in science education has focused on instruction that is specific science content, specific instructional strategies and how they are related to biology learning contexts and instructional outcomes. In the present scientific and technological age, the conventional teaching methods are not sufficient to arouse interest among the students and do not meet up to the intellectual, psychological and emotional needs of the students in the new millennium. The methods of teaching biology need to be changed.

In a vast country like India, enormous work is now being done in the field of education but it is still not possible to equip each and every higher and higher secondary school with all the facilities for teaching biology in the near future. Most of the higher secondary schools, both in rural and urban area are suffering from lack of modern science laboratories. They need equally advanced gadgets to support their education. Technology enables students get a live vision of life's aspects and scientific factors. Any diagram can be explained in detail with 3d effect, it helps the student to understand the lesson clearly. Keeping in mind the investigator felt it appropriate to use blended learning for the teaching of the concepts in biology topics included in the XI standard biology syllabus (Tamil Medium).

Blended Learning

Blended learning provides platform to attract the senses of the learner for easy and happy learning. Blended learning is a programme which integrates teaching learning process with different leaning environment. Its rapid growth facilitated by the internet and other emerging technology cloud computing and social networking. "Blended learning is the thoughtful fusion of face-to-face and online learning experiences. The basic principle is that face-to-face oral communication and online written communication are optimally integrated such that the strengths of each are blended into a unique learning experience congruent with the context and intended educational purpose."

Blended learning – an instructional practice that combines teaching methods from both face-to-face instruction and online learning, gives to educational institutions new approaches and strategies for addressing the challenges they face and for taking advantage of the exciting new learning opportunities that are now available.

Blended learning does not exclude the traditional learning methods, but adds new and modern methods as: IT tools (email, web, chat, online conferences, e-learning platforms), workshops, individual project groups, practical demonstrations, etc.

Objectives of the Study

The objectives of the study as follows

- To find out the effectiveness of blended learning programme for the teaching of biology at higher secondary level.
- To compare the effectiveness of blended learning programme in the teaching of biology with conventional method of teaching biology.

Hypotheses of the Study

The following null hypotheses have been formulated

- There is no significant difference between the experimental group and control group in the achievement of biology at pre test level.
- There is no significant difference between the experimental group and control group in the achievement of biology at posttest level.

- There is no significant difference between the pretest and posttest in the achievement of biology for the experimental group.
- There is no significant difference between the pretest and posttest in the achievement of biology for the control group.

Sample

The sample of the study consists of 100 students studying in XI standard under State Board syllabus at perambalur district. The sample includes both boys and girls.

Tools Used

The following tools had been used for the present study:

- An achievement test in biology constructed and validated by the investigators
- Blended learning programme was developed by the investigator for the teaching of the concepts in biology topics included in the XI standard biology syllabus.
- The progrmme was arranged logically based on the psychological principles of learning. Experimental design was adopted. For the experimentation pretest was conducted and sample was divided into two groups. The students of the experimental group were taught with the blended learning progrmme and the control group through the conventional method. After the treatment period the posttest was administered. The collected data were subjected to statistical analysis and the results obtained were interpreted.

Testing of Hypotheses

Hypothesis 1: There is no significant difference between the experimental group and control group in the achievement of biology at pre test level.

The't' test applied to test the significance of difference between the mean achievement test scores of the experimental group and control group of pretest level.

Table -1: Mean Achievement Test Scores of the Experimental Group Compared with that of the Control Group at Pretest level

Groups	N	Mean	S.D	't' value	Level of Significance at 0.05 level
Experimental	30	20.43	2.09	0.46	Not significant
Control	30	19.63	1.87		

The table indicates that the 't' value is not significant at 0.05 level. The students of the experimental group do not differ significantly from the students of the control group in the mean achievement test scores at pre test level.

Hypothesis 2: There is no significant difference between the experimental group and control group in the achievement of biology at posttest level

Th 't' test applied to test the significance of difference between the mean achievement test scores of the experimental group and control group of posttest level.

Table-2: Mean Achievement Test Scores of the Experimental Group Compared with that of the Control Group at Posttest level

Groups	N	Mean	S.D	't' value	Level of Significance at 0.01 level
Experimental	30	36.40	3.96	15.08	significant
Control	30	20.10	5.14		

The table indicates that the 't' value is significant at 0.01 level. Hence there is there is a significant difference between the two groups. As indicated by the mean value, it can be concluded that the students of the experimental group fared better in the achievement test than the students of the control group. This shows that learning with the help of blended learning programme will increase the achievement of the students better than learning through the conventional method.

Hypothesis 3: There is no significant difference between the pretest and posttest in the achievement of biology for the experimental group.

The 't' test applied to test the significance of difference between test scores of the pretest with that of the posttest for the experimental group.

Table -3: Mean Achievement Test Scores of Pretest Compared with that of the Posttest for the Experimental Group

Groups	N	Mean	S.D	't' value	Level of Significance at 0.01 level
Experimental	30	20.43	2.07	20.52	Significant
Control	30	37.40	3.96		

Table 3 indicates that the't' value is significant at 0.01 level. Hence, it could be concluded that there is a significant difference between the mean achievement test scores of the pretest and posttest for the experimental group. The higher mean value in the posttest shows that the students fared better in the posttest than in the pretest. This shows that the blended learning programme has helped the students to score more in the posttest.

Hypothesis 4: There is no significant difference between the pretest and posttest in the achievement of biology for the control group.

Table -4: Mean Achievement Test Scores of Pretest Compared with that of the Posttest for the Control Group

Groups	N	Mean	S.D	't' value	Level of Significance at 0.05 level
Experimental	30	19.76	1.87	0.034	Not significant
Control	30	20.00	5.06		

Table 4 indicates that the 't' value is not significant at 0.05 level. Hence, it could be concluded that there is no significant difference between the mean achievement test scores of the pretest and posttest for the control group.

Findings of the Study

There is no significant difference between the experimental group and control group in the achievement of biology at pretest level.

There is a significant difference between the experimental group and control group in the achievement of biology at posttest level. The students leaning with the help of blended learning programme fared better in biology than in students learning through the conventional method.

There is a significant difference between the mean achievement test scores of the pretest and posttest for the experimental group. This shows that the blended learning programme has helped the students to score more marks in the posttest.

There is a significant difference between the mean achievement test scores of the pretest and posttest for the control group. This shows that the conventional method of teaching will not help the students to score more marks in the posttest.

Conclusion

In the field of education is not possible to equip the teaching leaning in higher and higher secondary level because most of the higher secondary schools suffering from lack of modern methods of teaching, they still follow the conventional method of teaching in higher secondary level. This should be change in the modern era; they should follow the blended learning methods in their teaching learning methods because it supports the education department well in advance.

Reference

Barbour Michael, et al, (2012), Online and Blended Learning: A Survey of Policy and Practice of K-12 Schools Around the World, available at http://www.inacol.org/cms/wpcontent/uploads/2012/11/iNACOL_IntnlReport2011.pdf

Rogers Carl (1983), The Interpersonal Relationship in the Facilitation of Learning, London: Rutledge

The Oxford Group (2013), Blended Learning—Current Use, Challenges and Best Practices, report 2013, available at http://www.kineo.com/m/0/blended-learning-report-202013.pdf (accessed July 2013)

❐

9.

Implications of Multimedia in Teaching Economics with Special Reference to Higher Secondary Students in Chennai

Introduction

The computer has revolutionized the whole society overwhelmingly inclusive of all human activities especially those of education. The computer is changing the total educational system namely, content, methodology, learner participation learning process, teacher roles, curricular implication etc. "The computers are very powerful instructional media that enhance quality of instruction". By programming the subject of study in computers, teaching and learning become full of contexts and situations. The student can take his own time to learn the contents because they are individualized instructional situation. The performance of the student in instruction as well as in test will automatically record in the computer. The present study aims to find out the implications of multimedia in teaching economics with special reference to higher secondary education in Chennai. A samples of 155 samples selected randomly were studied. A questionnaire method of survey was used to find out the implications of multimedia in teaching economics. The data were collected by using questionnaire as an instrument. Primary data were collected by conducting direct structured interview using questionnaire. All the respondents were asked the same questions in the same fashion and they were informed the purpose of study. t-test, ANOVA and Correlation analysis were applied to test the hypotheses. The findings and observations are the result and outcome of the interpretations made during the study of analysis.

In 1965, Lorence settler and Danieal Davis[5] developed most complicated teaching process in which computer was used for presenting instruction in place of teacher. They divided the teaching process of the computer in two parts.

Pre-tutorial phase

Tutorial phase.

In the first phase, computer assisted instruction is given to the pupils to achieve the specific objectives on the basis of his entry behaviour. In the second phase instructing material is presented accordingly. The pupil is evaluated. After presenting the instruction, computer also controls it. It also provides reinforcement to the pupils.

In the modern age, the use of computers in the field of education, made in the following areas.

All the researches do all analytical tasks with the help of computers in the research work.

- Computers are also used in educational guidance and counseling.
- Remedial teaching of the pupils is also done by the computers.
- Computers help in sought for preparing the results of the examinations.

Learning with aid of computer through computer, aided instruction, computer simulation etc. It is a self learning strategy in teaching learning process. Students learnt their subjects at their own pace.

Internet is worldwide computer network that contains a large collection of information which could be made available to you on your computer. The person having internet connection can retrieve any information on individual interest. Purves, A.C.[6] (1998) says that, the internet is the abbreviation of inter network system. The internet is the name for a vast, worldwide system consisting of people, information and computers. It is also described as a network of networks because these are more than one lakh readily accessible through the Internet. Internet is the largest and most complete learning tool for a group of people with varied educational background and interests. Teachers, students, businessmen and other educators can share ideas instantly across vast distances. For scientific and research community, internet is an essential and indispensable tool. Through Internet scientist can gain and enjoy instant access to the world's most advanced research facilities and discuss their research problems with others, working in the same field.

Review of Literature

Coyne, Margaret Ann[17], Ed.D., (2006), in their paper "Emerging literacy Assisted parents to scaffold the emerging literacy skill of their pre-school-aged children through the used of electronic storybooks", reported that, that importance of parents reading to their young child is well supported by research (Health, 1986). However, Edwards (1989) found that parents whose own literacy skills are emerging have difficulty supporting the emerging literacy skills of their young children through storybook reading.

The development of a new paradigm, Universal Design for Learning (UDL) (Meyer & Rose, 1998 and 2002) provides a framework for the use of computer technology to support learning. Drawing on Vygotsky's (1978; 1986) socio constructive theory of learning and the latest advances in the neurosciences, UDL investigates how technology can support diverse learners. This study examined whether UDL –based technology might help parents who are themselves emerging readers support their children's literacy development.

When parents use of targeted storybook reading behaviours increased if their children's pre-intervention scores on language measures were below age-level, the children's scores on post-intervention measures improved to age-level or above. In addition, the children's scores on measures of story retelling and print knowledge improved.

BEABVIS C.,[18], Deakin University, Literacy and the new technologies in the middle years. (2006) This paper explores young people's textual engagements with electronic and other forms of popular culture, and the changing nature of literacy in the context of COM modification, mass marketing and the new technologies. Building on school based studies exploring computer games in the classroom and the Poke on phenomenon, it examines ways in which popular texts are read, and narrative and generic elements incorporated into the curriculum and into students' spoken and written texts. Drawing on Green's model of cultural, critical and opal dimensions of (technological) literacy, it examines issues of literacy and culture, identity and critique for teachers and students in the middle years, and their implications for constructions of literacy and curriculum.

BERRY L. and CHAPMAN E,[19] University of Sydney Effects of Background Information and Audiovisual Presentation Modes on Students' Attention Styles and Enjoyment in Listening to Unfamiliar Music.(2006) Research has indicated that students typically do not enjoy or engage with unfamiliar pieces of music. This is discouraging and puzzling to music educators who whish to introduce their students to a diverse range of musical genres. This study explored the effects of two factors on students' initial reactions to an unfamiliar Shakuhachi piece. Using a 2 by 2 crossed-factor design, 438 students in grades 9-11 were assigned at random to listen to the piece in either audio-only or audiovisual form, and with or without verbal background information.

Results indicated that while the provision of information significantly ($p<0.05$) increased students' enjoyment of the music and their interest in hearing more of the same kind of music, it had no effect on their listening attention styles (e.g., focusing on the melody or idiomatic details of the piece). Conversely, use of the audiovisual presentation mode significantly impacted on one aspect of students' attention styles (focus on idiomatic details) and perceived familiarity with the piece, but had only a marginally significant effect on their enjoyment or interest.

Implications of these results for the introduction of unfamiliar music to high school students will be discussed.

BLACKMORE J., JOHNSON R., WARREN W.[20], (2006) States that the potential of new learning technologies for transforming teaching and learning, and indeed the organization of schooling. Much has also been written about teacher responses to new learning technologies-how they resist, ignore, or innovate. A number of recent reports indicate a gap between policy, practice and the capacity of organizations to provide the conditions and resources sin schools to creatively use new learning technologies. Few of these discourses draw upon theories of educational change, in particular those which relate to the dissonance between attitudes and feelings about radical change, and how it impacts on teacher work identity with respect to learning technologies. Much of the literature has focused upon the technical aspects, the hardware and software, but not the 'warm ware', so critical to sound pedagogical practice. This paper draws from the Learning in New Environments Research Group action research project, a pilot study in a large metropolitan secondary college, which is exploring the social implications of new learning technologies for changing relations between students, between teachers and students, between teachers and between family and school. The paper draws from the first round of data collection from the teachers in an ongoing action research project in a region with a high level of socio-economic and cultural diversity.

It draws on concepts of Lieberman's notion of learning networks and Wenger's notion of communities of practice, as well as past research on the reception of gender equity reform in educational organizations, which focuses upon emotional aspects of professional work identity and organizational change.

Joseph Kacharayll[25] (2006) – "Suitability of colleges for Web Bases Learning" reported that Web based learning environment is expensive to establish, government and private managements should take necessary steps to provide adequate infrastructure facilities in colleges for web based learning. A proper utilization of available human resources would help improve web based learning. In order to overcome technical limitation, training has to be given to both teachers and learners to create flexible and uninterrupted learning environment. The training of material designers should be especially focused upon. Most of the colleges have not properly utilized the available web resources in their teaching learning strategies. There is only nominal technical support and assistance from technical staff and from government and private managements at the institutional level for web based learning. The author collected sample for the survey of 152 college lecturers was obtained through random sampling.

Objectives

- To find the effect on learning competency of the students by using Multi media for teaching economics
- To find the active participation of the teachers in using multi media for teaching economics.
- To find how the teaching of economics has been efficiently improved using the multi media.
- To find the importance of computers and internet in teaching economics.

Methodology

The investigator, for the present study adopts the survey method of research. It is a procedure in which data is systematically collected from a population through some form of direct solicitation such as face to face interview, questionnaire or schedule. The survey is extensive and cross sectional dealing with the relatively large number of cases of a particular time and yielding statistics that are abstracted from particular cases. It is the method of investigation which attempts to describe and interpret what exists at present in the form of conditions, practices, process, trends, effects, attitudes, and beliefs. Using this method the investigator had gathered information measure the Effect of Multi Media Aids in teaching economics for Higher Secondary Students in Chennai.

Sample

For the present study 155 Higher Secondary Students in Chennai.

Data Collection

Primary data, required for the present research work were collected by conducting direct interviews using questionnaire. All the respondents were given sufficient information about the study. These respondents were provided with the same questionnaires. They were also informed that they have to answer in the same fashion.

Statistical Tools for Analysis

The following tools statistical tools were used for the analysis of data. t-test, one way ANOVA and correlation analysis is used for the present study.

Analysis and Interpretation

Table 1: Six wise distribution of "t" value between the boys and girls of the higher secondary economics students using multimedia resources in their schools

Dimensions	Boys N = 55		Girls N = 100		Calculated value of "t"	Level of significance at 5% level
	Mean	S.D	Mean	S.D		
Working knowledge of computers	79.42	8.17	80.42	8.68	0.71	NS
Knowledge about internet	78.15	9.51	76.88	9.80	0.91	NS
Knowledge using A.V. Aids	79.76	7.48	76.26	10.79	2.37	S
Preparation of computer based study materials	76.40	7.97	74.77	11.04	1.06	NS
Assignment and project	81.75	6.31	78.35	10.18	2.56	S
Interaction with others through web	395.47	28.53	386.5	42.77	1.56	NS

(At5% level of significance, the table value of "t" is 1.96)

It is refereed from the above table that there is a significant difference between boys and of Higher Secondary Students of economics group in there, Knowledge in using A.V. Aids and Assignment and project but there is no significant difference between Male and Female Higher Secondary students of economics group in their Working knowledge of computers, knowledge about internet, Preparation of computer based study materials, interaction with others through web.

Table – 2 : Area wise distribution of "t" value between the urban and rural higher secondary economics students using multimedia resources in their schools

Dimensions	Urban N = 55		Rural N = 100		Calculated value of "t"	Level of significance at 5% level
	Mean	S.D	Mean	S.D		
Working knowledge of computers	79.42	8.17	80.42	8.68	0.71	NS
Knowledge about internet	78.15	9.51	76.88	9.80	0.91	NS

Knowledge using A.V. Aids	79.76	7.48	76.26	10.79	2.37	S
Preparation of computer based study materials	76.40	7.97	74.77	11.04	1.06	NS
Assignment and project	81.75	6.31	78.35	10.18	2.56	S
Interaction with others through web	395.47	28.53	386.5	42.77	1.56	NS

(At 5% level of significance, the table value of "t" is 1.96)

It is referred from the above table that there is no significant difference between urban and rural Higher Secondary Students of economics group in there, Knowledge in using A.V. Aids, Assignment and project, Working knowledge of computers, Knowledge about internet, Preparation of computer based study materials, Interaction with other through web.

Table – 3: "F" value among the boys and girls of Higher Secondary economics Group Students in Using Multimedia resources

Dimensions	df= 2,152			Calculated "f" Value	Remarks at 5% Level
	Source of variation	Sum of squares	M.S.V		
Working knowledge of computers	Between With in	118.75 11110.63	59.38 73.10	0.81	NS
Knowledge about internet	Between With in	7.94 14650.81	3.97 96.39	0.04	NS
Knowledge in using A.V. Aids	Between With in	23.44 15123.38	11.72 99.50	0.12	NS
Preparation of computer study materials	Between With in	155.56 15619.63	77.78 102.76	0.76	NS
Assignment and project	Between With in	164.39 12793.88	82.19 84.17	0.98	NS
Interaction with others through web	Between With in	216.00 23034.00	108.00 1515.39	0.07	NS

(For 2,152 df. At 5% level of significance, the table value of "f" is 3.06)

It is inferred from the above table that there is no significance difference among the boys and girls of Higher Secondary economics group students in using Multimedia resources in the Higher Secondary schools of Chennai.

Table – 4: "F" value among the Rural and Urban Higher Secondary Students of economics Group in Using Multimedia source in Chennai

Dimensions	df= 2,152			Calculated "f" Value	Remarks at 5% Level
	Source of variation	Sum of squares	M.S.V		
Working knowledge of computers	Between With in	39.50 11189.88	19.75 73.62	0.27	NS
Knowledge about internet	Between With in	394.39 14264.50	197.16 93.85	2.10	NS
Knowledge in using A.V. Aids	Between With in	130.31 15016.50	65.16 98.79	0.66	NS
Preparation of computer study materials	Between With in	444.44 153330.75	222.22 100.86	2.20	NS
Assignment and project	Between With in	364.69 12593.56	182.32 82.85	2.20	NS
Interaction with others through web	Between With in	5628.00 224924.00	2814.00	1.90	NS

(for 2,152 df.at 5% level of significance, the table value of "f" is 3.06)

It is inferred from the above table that there is no significance difference among the Rural and Urban Higher Secondary students of economics group in using Multi media resource in the Higher Secondary Schools of Chennai.

Table – 5: "F" value among the Higher Secondary Students of economics Group in Using Multimedia source in Government and Private Higher Secondary Schools in Chennai

Dimensions	**df= 2,152**			**Calculated "f" Value**	**Remarks at 5% Level**
	Source of variation	**Sum of squares**	**M.S.V**		
Working knowledge of computers	Between With in	39.50 11189.88	19.75 73.62	0.27	NS
Knowledge about internet	Between With in	394.39 14264.50	197.16 93.85	2.10	NS
Knowledge in using A.V. Aids	Between With in	130.31 15016.50	65.16 98.79	0.66	NS
Preparation of computer study materials	Between With in	444.44 153330.75	222.22 100.86	2.20	NS
Assignment and project	Between With in	364.69 12593.56	182.32 82.85	2.20	NS

Interaction with others through web	Between With in	5628.00 224924.00	2814.00	1.90	NS

(For 2,152 df. at 5% level of significance, the table value of '' is 3.06)

It is inferred from the above table that there is no significance difference among the Government and Private Higher Secondary students of economics group in using Multimedia resource in the Higher Secondary School of Chennai

Table – 6 : The Correlation value between the Male and Female Higher Secondary Students in using multimedia resources in the Higher Secondary Schools of Chennai

Category	?X	?X^2	?Y	?Y^2	?XY	Calculated	Remarks
Boys	683	8595	545	5495	6775	.68	NS
Girls	1199	14757	970	9584	11740	.425	S
Total	1882	23354	1515	15079	18515	.325	S

(Table value of Correlation Co-efficient at 5% level of Significance is 0.161)

It is inferred from the above table that there is no significant relationship between the rural and high secondary economics group boys in using multimedia resources and there is a significant relationship between rural and urban high secondary economics group girls in using multimedia resources.

Findings

There a significant difference among the higher secondary commence group students of boys and girls, higher secondary commence students of government and private schools, higher secondary commence group students of rural and urban schools, in their interest towards learning commence through multimedia resources in Chennai.

There is significant difference among the higher secondary economics group students in their levels of using multimedia shows moderate knowledge except interaction with others through web and no significant difference in low of using multimedia except interaction with other through web and no significant difference in higher level knowledge of using multimedia.

There is no significant difference among the higher secondary economics group boys in their level of using multimedia shows moderate knowledge and higher level of using multimedia and there is a significant difference low of using multimedia at the area of assignment and project, interaction with others though web.

There is no significant difference among the secondary economics group girls in all the levels of using multimedia resources. There is no significant difference among the higher secondary economics group students of government school in their level of using multimedia shows moderate knowledge and there is a significant difference in low level of interaction with others though web and shows significant difference in higher level of in knowledge about internet, knowledge in using AV aids and in the preparation of computer based study materials.

There is no significant difference among the higher secondary economics group students of private school in their level of using multimedia shows moderate knowledge and higher level knowledge of using multimedia and there is a significant difference in low level of using multimedia at the area of working of computer and in interaction with others though web.

There is no significant difference among the higher secondary economics group of rural school in their level of using multimedia shows moderate knowledge and there is a significant difference in low level of preparation of computer in high level of using multimedia at the is a significant difference in high level of using multimedia at the area of working knowledge of computer and in interaction with others with through web.

There is no significant difference between boys and girls or higher secondary students of economics group in their, knowledge in using A.V aids and assignments and project but there is no significant differences between male and female higher secondary of economics group in their working knowledge of computers, knowledge about internet, preparation of computer based study materials with others thought web.

There is no significant difference between urban and rural higher secondary of economics in their, knowledge in using A.V aids, assignment and project, working knowledge of computer knowledge about internet preparation of computer based study martial interaction with others web.

There is no significant difference among the Male and female higher secondary schools of economics group in using multimedia resource in the Higher secondary schools of Chennai.

There is no significance difference among the Rural and urban higher secondary students of economics group in using Multimedia resource in the higher secondary of Chennai.

There is n no significant difference among the Government and private Higher Secondary students of economics group in using Multimedia resource in the higher schools of Chennai.

There is no significant relationship between the Rural and urban high secondary group boys in using multimedia resources and there is a significant relationship between Rural and Urban high secondary economics group girls in using multimedia resources.

The research overwhelmingly demonstrates that usages of multimedia will definitely improve the quality of teaching economics in higher secondary classes.

The research found that the students are actively involved in learning part if the multimedia is introduced in classroom teaching.

The research shows the students are highly motivate towards the subject by using multimedia teaching aids and they are attracted more and improve their understanding and memory power in various economics topics like advertising, banking, etc. While using multimedia resources.

It is concluded that there is a positive effect of using multimedia aids in the economics achievement of the students in economics in Chennai.

Conclusion

The present study aims to find out the implications of multimedia in teaching economics with special reference to higher secondary. The researcher framed objectives and hypotheses on the basis of the above context. The research was carried out in 155 samples based randomly. A questionnaire constructed by R was used to collect the relevant data. After collecting the data they were analyzed using statistical tools such as t-test, ANOVA and Correlation analysis. The result concluded that students have average implications of multimedia in teaching at Higher Secondary level.

Reference

Beavis C. (2006), popular culture, textual practice and identify and identify: literacy and the new technologies, in the midde years

Berry l. And Chapman e, (2006); Effect of Background Information and Audiovisual Presentation Modes on Students' Attention style and enjoyment listening to Unfamiliar Music.

Blackmork j., Johnson R., Warren W. (2006), A handbook of Education Technology.

Bruce B.C (2004); Diversity and critical social engagement: How changing technologies enable new modes of literacy in changing circumstances. IN D.E. Alvermann (E.d), Adolescents and illiteracies in a digital world (pp. 1-18). New York: Peter Lang publication.

Chisamore, chris (2006), Multimedia and Education today.

Coyne, Margaret Ann (2006), Emerging Literacy: Assisting Parents to scaffold the emerging literacy skills of their preschool aged children through the use of electronic story books.

Lanksherar, C and Knoble, M (2003); New literacies: changing Knowledge and classroom learning. Philadelphia: Open university press.

Lewis, C and Finders, M. (2004); implied adolescents and implied teachers; A generation gap for new times. D.E Alvermann (Ed.), Adolescents and literacies in adugital world (pp.101-113).New York: peter Lang publishing.

❐

10.

Awareness towards Utilizing Cell Phones among the Higher Secondary School Students

Introduction

The invention of the fixed telephone in the late 19th century in the United States changed the way that people interacted and communicated. This has been paralleled in the early 21st century by the advent of the mobile phone. The mobile phone was originally created for business use. In the last few years extraordinary growth has taken place worldwide Information and Communication Technologies (ICT) and especially in the ICT sector tied to mobile communications, as evidenced by the more than two billion mobile phones handsets sold around the world in 2013. Mobile and light weight devices that are sometimes small enough to fit in a pocket or in the palm of one's hand are part of everyday life.

Mobile Learning

Nine in ten people (more than 5 billion individuals) around the world are carrying a powerful computing device in their pockets and purses. They don't realize it, but today's mobile phones have the computing power of a personal computer from the mid-nineties, while consuming a fraction of the energy and are made at significantly lower cost. In India, the mobile phone has revolutionized communication and India is now one of the faster growing markets for mobile phone service, with growing usage and increasing penetration. According to TRAI, there are 286 million wireless subscribers in India, June 2008, of which 76 million were capable of accessing data service. The increasing ubiquity of the mobile phone begs for it to be used as a learning tool.

Mobile Internet Browsers

Internet browsers are now built into an increasing number of phones, especially those that take advantage of 3G or enhanced data networks such as GPRS. Having a browser on the phone opens up all the learning resources available on the web, including Google, LMS applications, typical e-learning courseware and other tools/applications.

M-Learning in India

The Biju Patnaik University of Technology started a service in collaboration with SMS Gup Shup called the BPUTALERT, which distributes information, academic notice and calendars through SMS to students. Voice tap is another service using which people can send their queries through SMS, and the company messages back names of experts on the subject, and then users can connect to the right expert. The field mobile learning is in its infancy, and developers are still fumbling with products.

Mobile Communication between Parents, Teachers and Students

The new mobile technologies can be used in mediate the relationships between schools and parents. The discourses of the participants for what regards the new mobile technologies have been analyzed in order to mediate the relationships between the school and the parents, leaving the possibility of discussing more general topic to the parent school relationship.

Scope of the Study

To Study the attitude of teenagers towards cellular phones.

Enumerate the usage patterns and arrive at peculiarities.

Examine the way young people relate to the functionality of mobile phones as well as asses observable phenomena.

In this context the investigator attempts to study the influence and awareness towards utilizing cell phones among the higher secondary school students.

Need of the Study

Most of the people are using mobile phones in their daily life. Mobile phones are using to send the message and communicate the information's easily. Also college students are using the mobile for clearing the doubts on their subjects from teachers and pears. Hence this study is most important to identify the awareness of the mobile phones among the higher secondary school students.

Review of Literature

According to Guerra (2007), although most of the people are frequent textures, not all of them apply shorthand texting when writing. She said that students say it does affect their writing proficiency, and it has no impact at all. Nevertheless, texting is still a problem to most people.

Edwards (2009) said that texting contributes to people's indolence when it comes to writing. In his own experience, he himself developed changes on his writing abilities ever since he engaged in text messaging. According to him, it helps in speeding up communication. And because of frequent usage of shortened messages in texting, it becomes a "habit". He sometimes caught himself using the shorthand method of writing even in doing his projects in school, which goes to show that text messaging has really affected his writing ability. When he researched in the internet, he discovered that many people also believed that texting affects the writing skills of students. Edwards always feel that using the "original way" of writing when doing his school project is more difficult than using the "text messaging language". Because of this, he became lazier. He also said that most people are hooked up to texting that they send text messages even when they're doing several activities like driving, when in a funeral, or in a graduation ceremony. Myhra (2010) concluded that frequent sending of text messages could affect the student's way of writing. Students have developed the habit of writing in shorthand form, which caused them to write informally. Texting has affected the students writing and grammar proficiency negatively.

Objectives of the Study

- To find out the level of significant difference between Boys and Girls higher secondary school students among the awareness towards utilizing Cell phones.
- To find out the level of significant difference between Rural and Urban higher secondary school students among the awareness towards utilizing Cell phones.
- To find out the level of significant difference between Government, Government Aided and Private higher secondary school students among the awareness towards utilizing Cell phones.

Hypothesis of the Study

The null hypotheses were made with above objectives of the study.

Methodology

Normative survey method was used for the present study.

Samples for the Study

The investigator used random sampling technique for the selection of sample. 160 students were selected as sample of the present study. Out of these 160 students 75 of them are boys and 85 of them are girls.

Tool Used for the Study

To assess the awareness of utilizing cell phones among the students the tool ATUCP (Awareness towards Utilizing Cell Phones) was consists of 50 statements with four point rating scale was used. This was developed and standardized by the investigator.

Scoring Procedure

The students were asked to show their responses by placing (✓) tick marks. The tool consists of 28 positive statements and 22 negative statements. The negative statements were scored as 1/2/3/4 and positive statements were scored as 4/3/2/1 they are Strongly Agree, Agree, Disagree and Strongly Disagree.

Statistical Techniques Used

For the analysis of data following statistical techniques were adopted. They were, Arithmetic Mean

Standard Deviation and

't'-test

Analysis of the Data

The result of the Analyzed Data is presented below.

Table–1: Significant difference between Boys and Girls higher secondary school students' on the Awareness towards utilizing cell phones

Gender	N	Mean	S.D	t' Value'	Significance at 0.05 Level
Boys	75	77.85	7.07	1.56	**1.97
Girls	85	79.70	7.84		

**No Significant

The above table-1 shows that the calculated't' value is less than the tabulated't' value at 0.05 level of significance. Hence the null hypothesis is accepted, so there is no significant difference between Boys and Girls higher secondary school students' on the awareness towards utilizing cell phones.

Table–2: Significant difference between Rural and Urban higher secondary school students on the Awareness towards utilizing cell phones

Locality	N	Mean	S.D	t' Value'	Significance at 0.05 Level
Rural	90	77.72	8.35	2.09	*1.97
Urban	70	80.07	6.12		

* Significant

The above table-2 shows that the calculated 't' value is more than the tabulated 't' value at 0.05 level of significance. Hence the null hypothesis is not accepted. So there is significant difference between Rural and Urban higher secondary school students on the awareness towards utilizing cell phones.

Table–3: Significant difference between Goverr ment and Private higher secondary school students on the Awareness towards utilizing cell phones

Types of School	N		S.D	t'' Value	Significance at 0.05 Level
Government	50	75.70	9.05	3.77	*1.98
Aided	50	81.50	6.02		
Aided	50	81.50	6.02	1.82	**1.98
Private	60	79.35	6.32		
Private	60	79.35	6.32	2.41	*1.98
Government	50	75.70	9.05		

* Significant ** No Significant

The above table-3 shows that the Government and Aided schools students and Government and Private schools students are differed on the awareness towards utilizing cell phones. But Aided and Private schools students 't' value is less than the table value. So there is no significant difference between Aided and Private Students.

Major Findings of the Study

There is no significant difference between Boys and Girls and Aided and Private Higher Secondary School Students on the awareness towards utilizing Cell phones.

There is significant difference between Rural and Urban, Government and Aided and Private and Government Higher Secondary School Students on the awareness towards utilizing Cell phones.

Discussion

Awareness towards Utilizing Cell phones are more by the Girls than the Boy Students. Because, the Girls are more enthusiastic to work and use of cell phones.

Awareness towards Utilizing Cell phones are more by the urban students than the rural students. Because, the urban students are having more opportunities to use the Cell phones. But, the rural students are having less opportunity to use the Cell phones.

Awareness towards Utilizing Cell phones are more among Aided and Private School students. Because most of the Aided and Private Schools are mostly connected with the Parents on the progress, fees, results, attendance and relevant information's. So they have more awareness than the Government School students.

Regarding the review of literature past research's are in using the cell phones. But this research is known about awareness on the utilizing cell phones. So it is different from the review and the results are also new one.

Educational Implication of the Study

More measures are to be taken at Rural and Government School Students to create awareness of utilizing cell phones.

More programmes are to be conducted to create awareness of using cell phones for the benefit of higher secondary school students, parents and teachers.

The Teachers may be trained to teach their lessons by using the cell phones.

Government should introduce the curriculum about awareness of utilizing cell phones.

Conclusion

In the past three years, we have gone from a smattering of mobile to an abundance of useful information. But there's still a long way to go, there are still huge gaps in our knowledge to utilize the cell phones. It has been predicted that by the end of 2014 the number of mobile phone users in India will reach 1 billion. In the world every 100 citizens 97 are have mobiles. In India 90.47 have mobiles. In future M - teaching and learning is a new creative approach and technique to apply in Education for futuristic developments and requirements of the society.

References

Cruse, Alan D. (2000). Meaning in Language: An Introduction to Sematics and Pragmantics. United States: Oxford University Press Inc.

Quattrini,J.A.(1985).Brushing Up Your Writing Skills. 215 Park Avenue South, New York, N.Y.10003: Arco Publishing, Inc.

Montiel, C.J. and Estuar, M.R.(2006), Revolutionary Text: Social Psychology of Cellphone Texting during People Power II. Ateneo de Manila University.

Shidle, N.(1965).The Art of Successful Communication, USA: McGraw-Hill, Inc.

Edwards, Corban. (2009).Text Messaging Effects on Writing. Retrieved December 31, 2010 from htt://personal.georgiasouthern.edu/~ce00988/.

Myhra, John.(2010).Negative Effects of Texting in the Classroom. Retrieved January 21, 2011 from http://www.56wrtg1150.wikidot.com/ negative-effects-of-texting-in-the-classroom.

❒

11.

Perception of Prospective Teachers on Designing Learning Environment of Tomorrows Classroom

Introduction

Teaching and learning process in the 21st century has undergone a vast change from the narrow and teacher – centric method to a more liberal and student – centric one. Research studies on student's characteristics, teacher characteristics, learning environment both at the school and home, role of parents, peer group, nature and demand of the curriculum, mode of transaction of curriculum and assessment reveals the continuous changing process of teaching and learning. Of course the development of science and technology over a period of hundreds and thousands of years dramatically changed the process of teaching and learning with reference to individual and social demands, national and global demands from localization of education to globalization of education, from face to face mode of education to distance mode of education, from stereo type of learning to multimedia approach of learning etc. Therefore it is evident that there are host of factors that determine the effectiveness of teaching and learning. Among them, the classroom environment is the basis and foremost important one that facilitate for the smooth transaction of curriculum in such a manner to make the learning less hard, joyful, unforgettable and concrete one.

Learning Environment - Concept and Meaning

Learning environment means the support system that organize the condition in which human learn best system that accommodate the unique learning needs of every learner and support the positive human relationship needed for effective learning. The learning environment are the physical spaces, tools and learning communities that encourage and enable students and educators to attain the skill – set that the future century requires. This includes a number of important elements such as the physical environment, a school's daily operations including scheduling course and available activities, technology infrastructure, school culture, community involvement and school leadership.

Learning Environment - Definition

According to MC Robbie, Roth and Lucus (1997), "The nature of the classroom learning environment and psycho – social interactions can make a difference in how the students learn and achieve their goals". As cited by Khine and Chiew (2001) from Wilson (1996), "Classroom learning environment refers to a space on a place where learners and teachers interact with each other and use a variety of tools and information resources in their pursuit of learning activities". B.Wilson. (1996) remarks, learning environment is a place or community where people can draw upon resources to make sense out of things and construct meaningful solutions to problems".

Need for the Study

In the emerging trend of classroom context of the digital age, students leaning cannot be restricted and completed with just making them to sit in the classroom and listening to the teachers. But learning is a continuous process and has no limits, as referred by the researchers learning includes so many aspects and more connected with cognitive, affective and phycho-motor domains.

Classroom environment is the most important basis for effective transaction of teaching and learning process. It is determined by innumerable factors such as the physical environment of the classroom, learning resources, opportunities to explore the learning possibilities, interactions between students, interactions between teachers and students, learners' behavior, teachers' behaviour. However the traditional learning environment of the classroom has been thoroughly modified in the modern age of science and technology, especially by the application of digital technology. In this context, the educational administrators, curriculum framers, teachers, parents, students and other stakeholders of education should know the expectations of the learners, either in face to face mode of education or open distance learning. Hence the researcher felt the need for a study on the learning environment at different levels of education.

Statement of the Problem

The problem identified by the investigator is entitled as "Perception of Prospective Teachers on Designing of Learning Environment of Tomorrows Classroom".

Operational Definition of Key Terms

1. **Perception:** In this research, perception refers to the B.Ed students ability or capacity to perceive the future classroom learning environment based on the total score obtained by them, on the Learning Environment Inventory, a self-developed five-point rating scale.

2. **Prospective Teachers:** In this study, this refers to the B.Ed., students undergoing the course of study during the academic year 2013 – 2014.

3. **Designing of Learning Environment:** In this investigation, this refers to the total score obtained by the subjects of the study on the Perception of designing Classroom Learning Environment Inventory a self-developed five- point scale.

4. **Tomorrows Classroom:** In this study, it refers to the future classroom environment.

Objectives of the Study

The researcher intended to carry out the present study with the follow objectives.

- To find out the nature of perception of prospective teachers on the designing of learning environment of tomorrows classroom.
- To develop a suitable tool to study the perception of prospective teachers on the designing of learning environment of tomorrows classroom.
- To find out the significant difference in the perception of prospective teachers on the designing of learning environment of tomorrows classroom with respect to gender.
- To find out the significant difference in the perception of prospective teachers learning environment of tomorrows classroom with respect to subject group.
- To find out the significant difference in the perception of prospective teachers on the designing learning environment of tomorrows classroom with respect to educational qualification.

Hypotheses

- The present study is planned to be carried out with the following hypotheses.
- The nature of perception of prospective teachers on the designing of learning environment of tomorrow's classroom.
- There is no significant difference in the perception of prospective teachers on the designing
- Learning environment of tomorrow's class room with respect to gender.
- There is no significant difference in the perception of prospective teachers on the designing of learning environment of tomorrow's class room with respect to subject group.
- There is no significant difference in the perception of prospective teachers

on the designing of learning environment of tomorrow's class room with respect to educational qualification.

Methodology

The present study is conducted to a randomly selected 100 prospective teachers (i.e B.Ed students) from five different Colleges of Education, Chennai city, who are undergoing the B.Ed., Course during the academic year 2013 -2014.b To collect data from the selected sample an Information Schedule' was used in addition to a self -made five-point scale, 'Perception of Designing Classroom Learning Environment Inventory', which includes five dimensions with four items under each dimension thus making into 20 statements altogether. All the 20 statements are positive in nature the maximum possible score is 100 and the minimum will be 20. The tool was validated by test-retest method. The statistical techniques such as descriptive analysis and differential analysis are used.

Table 1: Designing of Learning Environment as perceived by the B.Ed Students

Variable	No. of Samples	Level	Frequency	Percentage
Perception of Designing of Learning Environment of Classroom	100	Poor	3	3.00
		Average	33	33.00
		High	64	64.00
		Total	100	100.00

Inference

From the above table, it is observed that majority of the B.Ed., students have shown high level of perception of designing of learning environment of tomorrows classroom (64.00%), about one third them (33.00%), have shown average level of perception of designing of learning environment and the remaining students (3.00%), have shown poor perception.

Table 2: Mean, Standard Deviation, Critical Ratio on Perceived Learning Environment of B.Ed students with regard to gender.

Variable	Gender	N	Mean	SD	Critical Ratio	Level of Significance
Physical Aspects	Male	20	17.85	2.834	2.534	0.05
	Female	80	18.92	1.281		
Social Aspects	Male	20	16.60	2.210	2.200	0.05
	Female	80	17.68	1.888		
Instructional Aspects	Male	20	17.75	1.970	2.127	0.05
	Female	80	18.59	1.464		
Teacher Characteristics	Male	20	17.05	2.328	2.484	0.05
	Female	80	18.12	1.554		
Student Characteristics	Male	20	17.00	2.991	3.055	0.01
	Female	80	18.72	2.044		
Overall Perception of Learning Environment	Male	20	92.90	4.471	1.551	N.S*
	Female	80	90.35	6.987		

*Not significant at 0.05 level.

Inference

From the above table, it is noted that there exist no significant difference on the overall perception of designing of learning environment of tomorrow's classroom among the B.Ed student with regard to gender at 0.05 level. However, the male and female teacher-trainees significantly differ on the perception of learning environment dimensions – Physical Aspect, Social Aspect, Instructional Aspects and Teacher Characteristics at 0.05 level. They also significantly differ on the dimension-Student Characteristics at 0.01 level. In these aspects, the female students have more mean score, when compared to the male students. But, in the case of overall perception of designing of learning environment, the male teacher-trainees have more mean score than the female teacher- trainees.

Table 3: Mean, Standard Deviation, Critical Ratio on Perceived Learning Environment of B.Ed students with regard to subject group

Variable	Subject	N	Mean	SD	Critical Ratio	Level of Significance
Physical Aspects	Arts	39	19.21	1.06	2.322	0.05
	Science	61	18.39	2.01		
Social Aspects	Arts	39	17.33	1.96	0.507	N.S*
	Science	61	17.54	2.02		
Instructional Aspects	Arts	39	18.38	1.74	0.176	N.S*
	Science	61	18.44	1.52		
Teacher Characteristics	Arts	39	17.64	1.88	1.214	N.S*
	Science	61	18.08	1.69		
Student Characteristics	Arts	39	18.36	2.55	0.071	N.S*
	Science	61	18.39	2.24		
Overall Perception of Learning Environment	Arts	39	89.41	6.03	1.77	N.S*
	Science	61	91.79	6.86		

*Not significant at 0.05 level.

Inference

From the above table, no significant difference is noted that on the overall perceived learning environment of tomorrow's classroom and also in all its dimensions except on the dimension of Physical Aspects. In Physical Aspects, the arts group B.Ed students have more mean score (M= 19.21) when compared to the science group B.Ed (students (M= 18.39).

Table 4: Mean, Standard Deviation, Critical Ratio on Perceived Learning Environment of B.Ed students with regard to educational qualification.

Variable	Educational Qualification	N	Mean	SD	Critical Ratio	Level of Significance
Physical Aspects	UG	81	18.72	1.84	0.071	N.S*
	PG	19	18.68	1.25		
Social Aspects	UG	81	17.27	2.02	1.98	0.05
	PG	19	18.26	1.66		
Instructional Aspects	UG	81	18.36	1.68	0.797	N.S*
	PG	19	18.68	1.20		
Teacher Characteristics	UG	81	17.85	1.84	0.674	N.S*
	PG	19	18.16	1.46		
Student Characteristics	UG	81	18.43	2.02	0.456	N.S*
	PG	19	18.16	3.52		
Overall Perceived Learning Environment	UG	81	90.52	6.91	1.07	N.S*
	PG	19	92.32	5.13		

*Not significant at 0.05 level.

Inference

From the above table, no significant difference is noticed at 0.05 level, on the perceived learning environment of tomorrow's classroom and also in all its dimensions expect the dimension of Social Aspects at 0.05 level among the B.Ed students with regard to educational qualification. In Social Aspects, the B.Ed students with post graduate qualification have more mean score (Mean = 18.26) when compared to the students with under graduate qualification (Mean = 17.27).

Major Findings of the Study

Majority of the B.Ed students involved in this study express more perception, on the designing the learning environment of tomorrows class room.

The B.Ed students do not differ significantly on the overall perception of designing the learning environment of tomorrow's classroom at 0.05 level with regard to gender. But they differ significantly on the entire five dimension – Physical Aspects, Social Aspects, Instructional Aspects, Teacher Characteristics and Student Characteristics. In all these dimensions the female students have more mean score when compare to the male students.

No significant difference is noticed among the B.Ed students on the overall perception of designing of learning environment of tomorrow's classroom and also in all its dimensions except the dimension the Physical Aspects with regard to subject group at 0.05 level. Further they significantly differ at 0.05 level on the dimension – Physical Aspects. In which, the Arts group student have more mean score (M=19.21) when compare to the Science group students (M=18.39).

No significant difference is noted among the B.Ed students on the overall perception of designing the learning environment of tomorrow's classroom and also in all its dimensions except the dimension of Social Aspects with regard to educational qualification at 0.05 level. In the dimension of Social Aspects the post graduate students have more mean score when compared to the undergraduate students.

Educational Implication

The present study reveals high level of perception of prospective teachers (B.Ed students) on designing of the learning environment of tomorrows classrooms. Accordingly the new class room atmosphere for effective teaching and learning need to be created with the help of all stakeholders of education. Even though the B.Ed male and female students did not differ significantly on the overall perception of designing the learning environment, the female students have high level of perception as compared to the male students. Therefore the male students need to be given necessary orientation to make use of the classroom environment for effective learning. Though the B.Ed students of Arts and Science group of optional subject did not differ significantly on the overall perception of designing the learning environment of tomorrows classroom, the students of Arts group need to be given necessary inputs on the importance of favourable transaction of teaching learning process. Further the B.Ed students with U.G and P.G qualification although did not differ significantly on the designing of the learning environment of tomorrows classroom they need to realize that suitable learn environment is the basis for the curriculum transaction at all levels of education.

Suggestions for Further Study

- The researcher has recommended the following for further research.
- This study may be extended to school and other college students.
- This study may be extended to the teachers of all levels of education.
- This study may be conducted to more number of samples.
- The area of the study may be extended to other places.

Conclusion

Learning environment plays an important role infringing total success of all activities at all levels of education. As the classroom environment is determined by many factors, the B.Ed students who are the future architects of modern India needs to have a thorough knowledge and mind set to create conducive atmosphere to accomplish the teaching and learning process a successful one.

References

Androw M. Colman (2001). A Dictionary of Psychology. New York: Oxford University Press.

Erkenberg, Jorma. (1995). Complex technology – based learning environment, Automating Instructional Design: computer based development and delivery tool, (245-264). NATU AS1 Series.

Magbool Ahmed (2008). Comprehensive Dictionary of Education. New Delhi: Atlontic Publishers & Distributers.

Torsten Husen(Eds) (1994). The International Encyclopedia of Education. (Second Edition). Great Britain: Pergamon.

❐

12.

An Assessment of Edu Digital Skills among Teachers in Namakkal District

Introduction

Teacher is an ideal personality whose knowledge and skill play a major role in the development of the nation to the global standard education in general and tapping the potentialities of students to the maximum extent in particular. Teachers are expected to learn forever to withstand the innovations in teaching and updating the knowledge and widen the clarity of the conceptual framework of the subject of specialization too. Unless and until the teachers prepared to meet the requirements and challenges, the dream and purpose of education will not be fulfilled. Nowadays the system of education has assumed the character which involves more students' participation and student centric which is highly enabled through the application of various educational technologies. Edu - digital skills is considered prerequisite for all teachers teaching for nursery to doctorate scholars. 21st century school curriculum has been enriched to meet the demands of world requirements of quality. Communication, collaboration, critical thinking, problem solving, creativity, invention, information and technology literacy and self direction will facilitate the achievement of aims and objectives of education. Teachers of 21st century are expected to equip themselves with modern technology application in teaching and learning process. A paradigm shift has happened to meet the demands of gen y and z learners which require innovative, explorative and interesting approach in teaching and learning. The curriculum will need withstand the futuristic vision for the global scenario. At this juncture the teachers of today should be enthusiastic to update their knowledge and skills forever in order to keep young to the youngest generation whom they meet and it may also be emphasized greatly as the professional ethics. This study has been attempted to assess the knowledge and skills of teachers in the field of information and communication technology which a teacher necessarily possess in the digital world.

Educational Digital Skills

It is mentioned that in order to thrive in a digital economy, students will need digital age proficiencies. It is important for the educational system to make parallel changes in order to fulfill its mission in society, namely the preparation of students for the world beyond the classroom. Therefore, the educational system must understand and embrace the following 21st century skills within the context of rigorous academic standards.

The 21st Century Literacy Summit (2002) contends that "the explosive growth of technology in every aspect of society offers us a unique opportunity to engage our citizens in economic and civic life" The report further states that to take advantage of this opportunity, we must continually acquire and develop new knowledge and skills. Summit participants noted "Information and communication technologies are raising the bar on the competencies needed to succeed in the 21st century, and they are compelling us to revisit many of our assumptions and beliefs" The sheer magnitude of human knowledge, world to technology necessitates a shift in our children's education - from plateaus of knowing to continuous cycles of learning. Therefore, policymakers and educators alike must define 21st century skills, highlighting the relationship of those skills to conventional academic standards. As they do so, they must also recognize the need for multiple assessments to measure these skills within the context of academic standards, evaluating their application to today's technological and global society.

Technological Literacy

Demonstrate a sound conceptual understanding of the nature of technology systems and view themselves as proficient users of these systems. Understand and model positive, ethical use of technology in both social and personal contexts. Use a variety of technology tools in effective ways to increase creative productivity. Use communication tools to reach out to the world beyond the classroom and communicate ideas in powerful ways. Use technology effectively to access, evaluate, process and synthesize information from a variety of sources. Use technology to identify and solve complex problems in real-world contexts have been considered as Technological Literacy

Information Literacy

Before Accessing Information one should determine what is known and what is needed for problem solving, identify different sources of information, including text, people, video, audio, and databases and prioritize sources based on credibility and relevance. When Accessing Information one need identify and retrieve relevant information from sources and use technology to enhance searching. Revise information-gathering strategies that prove to be in effective when understands how information retrieved does or does not address original problem, evaluate information in terms of credibility and know what are the social, economic, political, legal, and ethical issues that may impact it to facilitate to use technology for evaluation. After Information is extracted, using retrieved information to accomplish a specific purpose, present information clearly and persuasively by using a range of technology tools and media and evaluate the processes and products of these activities have here been considered essential to assure one to be Literate in information.

Global Awareness

Global awareness is knowledge about the connectedness of the nations of the world historically, politically, economically, technologically, socially, linguistically, and ecologically and understand that these interconnections of positive benefits and negative consequences too. The ability to recognize, analyzes, and evaluates major trends in global relations and the interconnections of these trends with both their local and national communities. Participate in the global society by staying current with international news and by participating in the democratic process.

Objectives of the Study

To find the level of Edu-digital skill among school teachers and find whether there is significant different exist among them in relation to their personal variables such as sex, Age, Educational Qualification, Area of Residence, Management of the Institution, Subject of Specialization and the Location of the School.

Research Question

What is the level of educational digital Skills of School Teachers? Is there any Significant Difference Exists among them with respect to their Personal Variables?

Research Methodology

A Normative Descriptive Method of study has been attempted to assess the level of Educational Digital Skills among the School Teachers in Namakkal District

Population, Sample and Sampling Technique of the Study

All teachers who teach in school education are the population of the study and the sample of the study has been chosen from teachers work in Namakkal district only and the sample was taken by stratified random sampling technique which consists of 250.

Tools and Technique of Data Collection

A tool consisted of 24 items related to some basic skills necessary for adopting computer enabled teaching technology, using internet connection which will benefit students to gain knowledge, understand the concept better, improve the critical thinking, problem solving ability, creativity and to enhance their communication skill and appropriate application of the knowledge gained for the betterment of himself and to the society. The scope of this study extent all teachers who teach in the classroom from kindergarten to plus two levels. The questionnaire has dimensions of using the computer for retrieving useful information via internet, knowledge about various search engines, and preparation of effective PowerPoint materials, video clippings, software package application, audio recording, connecting to virtual classroom and the facilities to publish the students works in internet. Knowledge and the application of MS word, Excel format, mobile for teaching and learning purpose and the ability to set ready LCD, mike and arrange show in the smart classroom and the application of social media in education have also been taken for assessing.

Scoring Procedure & Statistical Tools Used

The Questionnaire used in the study has five point scale of the level of skill of the respondents in relation to their digital skill hence it has five options of known very well, known, moderately known, known little and Unknown which scored as 5, 4,3,2 and 1 respectively.

SPSS package has been used to analyze the data and the percentage analysis and the differential analysis have been used to describe and infer the details pertaining to the research question formulated for the study.

Teachers have necessary in Skill and knowledge in the application of MS office, Mobile technology in teaching and learning, information retrieval system from online resource centre but the majority teachers have moderate and least knowledge about e-content preparation, application of social media, and security issues in web mails, various learning management system and efficient use of ICT in teaching

Table -1: Significance of Difference in Edu-Digital Skill of Teachers

Demographic Variables	P Value	L - level of Sig.
Sex	0.153	NS
Area of Residence	0.104	NS
Location of the School	0.214	NS
Teaching Experience	0.098	NS
Educational Qualification	0.521	NS
Management of the School	0.021*	S
Subject of Specialization	0.001**	S

There is no significant difference exist among the respondents in their Educational digital skill in relation to their personal variables of Sex, Area of Residence, Location of the School, Teaching Experience and their educational qualification. But the statistical report of analysis shows that there is significant difference exist among the sample in relation to their management of the school and their subject of specialization.

Educational Implications

Teacher Education curriculum should emphasize the ICT enabled education in B.Ed program

Workshops need to be conducted for B.Ed program in the practical application of ICT and training program can be organized for E- content preparation

Orientation and Refresher courses for the teachers in schools should be conducted frequently to enable teachers to facilitate them in the efficient use of ICT in teaching and learning environment

Collaborative Approach should be made in integrating ICT in education

Conclusion

Teachers are the forerunner of all developments and growth of the nation and the world; they play a significant role in bringing desirable outcome in the world with their adaptability and their ever learning behavior of updating knowledge and skills in any field. No technology can replace the teacher in any period of time but the teacher needs possess skills in the application of technology which facilitate desirable educational outcome in the field of education.

References

Felix.A & Jahitha Begum (2011) “An Awareness of E-resources related to ICT and Educaation among M.Ed Students and M.Phil Scholars” ICT in teaching and learning, APH Publishing Corporation, New Delhi, p.169

Nagarajan .K (2009) “Educational Innovations and Management” Ram Publishers, Chennai. Pp.135-185.

Natchimuthu.K (2012), “Need of E-Content Development in Education Today” APH Publication Corporation, New Delhi. P.76.

Rangarajan. P & Senthilnathan.S (2012) “Teacher Educators Attitude towards E Learning” Edutracks, Vol.No.12 No.1 pp. 21-32.

❐

13.

Access to Teaching Learning Materials among the General and Special Education Teachers in the School System

Introduction

Teaching Learning Materials (TLM) are the supportive sources for the learners to learn the contents. Some of the TLMs are customized where as others are readily available in the markets. Teachers are innovating and developing TLM according to the needs of the learners. The intension of this study is to find out the availability and accessibility of TLM with general and special education teachers in the school system. This study reveals that the customized materials are access to both general and special education teachers. The specific TLM or supportive materials are access to Special education teachers. The use of high technology like computer and laptops are access to the general education teachers.

Teaching Learning Materials (TLM) are the supportive sources for the learners to learn the contents. Some of the TLMs are customized where as others are readily available in the markets. Teachers are innovating and developing TLM according to the needs of the learners.

Learners should be the center of instruction and learning. The role of teachers is to help learners to learn. Teachers have to follow the curriculum and provide, make, or choose materials. They may adapt, supplement, and elaborate on those materials and also monitor the progress and needs of the students.

Materials include textbooks, video and audio tapes, computer software, and visual aids. They influence the content and the procedures of learning. The choice of deductive vs inductive learning, the role of memorization, the use of creativity and problem solving, production vs. reception, and the order in which materials are presented are all influenced by the materials.

Teaching materials is a generic term used to describe the resources teachers use to deliver instruction. Teaching materials can support student learning and increase student success. Ideally the teaching materials will be tailored to the content in which they are being used to the students and the teacher in the class. Teaching materials come in many shapes and sizes, but they all have in common the ability to support student learning.

Teaching materials here refers to teaching aids used when teachers carryout their activities in class room such as chalk ,writing board, charts, apparatus , specimens , concrete materials, photographs, pictures , maps ,globes , cassettes , video recording, transparencies , projectors and computers.

Materials in the typical general Education Classroom tend to be limited. Text books, work books and work sheets are the materials commonly available in the class room. Globe, Videos, soft ware and internet resources are rarely available with many of the class rooms. Braille texts, large print texts, CDs with Audio output, sign and symbols are the materials required for children having certain limitations to learn the subjects. Universally Design Learning Materials gives students the multiple means of representation of concepts and multiple means of expression for the students to demonstrate what they have learned. Instruction is flexible and provides accessibility for all students. Every learning material we develop will be an asset for us. An investment of time or money in good teaching materials is an investment in good teaching. This study will focus on magnitude of availability and accessibility of teaching learning materials with the teachers who are interacting with the students including children with special needs.

Review of Literature

Halil Eksi (2008) conducted a case study on the use of materials by classroom teachers at primary education level. They stated that they carryout various activities for an efficient and effective education and teaching, the teachers use different materials in lesson in order to create a multi learning setting for students. They face many problems while using the materials. They also reported that the newly adapted education programme requires more material use. They also reported that the insufficient materials will create problem in future.

Nelson(2006) reported that every student needs and has the right to access the curriculum regardless of disabilities or differentiated learning styles.

Pisha and Coyne (2001) identified an approach called "Smart from the start" that is Universally Designed Learning Materials (UDL) should be part of the Curriculum Learning Environments and assessments.

Prema P (2009) Conducted an impact study on instructional and nurturing effect of Activity Based Learning on selected districts in Tamil Nadu and reported that the ABL method of learning influences the children's overall academic performance , improvement in reading ,writing and numerical skills.

Rose Meyer &Hitchcock ,(2006) reported that the Alternative formats of basic materials can also be provided for students with disabilities. Such as Braille text for students with Visual Impairments , large print text for students with low vision , and CD s with audio output for students with dyslexia.

Santhanam.P (2005) conducted a study on remedial programmers for children with learning difficulties in Chennai ,Thiruvallur and Kancheepuram District of Tamil Nadu and reported that the intellectual capacity of the children with learning ability is significantly higher than those with learning disability. The children with learning disability show better academic performance after remedial programme. Awareness on remedial programme about learning disabilities to be conducted through print and electronic media

Aim and Objective

- The main aim is to find out the accessibility of teaching learning materials to the general and special education teachers
- To find out the availability of teaching and learning materials in the class room for general and special education teachers
- To find out the accessibility of teaching learning materials in the class room to teach the children.
- To find out the incidence of using the teaching learning materials in the class room by general and special education teachers

METHOD

Survey method

Samples

Purposive sampling 149 teachers consisting of 82 General Education Teachers from 5 different schools and 67 Special Education Teachers working in SSA Projects up to secondary level were selected for this study.

Tool

A questionnaire consisting of 28 teaching learning materials widely used in general education and special education programme is constructed and administered with the guidelines of scoring each items on Available and used frequently (2) Available but used rarely (1) Not available (0) Refer - Appendix (A)

Procedure

The tool was constructed and administered on the general and special education teachers working in public school by indicating their choice on each items of Teaching Learning Material in the following manner Available and used frequently (2) Available but used rarely (1) Not available (0). The confidentiality on their response is promised by the author.

Result and discussion

After collecting information from the teachers the scores were tabulated and interpreted for the study. Refer Table I

From the table it is learnt that the materials of Chalk and board, Chart &flash cards models, work book, poster and text are commonly available and frequently used by both general and special education teachers.

Computer, laptop is available and frequently used by the general education teachers where as ABL materials, mobility aids and sign languages are frequently used by the special education teachers.

Pictures/Icons, graphics are rarely used materials by the general education teachers where as video, TV, tape, laptop, signature guide; adapted pencils are used rarely by the special education teachers.

Braille, Abacus, mobility cane, sign language and ABL materials are not used by general education teachers. Whereas Computers, laptop, animation, graphics, film and slides are not used by the special education teachers.

Films and graphics are not used by general and special education teachers respectively.

Table I: Access to TLM among the general and special education teacher's Frequency distribution

Sl. No.	variable	Access to TLMs by the Educators			Access to TLMs by Special educators			Total
		Not used	Rarely used	Frequently used	Not used	Rarely used	Frequently used	
1	Chalk board	0	3	79 96%		2	65 97%	149
2	Chart and flash card	6	0	76 92%	1	7	59 88%	149
3	Models	6	11	65 79%	9	19	39 58%	149
4	Video	71	5	6 7%	16	42	9 13%	149
5	Television	73	5	4 4%	16	32	19 28%	149
6	Film	77	5	0	39	22	6 8%	149
7	audio	58	10	14 17%	20	29	18 26%	149
8	Slide	67	4	11 13%	35	26	6 8%	149
9	Tape	51	15	16 19%	19	29	19 28%	149
10	Work Book	12	7	63 76%	9	18	40 59%	149
11	Poster	19	12	51 62%	29	22	16 23%	149
12	Text	10	01	71 86%	16	15	36 53%	149
13	Braille	57	04	21 25%	29	30	08 11%	149

14	Abacus	63	03	16 19%	27	24	16 23%	149
15	Mobility Can	75	02	05 6%	25	29	13 19%	149
16	Sign language	64	03	15 18%	12	23	32 47%	149
17	ABL	46	08	28 34%	09	08	50 74%	149
18	Mobility Aid	60	06	16 19%	23	18	26 38%	149
19	Book rest	47	08	27 32%	25	28	14 20%	149
20	Signature guide	19	28	35 42%	29	23	15 22%	149
21	stencils	40	22	20 24%	27	23	17 25%	149
22	Tripod pencil or pen	20	16	46 56%	23	23	20 29%	149
23	Computer	14	16	52 63%	25	23	19 28%	149
24	Adapted key board mouse	27	17	38 44%	35	19	13 19%	149
25	laptop	31	25	26 31%	28	28	11 16%	149
26	animation	36	30	16 19%	36	25	06 8%	149
27	Pictures/ Icon	20	41	21 25%	28	21	18 26%	149
28	Graphics	29	38	15 18%	60	7	0	149

The study shows that there is no significant difference in Accessing the TLM among the general and special education teachers except the use of signature guide.

Conclusion

Majority of the TLM which is used in the public schools are traditionally prepared in nature which are used regularly

The innovated materials which are available in the public school to teach the students with diversified needs are minimal and used rarely.

Use of computer for teaching and learning is more common with the general education teachers than the special education teachers.

Recommendation

Teachers working in the public school system need to understand the shift from using traditional materials to the innovated materials according to the needs of children with diversified in nature.

The materials need to be explored by the teachers and the students as well to optimize the learning.

Use of computer should be practiced by the special education teachers for successful mainstreaming.

The management may give the liberty to explore and innovate the materials according to the needs of the diversified group of learning.

In-service training may be organized to innovate and develop TLM to cater the diversified group of learners.

There is a need to conduct more study in this area to innovate and develop appropriate TLM which is access to all categories of learners and the teachers.

References

Allwright, R. L. (1990). What do we want teaching materials for? In R. Rossner and R. Bolitho, (Eds.), Currents in language teaching. Oxford University Press

Halil Eksi (2008) A case study on the use of materials by classroom teachers ,Kasim Yildirim

Educational Sciences Theory and Practice 8(1) January 2008 ,305-322

Pisha and Coyne (2001) Incorporating Universal Design for learning principles in to the class room design.

Prema P (2009) Instructional and nurturant effect of Activity Based Learning An impact study in selected districts of Tamil Nadu. SSA TN Report

Santhanam.P (2005). Remedial programmers for children with learning difficulties. SSA TN Report.

❒

14.

Students Attitude towards Audio-Visual Aids Used by the Teachers

Introduction

Graphs, Diagram, Posters, Maps, Comics, Cartoons, Charts, Globes, Display Board, Peg Boards, Hook and loop board, felt board, magnetic board, marker board, chalk board, bulletin board, models, Epidiascope, slight projector, over head projector (OHP), fields trips, excursion, exhibition, museums, radio, Television, Tape recorder, Video Caste Record VCR and Computers. By using audio visual materials in accessible process, materials givens objects changes in time, speed and space could easily be brought to the class. Audio visual aids can helps to imaginative teachers to solve the communication problems. It also helps to extend human experience. Use of audio visual aids results in greater acquisition of knowledge of facts and ensures longer retention of the information gained. It can provide effective substitutes for direct contact of students with environment-social and physical. It also adds an expected change in attitude and behaviour of the students. It can provide integrated experiences varying from abstract to concrete. It helps in to secure and retain to attention as well as develop the communication skills. It could be used to motivate and stimulate interest of students to gain further knowledge. Lastly, In a conventional teaching method teacher is the centre of attention and the primary sources of information.

An attitude is a mental state of readiness exerting directive or dynamic influence upon individual's response to all objects and situations with which it is related. Therefore if we can have some judgement about the attitude of an individual towards a specific thing or activity then we can have a fair idea as to whether the individual can be persuaded to participate in a particular thing or activity and whether he shall adopt it with interest and sincerity or not.

The attitude is the degree of positive or negative effect associated with some psychological objects namely institution, ideal, symbol, phrase, slogan, job or idea towards which people can differ with respect to positive or negative effect (Thurstone, 1946). The attitude is a dispositional readiness to respond to certain situations, persons, objects in a consistent manner which has been learnt and has become one's typical mode of response (Free Mann, 1950). According to Guild (1950) attitude is a tendency of individual to favour or not to favour some type of situation. The attitude may be considered as motivational perceptual states, which direct perceptions and predispose a person to act in accordance with perceptions (Allport, 1955). The attitudes are learnt pre-dispositions to respond positively to certain objects, situations, institutions, concepts or other persons (Aiken, 1979).

Review of Literature

Glee Harrah Cady and **Pat Mc Gregor (2005**) describes that "Internet is a network of network and the internet mostly connects network of computers".

Barry (2006) studied the relationship between students perceptions of their science class room learning environment and attitude to four different scores of scientific information experiments, books, promote positive attitude towards experiment as a source of information, while less favorable environment promoted more positive attitude to the more authoritarian sources of information.

Schafer (2007) compared third and fourth grade students using ESS units with students using laid low science serious on classification skills, science achievements and science attitudes. No achievement or classification skill different were noted but ESS students had more favorable attitudes.

Williams (2008), "Attitude of high school pupils towards general science and its relationship with achievement and its subjects". In her study it is found to examine if there are any differences among the different groups of students such as boys and girls. Rural school pupil and Urban school pupils in respect of their achievement in science, attitude towards science and attitude forwards science education.

Martis Anandi (2009) developed the test on scientific attitudes (TOSA), taking the point of view that attitudes must be inferred from the behavior of students. They developed a multiple – choice format test. The developed behavioral definitions of eight attitudes: (1) critical mindedness, (2) suspended judgment (3) Respect for evidence (4) Honesty, (5) Objectivity, (6) Willingness to change opinions, (7) Open – mindedness and (8) Questioning attitude. The behavioral definitions to these eight attitudes were used to develop items.

Mohanty Ajay Kumar (2010) investigated attitudes towards education, critical thinking ability and specific effective behavious of (1) Students who had studied, the BSCS nvironmental models "Investing your Environment" (IYE), (2) Those students using one of BSCS biological science version and (3) Those studying models of Biology. He found that the ability of students who had experienced BSCS Biological science was significantly increased but no other differences were found among the students on any of the other variables.

Objectives

The present study attempts to investigate the attitude towards Audio-visual aids used by the teachers.

Methodology

Methodology is an important aspect of any research work. There are different methods followed at various stages of any investigation. The details of methods followed in this study such as selection of tools, sample frame, collection of data, and analysis of data are involved in this research paper. The study has been designed with the students attitude towards Audio-visual aids used by the teachers achievement. The major aim of the present study is to determine the students Audio-visual aids used by the teacher.

Method of data collection

The investigator personally distributed the questionnaires to each member of the randomly selected sample. They were requested to answer the items in the booklet as per the instructions provided at the beginning of each questionnaire. Confidentiality of response was assured. The questionnaires were collected by the investigator from the employees. The responses were scored as per the scoring key of the respective questionnaire. Then the results were tabulated, analysed and discussed.

Sample

A sample is a finite number of observations (or) cases in a particular universe of which it is a pat (Good 1952). The investigator prepared a representative random sample of students studying VIII & IX standard in different schools at Coimbatore District. A sample of 100 students was finally selected

Hypothesis

Students have favourable attitude towards use of Audio Visual Aids in Coimbatore district school.

Nature of the Tool

The inventory contained general instruction for the students and information about bio data. In addition to that the specific instruction ware given to on the first page of the inventory. Space for collecting personal data like students name type of school, locality of the school, class, gender, community, religion, group, medium of instruction, birth order of the child and parental literacy.

Data Processing

The collected data were analysed using appropriate statistical techniques. The descriptive statistics such as mean and S.D, t-ratio were computed. In order to study the functional dependencies to indicate the likelihood of causal relationships between the variables, inferential statistical techniques of ANOVA and Percentage analysis were computed.

Analysis And Interpretation

Table 1: Showing Mean, SD and t-test for respondent about students attitude towards audio visual aids used by the teachers on the basis of type of the school.

Types of the school	N	Mean	SD		LS
Government	62	70.48	6.50	2.78	0.01
Private	38	73.30	10.33		

Hypothesis 1: Students do not differ in their students attitude towards audio visual aids used by the teachers on the basis of types of the school.

The calculated t-value (2.78), which is significant at 0.01 level, confirms that there is a significant difference in student audio visual aids on the basis of type of the school. Hence the stated hypothesis is rejected. So government students have high level of audio visual aids than private school students.

Table 2: Showing Mean, SD and t-test for respondent about students attitude towards audio visual aids used by the teachers on the basis of locality of the school.

Locality of the school	N	Mean	SD	t-value	LS
Urban	74	72.24	8.11	1.07	NS
Rural	26	71.14	9.19		

Hypothesis 2: Students do not differ in their students attitude towards audio visual aids used by the teachers on the basis of locality of the school.

The calculated t-value (1.07), which is not significant at 0.05 level, confirms that there is no significant difference in their audio visual aids on the basis of locality of the school. Hence the stated hypothesis is accepted.

Table 3: Showing Mean, SD and t-test for respondent about students attitude towards audio visual aids used by the teachers on the basis of Gender.

Gender	N	Mean	SD	t-value	LS
Male	74	70.97	7.41	1.85	NS
Female	26	72.90	9.89		

Hypothesis 3: Students do not differ in their students attitude towards audio visual aids used by the teachers on the basis of gender.

The calculated t-value (1.85), which is not significant at 0.05 level, confirms that there is no significant difference in their audio visual aids on the basis of gender. Hence the stated hypothesis is accepted.

Table 4: Showing Mean, SD and t-test for respondent about students attitude towards audio visual aids used by the teachers on the basis of group.

Group	N	Mean	SD	t-value	LS
Arts	56	69.19	5.37	5.58	0.01
Science	44	74.58	10.37		

Hypothesis 4: Students do not differ in their attitude towards audio visual aids used by the teachers on the basis of group.

The calculated t-value (5.58), which is significant at 0.01 level, confirms that there is a significant difference in student audio visual aids on the basis of group. Hence the stated hypothesis is rejected. So science students have high level of audio visual aids than art students.

Table 5: Showing Mean, SD and F-ratio for students attitude towards audio visual aids used by the teachers on the basis of medium of instruction.

Medium of instruction	N	Mean	SD	F-ratio	LS
Hindi	50	70.20	9.64		
English	30	71.75	4.19	6.49	0.01
Kannada	20	75.00	11.60		
Total	100	71.78	8.58		

Hypothesis 5: Students do not differ in their attitude towards audio visual aids used by the teachers on the basis of medium of instruction.

The calculated F-ratio (6.49), which is not significant at 0.05 level, confirms that there is a significant difference in students attitude of audio visual aids on the basis of medium of instruction. Hence the stated hypothesis is rejected.

Table 6: Regression for student demographic characters and their attitude towards audio visual aids used by the teachers.

MODEL SUMMARY

Model	R	R Square	Adjusted R Square	Std. Error of the Estimate
1	436[a].	190.	159.	7.87

a. Predictors: (Constant)

ANOVA[B]

Model	Sum of Squares	df	Mean Square	F	.Sig
	4189.756.	11	380.887	6.155	000[a].
Residual	17821.724	88	61.881		
Total	22011.480	99			

a. Predictors: (Constant)

b. Dependent variable

C efficients [a]

Model	Unstandardized Coefficients		Standardized Coefficients	t	Sig.
	B	Std. Error	Beta		
Name of the school	58.979	4.376		13.477	.000
Type of the school	2.387	1.116	.139	2.139	.033**
Locality of the school	-1.000	1.005	-.058	-.995	.320
Class	-.500	1.046	-.028	-.478	.633
Gender	1.989	1.052	.115	1.891	.060
Community	-1.365	.422	-.190	-3.233	.001**
Religion	.757	.627	.068	1.208	.228
Groups	5.255	.947	.306	5.548	.000**
Medium of instruction	2.183	.649	.191	3.365	.001**
Birth order of the child	-9.11	1.032	-.001	-.009	.993
Parental literacy (Father)	-.143	1.003	-.008	-.143	.887
Parental literacy (Mother)	-.585	.955	-.033	-.612	.541

a. Dependent Variable: Attitude towards Audi visual aids

** Significant at 0.01 level

According to the regression result it is known that the demographic variables are influenced nearly 19 per cent to measure their attitude towards audio visual aids. This is proved by the obtained r square value (0.19).

Further the calculated F-value (6.15) also significant at 0.01 level. It indicates that there is a significant influence between students demographic characters and their attitude towards audio visual aids.

Also from the obtained t- values the demographic variables such as type of school, community, group studied and medium of instructions the students studied are significant at 0.01 level. So it is concluded that there is a significant difference regarding attitude towards audio visual aids on the basis of these variables.

Conclusion

Audio Visual aids or graphic aids are the form of visuals that are represented on plane surface. The subject – matter areas that are represented in Audio Visual aids or graphic aids are in an abridged and easily understandable form. They convey meaning mainly through relatively conventionalized symbols that are nearer to reality perceptually than verbal symbols. They secure the attention of the pupils by their attractive format and simplicity of layout. They convey the expected message by combination of visual and pictorial message made meaningful by suitable captions. Pictures and words blended in harmony deliver the required information. The idea conveyed by any graphic aid should be a single concept. The layout and words should not be complicated so as to puzzle the viewer and make him lose interest in the same. The statement "one good visual which can secure and maintain attention and educate the viewer in the desired area is worth a thousand words" is quite correct. Graphics could be truly considered as the shorthand language of the idea presented. The criteria for good graphics are that they should be simple, bold, legible, brief and have adequate margins.

Findings of the study

Based on the results that students do not differ in their audio visual aids on the basis of types of the school

From the calculation that students do not differ in their audio visual aids on the basis of locality of the school

Based on the results that students do not differ in their audio visual aids on the basis of gender

Based on the results that students do not differ in their audio visual aids on the basis of group

From the analysis that students do not differ in their audio visual aids on the basis of medium of instruction

Discussion

Audio visual aids a process of inward journey to unravel the hidden potentialities of a being. It helps an individual to develop ones personality. A systematic approach of Audio visual aids helps an individual to see the all around development at physical, mental, intellectual and emotional level. The practice of use of audio visual aids makes an individual perfect. It removes the unwanted elements in the mind of the learner. It improves concentration and brings mental stability. Audio visual aids are an essential tool for students to achieve higher score in their studies as if improves concentration, memory and skills. The present study clearly indicates and recommends the students to use of audio visual aids as to develop positive attitude towards everything in their life which helps to excel themselves in their studies. The entire study concluded reveals that the use of audio visual aids has high achievement and expressed more favourable attitude.

Educational Implications

Audio-visual aids are very important and useful aids for teaching. As well as it creates high interest among the students to learn the subjects. So, the department of education shall take a steps to implement the latest audio-visual aids to all the school and colleges for teaching purpose.

For self-learning, these type of aids are very helpful to the students. Also students are very much interested in using latest technologies such as computers and internet. In internet lot of facilities are there to learn new information with visual appearance. From that students are also get more interest to use that. In the case of teaching, in older days teachers follow interactive methods and oral demonstration. But these are not creating much interest. In order to create interest and attention audio-visual aids are highly useful. So, the concerned educational institution tries to provide these facilities. So that teachers and students get benefited.

Conclusion

The present study attempted to identify the students attitude towards audio-visual aids used by the teachers. For that the researcher framed some objectives. On the basis of objectives, a questionnaire is framed. After framing the questionnaire, these are circulated to the selected samples. 100 samples were selected randomly. The responses were collected and coded using computerized. To test the hypotheses and characteristics of the data, some standard statistical tools were used. The statistical tools such as t-test, F-ratio and correlation were used. From the analysis the result concluded that the students have positive attitude towards audio-visual aids used by the teachers.

References

Glee Harrah Cady and Pat Mc Gregor (2005) "Internet is a network of network and the internet mostly connects network of computers". Journal of research in science teaching.

Barry (2006) "Relationship between students perceptions of their science class room learning environment and attitude", Journal of Educational Research.

Williams (2008), "Attitude of high school pupils towards general science and its relationship with achievement and its subjects". Journal Community and Guidance.

Martis Anandi (2009), in test on scientific attitudes (TOSA), taking the point of view that attitudes must be inferred from the behavior of students, Journal of All India Association for Educational Research, Vol.17, Nos. 1 & 2, March & June.

Mohanty Ajay Kumar (2010), Attitudes towards education, critical thinking ability and specific effective behavious, Journal of all India Association for Educational Research, Vol.14, Nos.3 & 4

❐

15.

Aching of Biological Science Education

Introduction

The development of Science and Technology, especially the application of information and communication technology (ICT) in the new era has greatly influenced teaching and learning in education. In the present era of knowledge explosion, adopting modern tools for teaching is one of the predominant needs of the hour. Instructional technology in the third world is changing rapidly. Knowledge packaging in electronic form or e-content is a powerful technique for teaching all subjects. ICT have become handy in class room teaching which has the potential to engage the students throughout the period and make learning easy and effective through, visual aids, animations and simulations.

Need for the Study

New innovations are coming to the fields of education in terms of technology which promises to change the process of teaching and learning. Training of competent teachers is very important because they directly or indirectly influence the quality and the quantity of educational services. Without adequately trained teacher cadre the institution cannot aim to expand the educational facilities.

E-Content

The term 'e-content' refers to that form of knowledge or content which is packed in an electronic form. It includes text, audio, video, animations, images etc. An innovative application of computer in the teaching and learning process is e-content. E-content is the advancement of technology to design, deliver, select, administer and extend learning.

Objectives of the Study

To prepare e-content for particular topic in Teaching of Biological Science Education at B.Ed., level.

To find out whether there is any significant difference in achievement means score between control group and experimental group in learning Teaching of Biological Science Education by the B.Ed., student teachers.

Methodology

The investigator followed the experimental method for the present study. The data thus collected were put into appropriate statistical analysis: Mean, t-test, standard deviation.

Sampling Procedure

The present study is concerned only with B.Ed student teachers in J.J. College of Education and Oxford College of Education, Trichy. Hence the college selected could be considered as a representative college. Eighteen students have been selected for experimental group and another eighteen students for control group by using purposive sampling method.

Hypotheses of the Study

The following hypotheses were formulated based on the objectives of the study

There is no significant difference in the Posttest achievement mean scores between control group and experimental group.

There is significant difference in the achievement mean scores between the Pre and Post test of experimental groups who learnt through e-content.

Table 1: The table shows the comparison of Post-test achievement mean scores of Experimental group and control group.

Group Compared	N	M	**SD**	**t value**	**df**	Level of significance
Control Group	18	8.72	1.127	9.22	34	**Significant**
Experimental Group	18	13.33	1.910			

The calculated t-value 9.22 is greater than the critical value 2.704 corresponding to the 0.01 level of significance. This implies that the control group and experimental group differ significantly in their achievement in the post-test. Hence the null hypothesis is not accepted.

Table – 2: The table shows the difference between the Pre-test and Post-test achievement mean scores due to treatment for the experimental group.

Experimental Group	No of students	Mean	SD	't' value	df	Level of significance
Pre – test	18	10.72	1.364	8.040	34	**Significant**
Post - test	18	13.33	1.910			

The calculated t-value 8.040 is greater than the critical value 2.704 corresponding to the 0.01 level of significance. This shows that experimental group is highly significant in their achievement in post-test. Hence the null hypothesis is accepted.

Major Findings of the Study

The major findings which have emerged from the study are as follows:

An Achievement test was conducted to access the effectiveness of the e-content. While analyzing the result, i.e., the performance of the students in the achievement test is better and it became clear that the e-content is effective.

The student teachers of experimental group who were taught through e-content achieved more in subject units than the control group student teachers.

It was found .that learning through e-content and learning through traditional lecture method are not similar and they differ significantly.

Educational Implications of the Study

New instructional techniques of assisting student through computer are to be explored by the teachers and researchers continuously.

Teachers of higher secondary schools can be given orientation as how to develop e-content.

The use of e-content is found to be valid in enhancing the achievement; it will diminish wastage and stagnation in school.

Conclusion

Based on the proceeding findings of the study, the following conclusions are arrived. The levels of performance of teacher trainees who learnt through e-content were greater the other part and hence it was evident that e-content is also an effective approach to teach Biological Science Education. The rise of e-learning and an electronic content (e-content) is a new paradigm for education and training in the knowledge society, empowered by technological advancements which give the modern instructional technology. The development of educational content in time with the changing times has become a major responsibility of the modern teacher who has to face a new learner in a new environment. More over the level of motivation, learning style and anxiety towards computer improves the efficiency of the student teachers and hence the e-content approach is having great scope in the instructional design of the student teachers.

References

Amutha. S. & Ramganesh. E e-content- An Inevitable Supplement for a Teacher Educator. Paper presented at the International conference on Quality Enhancement in Distance Education for Lifelong learning 26-27 March 2011, Edited by Dr.K.Anandhan, Bharathidasan University.

Jeya Shanmuga Raja. J, E-Content Development on Teaching method of Zoology at B.Ed Level., Paper presented at the International conference on Quality Enhancement in Distance Education for LifeLong Learning 26-27 March 2011, Edited by Dr.K.Anandhan, Bharathidasan University.

Suma.S.(2007). Development and Validation of e-content on the uses of the simple present tense in English at higher secondary level. M.Phil Thesis submitted to Bharathidasan University.

❐

16.

Implications of Multimedia in Teaching Economics with Special Reference to Higher Secondary Students in Chennai

Introduction

In 1965, Lorence settler and Danieal Davis[5] developed most complicated teaching process in which computer was used for presenting instruction in place of teacher. They divided the teaching process of the computer in two parts.

1. Pre-tutorial phase 2. Tutorial phase.

In the first phase, computer assisted instruction is given to the pupils to achieve the specific objectives on the basis of his entry behaviour. In the second phase instructing material is presented accordingly. The pupil is evaluated. After presenting the instruction, computer also controls it. It also provides reinforcement to the pupils. In the modern age, the use of computers in the field of education, made in the following areas.

All the researches do all analytical tasks with the help of computers in the research work.

- Computers are also used in educational guidance and counseling.
- Remedial teaching of the pupils is also done by the computers.
- Computers help in sought for preparing the results of the examinations.

Learning with aid of computer through computer, aided instruction, computer simulation etc. It is a self learning strategy in teaching learning process. Students learnt their subjects at their own pace.

Internet is worldwide computer network that contains a large collection of information which could be made available to you on your computer. The person having internet connection can retrieve any information on individual interest. Purves, A.C.[6] (1998) says that, the internet is the abbreviation of inter network system. The internet is the name for a vast, worldwide system consisting of people, information and computers. It is also described as a network of networks because these are more than one lakh readily accessible through the Internet. Internet is the largest and most complete learning tool for a group of people with varied educational background and interests. Teachers, students, businessmen and other educators can share ideas instantly across vast distances. For scientific and research community, internet is an essential and indispensable tool. Through Internet scientist can gain and enjoy instant access to the world's most advanced research facilities and discuss their research problems with others, working in the same field.

Review of Literature

Coyne, Margaret Ann, Ed.D., (2006), in their paper "Emerging literacy Assisted parents to scaffold the emerging literacy skill of their pre-school-aged children through the use of electronic storybooks", reported that, that importance of parents reading to their young child is well supported by research (Health, 1986). However, Edwards (1989) found that parents whose own literacy skills are emerging have difficulty supporting the emerging literacy skills of their young children through storybook reading.

The development of a new paradigm, Universal Design for Learning (UDL) (Meyer & Rose, 1998 and 2002) provides a framework for the use of computer technology to support learning. Drawing on Vygotsky's (1978; 1986) socio constructive theory of learning and the latest advances in the neurosciences, UDL investigates how technology can support diverse learners. This study examined whether UDL –based technology might help parents who are themselves emerging readers support their children's literacy development.

When parents use of targeted storybook reading behaviours increased if their children's pre-intervention scores on language measures were below age-level, the children's scores on post-intervention measures improved to age-level or above. In addition, the children's scores on measures of story retelling and print knowledge improved.

BEABVIS C., Deakin University, Literacy and the new technologies in the middle years. (2006) This paper explores young people's textual engagements with electronic and other forms of popular culture, and the changing nature of literacy in the context of COM modification, mass marketing and the new technologies. Building on school based studies exploring computer games in the classroom and the Poke on phenomenon, it examines ways in which popular texts are read, and narrative and generic elements incorporated into the curriculum and into students' spoken and written texts. Drawing on Green's model of cultural, critical and opal dimensions of (technological) literacy, it examines issues of literacy and culture, identity and critique for teachers and students in the middle years, and their implications for constructions of literacy and curriculum.

BERRY L. and CHAPMAN E, University of Sydney Effects of Background Information and Audiovisual Presentation Modes on Students' Attention Styles and Enjoyment in Listening to Unfamiliar Music.(2006) Research has indicated that students typically do not enjoy or engage with unfamiliar pieces of music. This is discouraging and puzzling to music educators who wish to introduce their students to a diverse range of musical genres. This study explored the effects of two factors on students' initial reactions to an unfamiliar Shakuhachi piece. Using a 2 by 2 crossed-factor design, 438 students in grades 9-11 were assigned at random to listen to the piece in either audio-only or audiovisual form, and with or without verbal background information.

Results indicated that while the provision of information significantly ($p<0.05$) increased students' enjoyment of the music and their interest in hearing more of the same kind of music, it had no effect on their listening attention styles (e.g., focusing on the melody or idiomatic details of the piece). Conversely, use of the audiovisual presentation mode significantly impacted on one aspect of students' attention styles (focus on idiomatic details) and perceived familiarity with the piece, but had only a marginally significant effect on their enjoyment or interest. Implications of these results for the introduction of unfamiliar music to high school students will be discussed.

BLACKMORE J., JOHNSON R., WARREN W., (2006) States that the potential of new learning technologies for transforming teaching and learning, and indeed the organization of schooling. Much has also been written about teacher responses to new learning technologies-how they resist, ignore, or innovate. A number of recent reports indicate a gap between policy, practice and the capacity of organizations to provide the conditions and resources sin schools to creatively use new learning technologies. Few of these discourses draw upon theories of educational change, in particular those which relate to the dissonance between attitudes and feelings about radical change, and how it impacts on teacher work identity with respect to learning technologies. Much of the literature has focused upon the technical aspects, the hardware and software, but not the 'warm ware', so critical to sound pedagogical practice. This paper draws from the Learning in New Environments Research Group action research project, a pilot study in a large metropolitan secondary college, which is exploring the social implications of new learning technologies for changing relations between students, between teachers and students, between teachers and between family and school. The paper draws from the first round of data collection from the teachers in an ongoing action research project in a region with a high level of socio-economic and cultural diversity.

It draws on concepts of Lieberman's notion of learning networks and Wenger's notion of communities of practice, as well as past research on the reception of gender equity reform in educational organizations, which focuses upon emotional aspects of professional work identity and organizational change.

Joseph Kacharayll, (2006) – "Suitability of colleges for Web Bases Learning" reported that Web based learning environment is expensive to establish, government and private managements should take necessary steps to provide adequate infrastructure facilities in colleges for web based learning. A proper utilization of available human resources would help improve web based learning. In order to overcome technical limitation, training has to be given to both teachers and learners to create flexible and uninterrupted learning environment. The training of material designers should be especially focused upon. Most of the colleges have not properly utilized the available web resources in their teaching learning strategies. There is only nominal technical support and assistance from technical staff and from government and private managements at the institutional level for web based learning. The author collected sample for the survey of 152 college lecturers was obtained through random sampling.

Objectives

- To find the effect on learning competency of the students by using Multi media for teaching economics
- To find the active participation of the teachers in using multi media for teaching economics.
- To find how the teaching of economics has been efficiently improved using the multi media.
- To find the importance of computers and internet in teaching economics.

Methodology

The investigator, for the present study adopts the survey method of research. It is a procedure in which data is systematically collected from a population through some form of direct solicitation such as face to face interview, questionnaire or schedule. The survey is extensive and cross sectional dealing with the relatively large number of cases of a particular time and yielding statistics that are abstracted from particular cases. It is the method of investigation which attempts to describe and interpret what exists at present in the form of conditions, practices, process, trends, effects, attitudes, and beliefs. Using this method the investigator had gathered information's measure the Effect of Multi Media Aids in teaching economics for Higher Secondary Students in Chennai.

Sample

For the present study 155 Higher Secondary Students in Chennai.

Data Collection

Primary data, required for the present research work were collected by conducting direct interviews using questionnaire. All the respondents were given sufficient information about the study. These respondents were provided with the same questionnaires. They were also informed that they have to answer in the same fashion.

Statistical Tools for Analysis

The following tools statistical tools were used for the analysis of data. t-test, one way ANOVA and correlation analysis is used for the present study.

Analysis and Interpretation

Table 1: Six wise distribution of "t" value between the boys and girls of the higher secondary economics students using multimedia resources in their schools

Dimensions	Boys N = 55		Girls N = 100		Calculated value of "t"	Level of significance at 5% level
	Mean	S.D	Mean	S.D		
Working knowledge of computers	79.42	8.17	80.42	8.68	0.71	NS
Knowledge about internet	78.15	9.51	76.88	9.80	0.91	NS
Knowledge using A.V. Aids	79.76	7.48	76.26	10.79	2.37	S
Preparation of computer based study materials	76.40	7.97	74.77	11.04	1.06	NS
Assignment and project	81.75	6.31	78.35	10.18	2.56	S
Interaction with others through web			386.5	42.77	1.56	NS

(At5% level of significance, the table value of "t" is 1.96)

It is refereed from the above table that there is a significant difference between boys and of Higher Secondary Students of economics group in there, Knowledge in using A.V. Aids and Assignment and project but there is no significant difference between Male and Female Higher Secondary students of economics group in their Working knowledge of computers, knowledge about internet, Preparation of computer based study materials, interaction with others through web.

Table – 2: Area wise distribution of "t" value between the urban and rural higher secondary economics students using multimedia resources in their schools

Dimensions	Urban N = 55		Rural N = 100		Calculated value of "t"	Level of significance at 5% level
	Mean	S.D	Mean	S.D		
Working knowledge of computers	79.42	8.17	80.42	8.68	0.71	NS
Knowledge about internet	78.15	9.51	76.88	9.80	0.91	NS
Knowledge using A.V. Aids	79.76	7.48	76.26	10.79	2.37	S
Preparation of computer based study materials	76.40	7.97	74.77	11.04	1.06	NS
Assignment and project	81.75	6.31	78.35	10.18	2.56	S
Interaction with others through web	395.47	28.53	386.5	42.77	1.56	NS

(At 5% level of significance, the table value of "t" is 1.96)

It is referred from the above table that there is no significant difference between urban and rural Higher Secondary Students of economics group in there, Knowledge in using A.V. Aids, Assignment and project, Working knowledge of computers, Knowledge about internet, Preparation of computer based study materials, Interaction with other through web.

Table – 3: "F" value among the boys and girls of Higher Secondary economics Group Students in Using Multimedia resources

Dimensions	**df= 2,152**			**Calculated "f" Value**	**Remarks at 5% Level**
	Source of variation	**Sum of squares**	**M.S.V**		
Working knowledge of computers	Between With in	118.75 11110.63	59.38 73.10	0.81	NS
Knowledge about internet	Between With in	7.94 14650.81	3.97 96.39	0.04	NS
Knowledge in using A.V. Aids	Between With in	23.44 15123.38	11.72 99.50	0.12	NS
Preparation of computer study materials	Between With in	155.56 15619.63	77.78 102.76	0.76	NS
Assignment and project	Between With in	164.39 12793.88	82.19 84.17	0.98	NS

Interaction with others through web	Between With in	216.00 23034.00	108.00 1515.39	0.07	NS

(For 2,152 df. At 5% level of significance, the table value of "f" is 3.06)

It is inferred from the above table that there is no significance difference among the boys and girls of Higher Secondary economics group students in using Multimedia resources in the Higher Secondary schools of Chennai.

Table – 4: "F" value among the Rural and Urban Higher Secondary Students of economics Group in Using Multimedia source in Chennai

Dimensions	df= 2,152			Calculated "f" Value	Remarks at 5% Level
	Source of variation	**Sum of squares**	**M.S.V**		
Working knowledge of computers	Between With in	39.50 11189.88	19.75 73.62	0.27	NS
Knowledge about internet	Between With in	394.39 14264.50	197.16 93.85	2.10	NS
Knowledge in using A.V. Aids	Between With in	130.31 15016.50	65.16 98.79	0.66	NS
Preparation of computer study materials	Between With in	444.44 153330.75	222.22 100.86	2.20	NS
Assignment and project	Between With in	364.69 12593.56	182.32 82.85	2.20	NS
Interaction with others through web	Between With in	5628.00 224924.00	2814.00 11479.76	1.90	NS

(for 2,152 df.at 5% level of significance, the table value of "f" is 3.06)

It is inferred from the above table that there is no significance difference among the Rural and Urban Higher Secondary students of economics group in using Multimedia resource in the Higher Secondary Schools of Chennai.

Table – 5: "F" value among the Higher Secondary Students of economics Group in Using Multimedia source in Government and Private Higher Secondary Schools in Chennai

Dimensions	df= 2,152			Calculated "f" Value	Remarks at 5% Level
	Source of variation	**Sum of squares**	**M.S.V**		
Working knowledge of computers	Between With in	39.50 11189.88	19.75 73.62	0.27	NS
Knowledge about internet	Between With in	394.39 14264.50	197.16 93.85	2.10	NS
Knowledge in using A.V. Aids	Between With in	130.31 15016.50	65.16 98.79	0.66	NS
Preparation of computer study materials	Between With in	444.44 153330.75	222.22 100.86	2.20	NS
Assignment and project	Between With in	364.69 12593.56	182.32 82.85	2.20	NS
Interaction with others through web	Between With in	5628.00 224924.00	2814.00 11479.76	1.90	NS

(For 2,152 df. at 5% level of significance, the table value of '' is 3.06)

It is inferred from the above table that there is no significance difference among the Government and Private Higher Secondary students of economics group in using Multimedia resource in the Higher Secondary School of Chennai

Table – 6: The Correlation value between the Male and Female Higher Secondary Students in using multimedia resources in the Higher Secondary

SCHOOLS OF CHENNAI

Category	?X	?X²	?Y	?Y²	?XY	Calculated	Remarks
Boys	683	8595	545	5495	6775	.68	NS
Girls	1199	14757	970	9584	11740	.425	S
Total	1882	23354	1515	15079	18515	.325	S

(Table value of Correlation Co-efficient at 5% level of Significance is 0.161)

It is inferred from the above table that there is no significant relationship between the rural and high secondary economics group boys in using multimedia resources and there is a significant relationship between rural and urban high secondary economics group girls in using multimedia resources.

Findings

There a significant difference among the higher secondary commence group students of boys and girls, higher secondary commence students of government and private schools, higher secondary commence group students of rural and urban schools, in their interest towards learning commence through multimedia resources in Chennai.

There is significant difference among the higher secondary economics group students in their levels of using multimedia shows moderate knowledge except interaction with others through web and no significant difference in low of using multimedia except interaction with other through web and no significant difference in higher level knowledge of using multimedia.

There is no significant difference among the higher secondary economics group boys in their level of using multimedia shows moderate knowledge and higher level of using multimedia and there is a significant difference low of using multimedia at the area of assignment and project, interaction with others though web.

There is no significant difference among the secondary economics group girls in all the levels of using multimedia resources.

There is no significant difference among the higher secondary economics group students of government school in their level of using multimedia shows moderate knowledge and there is a significant difference in low level of interaction with others though web and shows significant difference in higher level of in knowledge about internet, knowledge in using A.V.aids and in the preparation of computer based study materials.

There is no significant difference among the higher secondary economics group students of private school in their level of using multimedia shows moderate knowledge and higher level knowledge of using multimedia and there is a significant difference in low level of using multimedia at the area of working of computer and in interaction with others though web.

There is no significant difference among the higher secondary economics group of rural school in their level of using multimedia shows moderate knowledge and there is a significant difference in low level of preparation of computer in high level of using multimedia at the is a significant difference in high level of using multimedia at the area of working knowledge of computer and in interaction with others with through web.

There is no significant difference between boys and girls or higher secondary students of economics group in there, knowledge in using A.V aids and assignments and project but there is no significant differences between male and female higher secondary of economics group in their working knowledge of computers, knowledge about internet, preparation of computer based study materials with others thought web.

There is no significant difference between urban and rural higher secondary of economics in there, knowledge in using A.V aids, assignment and project, working knowledge of computer knowledge about internet preparation of computer based study martial interaction with others web.

There is no significant difference among the Male and female higher secondary schools of economics group in using multimedia resource in the Higher secondary schools of Chennai.

There is no significance difference among the Rural and urban higher secondary students of economics group in using Multimedia resource in the higher secondary of Chennai.

There is n no significant difference among the Government and private Higher Secondary students of economics group in using Multimedia resource in the higher schools of Chennai.

There is no significant relationship between the Rural and urban high secondary group boys in using multimedia resources and there is a significant relationship between Rural and Urban high secondary economics group girls in using multimedia resources.

The research overwhelmingly demonstrates that usages of multimedia will definitely improve the quality of teaching economics in higher secondary classes.

The research found that the students are actively involved in learning part if the multimedia is introduced in classroom teaching.

The research shows the students are highly motivate towards the subject by using multimedia teaching aids and they are attracted more and improve their understanding and memory power in various economics topics like advertising, banking, etc. While using multimedia resources.

It is concluded that there is a positive effect of using multimedia aids in the economics achievement of the students in economics in Chennai.

Conclusion

The present study aims to find out the implications of multimedia in teaching economics with special reference to higher secondary. The researcher framed objectives and hypotheses on the basis of the above context. The research was carried out in 155 samples based randomly. A questionnaire constructed by R was used to collect the relevant data. After collecting the data they were analyzed using statistical tools such as t-test, ANOVA and Correlation analysis. The result concluded that students have average implications of multimedia in teaching at Higher Secondary level.

Reference

Beavis C. (2006), popular culture, textual practice and identify and identify: literacy and the new technologies, in the middle years

Berry l. And Chapman e, (2006); Effect of Background Information and Audiovisual Presentation Modes on Students' Attention style and enjoyment listening to Unfamiliar Music.

Best, (1982); J., Johnson R., Warren W. (2006), A hand book of Education Technology.

Blackmork j., Johnson R., Warren W. (2006), A handbook of Education Technology.

Bruce B.C (2004); Diversity and critical social engagement: How changing technologies enable new modes of literacy in changing circumstances. IN D.E. Alvermann (E.d), Adolescents and illiteracies in a digital world (pp. 1-18). New York: Peter Lang publication.

Chisamore, chris (2006), Multimedia and Education today.

Coyne, Margaret Ann (2006), Emerging Literacy: Assisting Parents to scaffold the emerging literacy skills of their preschool aged children through the use of electronic story books.

Joseph Kacharayll (2006); Educational Technology Year Book, 1998.

Lanksherar, C and Knoble, M (2003); New literacies: changing Knowledge And classroom learning. Philadelphia: open University press.

Lewis, C and Finders, M. (2004); implied adolescents and implied teachers; A generation gap for new times. D.E Alvermann (Ed.), Adolescents and literacies in adugital world (pp.101-113).New York: peter Lang publishing.

❒

17.

An Assessment of Edu Digital Skills of Teachers in Namakkal District

Introduction

Teacher is an ideal personality whose knowledge and skill play a major role in the development of the nation to the global standard education in general and tapping the potentialities of students to the maximum extent in particular. Teachers are expected to learn forever to withstand the innovations in teaching and updating the knowledge and widen the clarity of the conceptual framework of the subject of specialization too. Unless and until the teachers prepared to meet the requirements and challenges, the dream and purpose of education will not be fulfilled. Nowadays the system of education has assumed the character which involves more students' participation and student centric which is highly enabled through the application of various educational technologies. Edu - digital skills is considered prerequisite for all teachers teaching for nursery to doctorate scholars. 21st century school curriculum has been enriched to meet the demands of world requirements of quality. Communication, collaboration, critical thinking, problem solving, creativity, invention, information and technology literacy and self direction will facilitate the achievement of aims and objectives of education. Teachers of 21st century are expected to equip themselves with modern technology application in teaching and learning process. A paradigm shift has happened to meet the demands of gen y and z learners which require innovative, explorative and interesting approach in teaching and learning. The curriculum will need withstand the futuristic vision for the global scenario. At this juncture the teachers of today should be enthusiastic to update their knowledge and skills forever in order to keep young to the youngest generation whom they meet and it may also be emphasized greatly as the professional ethics. This study has been attempted to assess the knowledge and skills of teachers in the field of information and communication technology which a teacher necessarily possess in the digital world.

Teacher is an ideal personality whose knowledge and skill play a major role in the development of the nation to the global standard education in general and tapping the potentialities of students to the maximum extent in particular. Teachers are expected to learn forever to withstand the innovations in teaching and updating the knowledge and widen the clarity of the conceptual framework of the subject of specialization too. Unless and until the teachers prepared to meet the requirements and challenges, the dream and purpose of education will not be fulfilled. Nowadays the system of education has assumed the character which involves more students' participation and student centric which is highly enabled through the application of various educational technologies. Edu - digital skills is considered prerequisite for all teachers teaching for nursery to doctorate scholars. 21st century school curriculum has been enriched to meet the demands of world requirements of quality. Communication, collaboration, critical thinking, problem solving, creativity, invention, information and technology literacy and self direction will facilitate the achievement of aims and objectives of education. Teachers of 21st century are expected to equip themselves with modern technology application in teaching and learning process. A paradigm shift has happened to meet the demands of gen y and z learners which require innovative, explorative and interesting approach in teaching and learning. The curriculum will need withstand the futuristic vision for the global scenario. At this juncture the teachers of today should be enthusiastic to update their knowledge and skills forever in order to keep young to the youngest generation whom they meet and it may also be emphasized greatly as the professional ethics. This study has been attempted to assess the knowledge and skills of teachers in the field of information and communication technology which a teacher necessarily possess in the digital world.

Educational Digital Skills

It is mentioned that in order to thrive in a digital economy, students will need digital age proficiencies. It is important for the educational system to make parallel changes in order to fulfill its mission in society, namely the preparation of students for the world beyond the classroom. Therefore, the educational system must understand and embrace the following 21st century skills within the context of rigorous academic standards.

The 21st Century Literacy Summit (2002) contends that "the explosive growth of technology in every aspect of society offers us a unique opportunity to engage our citizens in economic and civic life" The report further states that to take advantage of this opportunity, we must continually acquire and develop new knowledge and skills. Summit participants noted "Information and communication technologies are raising the bar on the competencies needed to succeed in the 21st century, and they are compelling us to revisit many of our assumptions and beliefs" The sheer magnitude of human knowledge, world to technology necessitates a shift in our children's education - from plateaus of knowing to continuous cycles of learning. Therefore, policymakers and educators alike must define 21st century skills, highlighting the relationship of those skills to conventional academic standards. As they do so, they must also recognize the need for multiple assessments to measure these skills within the context of academic standards, evaluating their application to today's technological and global society.

Technological Literacy

Demonstrate a sound conceptual understanding of the nature of technology systems and view themselves as proficient users of these systems. Understand and model positive, ethical use of technology in both social and personal contexts. Use a variety of technology tools in effective ways to increase creative productivity. Use communication tools to reach out to the world beyond the classroom and communicate ideas in powerful ways. Use technology effectively to access, evaluate, process and synthesize information from a variety of sources. Use technology to identify and solve complex problems in real-world contexts have been considered as Technological Literacy

Information Literacy

Before Accessing Information one should determine what is known and what is needed for problem solving, identify different sources of information, including text, people, video, audio, and databases and prioritize sources based on credibility and relevance. When Accessing Information one need identify and retrieve relevant information from sources and use technology to enhance searching. Revise information-gathering strategies that prove to be in effective when understands how information retrieved does or does not address original problem, evaluate information in terms of credibility and know what are the social, economic, political, legal, and ethical issues that may impact it to facilitate to use technology for evaluation. After Information is extracted, using retrieved information to accomplish a specific purpose, present information clearly and persuasively by using a range of technology tools and media and evaluate the processes and products of these activities have here been considered essential to assure one to be Literate in information.

Global Awareness

Global awareness is knowledge about the connectedness of the nations of the world historically, politically, economically, technologically, socially, linguistically, and ecologically and understand that these interconnections of positive benefits and negative consequences too. The ability to recognize, analyzes, and evaluates major trends in global relations and the interconnections of these trends with both their local and national communities. Participate in the global society by staying current with international news and by participating in the democratic process.

Objectives of the Study

To find the level of Edu-digital skill among school teachers and find whether there is significant different exist among them in relation to their personal variables such as sex, Age, Educational Qualification, Area of Residence, Management of the Institution, Subject of Specialization and the Location of the School.

Research Question

What is the level of educational digital Skills of School Teachers? Is there any Significant Difference Exists among them with respect to their Personal Variables?

Research Methodology

A Normative Descriptive Method of study has been attempted to assess the level of Educational Digital Skills among the School Teachers in Namakkal District.

Population, Sample and Sampling Technique of the Study

All teachers who teach in school education are the population of the study and the sample of the study has been chosen from teachers work in Namakkal district only and the sample was taken by stratified random sampling technique which consists of 250.

Tools and Technique of Data Collection

A tool consisted of 24 items related to some basic skills necessary for adopting computer enabled teaching technology, using internet connection which will benefit students to gain knowledge, understand the concept better, improve the critical thinking, problem solving ability, creativity and to enhance their communication skill and appropriate application of the knowledge gained for the betterment of himself and to the society. The scope of this study extent all teachers who teach in the classroom from kindergarten to plus two levels. The questionnaire has dimensions of using the computer for retrieving useful information via internet, knowledge about various search engines, and preparation of effective PowerPoint materials, video clippings, software package application, audio recording, connecting to virtual classroom and the facilities to publish the students works in internet. Knowledge and the application of MS word, Excel format, mobile for teaching and learning purpose and the ability to set ready LCD, mike and arrange show in the smart classroom and the application of social media in education have also been taken for assessing.

Scoring Procedure & Statistical Tools Used

Questionnaire used in the study has five point scale of the level of skill of the respondents in relation to their digital skill hence it has five options of known very well, known, moderately known, known little and Unknown which scored as 5, 4,3,2 and 1 respectively.

SPSS package has been used to analyze the data and the percentage analysis and the differential analysis have been used to describe and infer the details pertaining to the research question formulated for the study.

Table -1: An Analysis of Edu Digital Skills among Teachers in Namakkal District

Items	Very well Known		Well Known		Moderately Known		Known Little		Unknown		Total
	F	%	F	%	F	%	F	%	F	%	
Information Retrieval	41	16.4	59	23.6	62	24.8	75	30	13	5.2	250
Power point preparation	52	20.8	67	26.8	53	21.2	60	24	18	7.2	250
Efficient use of Windows operating system	35	14	48	19.2	75	30	81	32.4	11	4.4	250
Connecting to the Online Teaching of World Classroom	15	6	20	8	39	15.6	116	46.4	60	24	250
Skill in make it work well of LCD mike screen view	15	6	26	10.4	77	30.8	114	45.6	18	7.2	250
Knowledge about E learning material preparation	21	8.4	15	6	27	10.8	129	51.6	58	23.2	250
Account in social networking sites like Face-book, twitter	22	8.8	36	14.4	74	29.6	12	4.8		42.4	250
Using of videos and computer games in teaching	19	7.6	29	11.6	55	22	85	34	62	24.8	250
Application of Virtual classrooms and chat rooms in teaching and learning	13	5.2	18	7.2	17	6.8	56	22.4		58.4	250
Application of documentary film in deliverance of the instructional objectives	51	20.4	60	24	41	16.4	31	12.4	67	26.8	250
Using of web- Camera in virtual interaction	16	6.4	41	16.4	27	10.8	71	28.4	95	38	250
Application of white Board in teaching	25	10	16	6.4	19	7.6	43	17.2		58.8	250

Items	Very well Known		Well Known		Moderately Known		Known Little		Unknown		Total
Safety and security issues in using webmail	17	6.8	39	15.6	90	36	70	28	44	17.6	250
Security Challenges in instant messaging	15	6	35	14	78	31.2	98	39.2	24	9.6	250
Application of iPod and tables in teaching	11	4.4	23	9.2	67	26.8	80	32	69	27.6	250
Application of Video conferencing for teaching and learning	32	12.8	24	9.6	71	28.4	90	36	33	13.2	250
Application of YouTube	49	19.6	86	34.4	55	22	62	24.8	38	15.2	250
Application of Flicker & Picasa	19	7.6	25	10	62	24.8	104	41.6	40	16	250
Application of mobile phone for transferring data of video	21	8.4	27	10.8	80	32	90	36	32	12.8	250
Application of mobile phone for transferring data of voice	22	8.8	33	13.2	76	30.4	81	32.4	38	15.2	250
Application of mobile phone for transferring data of text		74.8	46	18.4	3	1.2	9	3.6	5	2	250
Assessment of students performance through online	25	10	52	20.8	58	23.2	105	42	10	4	250
Application of learning Management System - LMS	11	4.4	21	8.4	37	14.8	57	22.8	15	6	250
Application of Video-recording	17	6.8	26	10.4	51	20.4	78	31.2	78	31.2	250

Majority of teachers have necessary in Skill and knowledge in the application of MS office, Mobile technology in teaching and learning, information retrieval system from online resource centre but the majority teachers have moderate and least knowledge about e-content preparation, application of social media, and security issues in web mails, various learning management system and efficient use of ICT in teaching

Table -2: Significance of Difference in Edu-Digital Skill of Teachers

Demographic Variables	P Value	.Level of Sig
Sex	0.153	NS
Area of Residence	0.104	NS
Location of the School	0.214	NS
Teaching Experience	0.098	NS
Educational Qualification	0.521	NS
Management of the School	*0.021	S
Subject of Specialization	**0.001	S

There is no significant difference exist among the respondents in their Educational digital skill in relation to their personal variables of Sex, Area of Residence, Location of the School, Teaching Experience and their educational qualification. But the statistical report of analysis shows that there is significant difference exist among the sample in relation to their management of the school and their subject of specialization.

Educational Implications

Teacher Education curriculum should emphasize the ICT enabled education in B.Ed program

Workshops need to be conducted for B.Ed program in the practical application of ICT and training program can be organized for E- content preparation

Orientation and Refresher courses for the teachers in schools should be conducted frequently to enable teachers to facilitate them in the efficient use of ICT in teaching and learning environment

Collaborative Approach should be made in integrating ICT in education

Conclusion

Teachers are the forerunner of all developments and growth of the nation and the world; they play a significant role in bringing desirable outcome in the world with their adaptability and their ever learning behavior of updating knowledge and skills in any field. No technology can replace the teacher in any period of time but the teacher needs possess skills in the application of technology which facilitate desirable educational outcome in the field of education.

References

Felix.A & Jahitha Begum (2011) "An Awareness of E-resources related to ICT and Education among M.Ed Students and M.Phil Scholars" ICT in teaching and learning, APH Publishing Corporation, New Delhi, p.169

Nagarajan .K (2009) "Educational Innovations and Management" Ram Publishers, Chennai. Pp.135-185.

Natchimuthu.K (2012), "Need of E-Content Development in Education Today" APH Publication Corporation, New Delhi. P.76.

Rangarajan. P & Senthilnathan.S (2012) "Teacher Educators Attitude towards E Learning" Edutracks, Vol.No.12 No.1 pp. 21-32.

www.educatorstechnology.com/2012/06/33-digital-skills-every-21st-century.htm

http://www.educatorstechnology.com/2013/07/the-8-digital-skills-students-need-for.html

❐

18.

Awareness of Flip Teaching among School Teachers

Introduction

The Flip classroom is the latest learning model to have taken the teaching and training world by storm. The investigator adopted the survey method and target population was the school teachers who are teaching in various boards such as Matriculation and CBSE in and around Madurai district. The size of the sample of the present study is 60 school teachers. The self made check list was used in the study and it consists of 20 items. Statistical technique used are Calculating mean value,' t' test. The Findings are there is no Awareness of flip teaching among school teachers in and around Madurai District and there is no significant difference in the awareness of flip teaching among school teachers with regard to the gender and Board of Institution.

"A Quality education has the power to transform societies in a single generation, provide children with the protection they need from the hazards of poverty, labor exploitation and disease and give them the knowledge, skills and confidence to reach their full potential". India needs multi-dimensional and broad based quality education to maintain its leader ship in the 21st century. Therefore India should show the concern over the quality in education as the education in India is not competitive in terms of the quality with other countries. The FLIP classroom is the latest learning model to have taken the teaching and training world by storm.

In a flipped classroom content normally delivered in lectures is covered by students in their own time, often through the use of video or readings. Face-to-face time is used for activities where the focus is on learning through experience. It allows teachers and trainers to flip through concepts, which in turn gives them more time to interact with students instead of lecturing. This is also known as backwards classroom, reverse instruction, flipping the classroom and reverse teaching. The flip classroom is ideal for adult education and training, where students are more self-motivated and focused. This model of learning compliments training objectives which are 'actionable' rather than passive objectives like 'awareness or comprehension'.

Significance of the Study

This study is undertaken to find out the awareness of flip teaching among school teachers in and around Madurai District. This study gave them the clear knowledge about Flip teaching is a form of blended learning in which students learn new content online by watching video lectures, usually at home, and what used to be homework (assigned problems) is now done in class with teachers offering more personalized guidance and interaction with students, instead of lecturing. This is also known as backwards classroom, flipped classroom, reverse teaching, and the Thayer Method

Background of the Study

This study was done in and around Madurai city. The need of today is quality of education. If the quality is maintained in all the above we can produce professionally skillful students who are going to the meet the future global citizens. So it is necessary to have innovative teaching methods or alternative methods in imparting knowledge among the students. The traditional pattern of teaching has been to assign students to read textbooks and work on problem sets outside school, while listening to lectures and taking tests in class.

Traditionally, the teacher engages with the students who ask questions — but those who don't ask tend to need the most attention. "We refer to 'silent failers,' " said one teacher, claiming that flipping allows her to target those who need the most help rather than the most confident. Flipping changes teachers from "sage on the stage" to "guide on the side", allowing them to work with individuals or groups of students throughout the session. The Investigator wanted to know whether there is awareness of flip teaching among school teachers in and around Madurai District

Objectives of the study

To measure and find out whether there is awareness of flip teaching among school teachers in and around Madurai District

To enable the teachers to sensitize the today's need to turn towards the flip teaching and classrooms.

Hypotheses

Awareness of flip teaching among school teachers in and around Madurai District are high

There is significant difference in the awareness of flip teaching among school teachers with regard to the board of institution. [Matriculation and CBSE]

There is significant difference in the awareness of flip teaching among school teachers with regard to the gender. [Male & Female]

Methodology used

The survey method was taken and target population is the school teachers who are teaching in various boards such as Matriculation and CBSE in and around Madurai district. The size of the samples of the present study is 60 teachers.

Tool Construction

The self made check list was used to find out whether there is awareness of flip teaching among school teachers in and around Madurai District. The checklist had 20 items

Administration of the Tool

The photocopies of the check-list were distributed to the teachers of four educational institutions in and around Madurai. The filled in questionnaires were corrected analyzed and interpreted.

Statistical Technique Used

Table shows the number of teachers from four schools

S.no	Name of the school	Institution	Total no	F	M
1)	S.S.V.Sala	Matriculation	15	15	-
2)	Le Chatlier	Matriculation	15		15
3)	PVK Academy	CBSE	15	8	7
4)	Vellammal	CBSE	15	7	8
		Total	60	30	30

Hypothesis: 1

Awareness of flip teaching among school teachers in and around Madurai District are high

Table Showing the Mean Value

Name of the school	Total no	Sex		Board	Over All Mean
		Female	Male		
S.S.V.Sala	15	15	-	Matriculation	7.5
Le Chatlier	15		15	Matriculation	9
PVK Academy	15	8	7	CBSE	8.5
Vellammal	15	7	8	CBSE	9.5

It is inferred from the above table that there is no Awareness of flip teaching among school teachers in and around Madurai District .All the mean scores indicated that they are less than the theoretical mean (10). Still there were no innovative teaching methods were followed to reach the global standard as well as to improve the low achievers.

Hypothesis: 2

There is significant difference in the awareness of flip teaching among school teachers with regard to the board of institution. [Matriculation and CBSE]

Table showing the difference between the variables

S.No	Variable	Mean	Std.dev	't'	Significance at 0.5 level
1	Matriculation	8.25	0.50	0.93	No Significant
2	CBSE	9	0.74		

It is inferred from the above table that the't' value is 0.93 is lesser than the't' value 1.96 at 0.5 level of significance. So the research hypothesis is rejected. The result indicated that there is no significant difference in the awareness of flip teaching among school teachers with regard to the board of institution. [Matriculation and CBSE]

Hypothesis: 3 : There is significant difference in the awareness of flip teaching among school teachers with regard to the gender. [Male & Female]

Table showing the difference between the variables

S.NO	Variable	mean	Std. dev	't'	Significance at 0.5 level
1	Female	8.5	1.25	0.98	No Significant
2	male	9	0.57		

It is inferred from the above table that the't' value is 0.98 is lesser than the't' value 1.96 at 0.5 level of significance. So the research hypothesis is rejected. The result indicated that there is no significant difference in the awareness of flip teaching among school teachers with regard to the gender. [Male & Female]

Hypotheses Verification

There is significant difference in the awareness of flip teaching among school teachers with regard to the board of institution. [Matriculation and CBSE] is rejected.

There is significant difference in the awareness of flip teaching among school teachers with regard to the gender. [Male & Female] is rejected.

Delimitation

The samples are taken from only from four schools in and around Madurai area and also restricted to the variable that is type of institution and gender alone. In this study the Investigator use only mean and‘t’ test as the statistical treatment .This was also delimitation.

Scope of the Study

This study can highlight the need for the alternative, creative, student friendly, user friendly and innovative methods of teaching. The flip classroom is the latest learning model to have taken the teaching and training world by storm. The flip teaching models are being incorporated by teachers of all subjects, for students of all ages. This mode of learning is now slowly making inroads into the teaching and training in India. The flip classroom is ideal for adult education and training, where students are more self-motivated and focused. This model of learning compliments training objectives which are ‘actionable’ rather than passive objectives like ‘awareness or comprehension’.

Suggestion for the Future

- We can take more schools for the study
- We can take so many variables
- We can also use extend all the boards of schools in future.

Educational Implications

This Study revealed that there is a need for considering another scenario where in students has already gone through a video lecture on the second conditional at their own time. They can rewind, pause and repeat the lecture as many times as they want. Additionally, they do graded exercises to practice the concept and take up an assessment to check their proficiency. Both the learner and the facilitator now know what to focus on and the class is much more productive for the learner. The facilitator only has to provide solutions for problem areas. Flip training can help overcome the constraints and make learning a focused and productive experience for the learner.

❒

19.

A Study of Online Teaching among School Students

Introduction

Blended Learning is a formal education program in which a student learns at least in part through online delivery of content and instruction with some element of student control over time, place, path, or pace. In the growing technology, this scenario plays a major role in teaching and learning. The Learners, Learning methods, learning approaches, Learning situations and the teachers all have to be accessed with the online learning or Teaching.

As all the Learners of all the fields are depending on the Information Technology in our day today life, one needs to have the knowledge about the blended learning for self development among all major fields of learning. Education plays a major role with this blended learning, as the class room is the place which determines the future of every child and the Nation. In this Y-Generation, everything is easily learnt though online. For example; Driving, Cooking, Marketing, Shopping and ticketing…etc

Review

The Concept of blended learning has been around for a longtime, but the terminology was not firmly established until 21st century. In 1999, the Interactive learning centers, announced its change of name to EPIC learning.

In 2006, the first handbook of Blended Learning by Book and Graham was published. Graham defined "blended as the learning system, combining of internet, digital media with established classroom forms that require the physical co presence of teacher and students.

In 2007, Clark & Westcott stated that Podcasting consists of listening to audio recordings of lectures. It can be used to review live lectures and to provide opportunities for students to rehearse oral presentations.

In 2009, Mc Garr and in 2009 again Steven & Teasley studied that Podcasts may also provide supplemental information to enhance traditional lectures.

In 2009, Callaway & Ewen said the Psychological researches suggest that university students who download podcast lectures achieve substantially higher exam results than those who attend the lectures in person.

Word Usage and Context

In current research literature, the word blended learning are often used interchangeably as, blended, Hybrid, Technology- Mediated Instruction, web-enhanced Instruction and Mixed-Mode Instruction...Etc however the united states use the term often blended learning and mixed mode instruction with more regularity in recent researches.

Objectives

- To study simultaneous independent and collaborative learning experiences.
- To study the incorporation of major contributions in lecture or teaching.
- To study the incorporation of information technology into the class project.
- To study the incorporation of communication between teachers and students.
- To study the evaluation of students understanding of course material
- To study the development of interest and creativity of students in online teaching.

Hypotheses

There is a simultaneous independent and collaborate learning experience would be in favorable mode for present days educational streamline

There is a significant relationship in blended learning on interest and success (achievement).

There is a relationship between lectures and students.

There is significant relationship in student understanding in online evaluation.

There is a significant relationship among interest and creativity of using information technology.

Methodology

The following questionnaire is prepared in order to study the use of online teaching and

learning among B.Ed Students.

How far the mobile / internet browsing help in you development?

Yes/Fair/No

How far the information technologies help in doing your project and homework?

Yes/Fair/No

Is getting education related information is easy to access from mobile internet?

Yes/Fair/No

Is getting educational related information is easy to access from computer internet?

Yes/Fair/No

How far the knowledge of computer helps you in initiating your creativity and interest?

Yes/Fair/No

How far the e-communication helps to learn?

Yes/Fair/No

Blended Learning Result Analysis

	Good	**Fair**	**No**
Total	555	190	55
Percentage(%)	69.375	23.75	6.875

Recommendations:

- For lower achievers and average students the online teaching method would be more useful as they can save the information and learn whenever they can but it is not possible with the teacher.
- Online teaching helps to develop the interest of all children through animation and graphics which the teacher or the Blackboard cannot provide.
- Self learning for lower achievers is more possible in online learning.
- Based on the level of learning, one can be promoted to the higher level of learning with their interest and area of knowledge.
- Time and place of learning or any other factors are not a limit for learning through online.
- Easy to access all information through online from any corner of the world.

Conclusion

Thus the Blended learning combines brick and mortar schooling with online delivery of content and instruction. Mobile devices provide support that enhances teaching and learning in a virtual class room environment and educational experiences. Blended learning takes the classroom out of a traditional brick and mortar setting. The students become the part of virtual communities used for collaboration. Blended learning transitions away from a traditional teaching environment to a customized and interactive web platform for the user. The proponents of blended learning cite the opportunities for data collections and customization of instruction and assessment as two major benefits of this approach. Schools with blended learning models may also choose to reallocate resources to boost student achievement outcomes.

❐

20.

Implications of Multimedia in Teaching Economics with Special Reference to Higher Secondary Students

Introduction

The computer has revolutionized the whole society overwhelmingly inclusive of all human activities especially those of education. The computer is changing the total educational system namely, content, methodology, learner participation learning process, teacher roles, curricular implication etc. "The computers are very powerful instructional media that enhance quality of instruction". By programming the subject of study in computers, teaching and learning become full of contexts and situations. The student can take his own time to learn the contents because they are individualized instructional situation. The performance of the student in instruction as well as in test will automatically record in the computer. The present study aims to find out the implications of multimedia in teaching economics with special reference to higher secondary education in Chennai. A samples of 155 samples selected randomly were studied. A questionnaire method of survey was used to find out the implications of multimedia in teaching economics. The data were collected by using questionnaire as an instrument. Primary data were collected by conducting direct structured interview using questionnaire. All the respondents were asked the same questions in the same fashion and they were informed the purpose of study. t-test, ANOVA and Correlation analysis were applied to test the hypotheses. The findings and observations are the result and outcome of the interpretations made during the study of analysis.

In 1965, Lorence settler and Danieal Davis[5] developed most complicated teaching process in which computer was used for presenting instruction in place of teacher. They divided the teaching process of the computer in two parts.

Pre-tutorial phase

Tutorial phase.

In the first phase, computer assisted instruction is given to the pupils to achieve the specific objectives on the basis of his entry behaviour. In the second phase instructing material is presented accordingly. The pupil is evaluated. After presenting the instruction, computer also controls it. It also provides reinforcement to the pupils.

In the modern age, the use of computers in the field of education, made in the following areas.

All the researches do all analytical tasks with the help of computers in the research work.

- Computers are also used in educational guidance and counseling.
- Remedial teaching of the pupils is also done by the computers.
- Computers help in sought for preparing the results of the examinations.

Learning with aid of computer through computer, aided instruction, computer simulation etc. It is a self learning strategy in teaching learning process. Students learnt their subjects at their own pace.

Internet is worldwide computer network that contains a large collection of information which could be made available to you on your computer. The person having internet connection can retrieve any information on individual interest. Purves, A.C.[6] (1998) says that, the internet is the abbreviation of inter network system. The internet is the name for a vast, worldwide system consisting of people, information and computers. It is also described as a network of networks because these are more than one lakh readily accessible through the Internet. Internet is the largest and most complete learning tool for a group of people with varied educational background and interests. Teachers, students, businessmen and other educators can share ideas instantly across vast distances. For scientific and research community, internet is an essential and indispensable tool. Through Internet scientist can gain and enjoy instant access to the world's most advanced research facilities and discuss their research problems with others, working in the same field.

Review of Literature

Coyne, Margaret Ann[17], Ed.D., (2006), in their paper "Emerging literacy Assisted parents to scaffold the emerging literacy skill of their pre-school-aged children through the used of electronic storybooks", reported that, that importance of parents reading to their young child is well supported by research (Health, 1986). However, Edwards (1989) found that parents whose own literacy skills are emerging have difficulty supporting the emerging literacy skills of their young children through storybook reading.

The development of a new paradigm, Universal Design for Learning (UDL) (Meyer & Rose, 1998 and 2002) provides a framework for the use of computer technology to support learning. Drawing on Vygotsky's (1978; 1986) socio constructive theory of learning and the latest advances in the neurosciences, UDL investigates how technology can support diverse learners. This study examined whether UDL –based technology might help parents who are themselves emerging readers support their children's literacy development.

When parents use of targeted storybook reading behaviours increased if their children's pre-intervention scores on language measures were below age-level, the children's scores on post-intervention measures improved to age-level or above. In addition, the children's scores on measures of story retelling and print knowledge improved.

BEABVIS C.,$_{18}$, Deakin University, Literacy and the new technologies in the middle years. (2006) This paper explores young people's textual engagements with electronic and other forms of popular culture, and the changing nature of literacy in the context of COM modification, mass marketing and the new technologies. Building on school based studies exploring computer games in the classroom and the Poke on phenomenon, it examines ways in which popular texts are read, and narrative and generic elements incorporated into the curriculum and into students' spoken and written texts. Drawing on Green's model of cultural, critical and opal dimensions of (technological) literacy, it examines issues of literacy and culture, identity and critique for teachers and students in the middle years, and their implications for constructions of literacy and curriculum.

BERRY L. and CHAPMAN E,,$_{19}$ University of Sydney Effects of Background Information and Audiovisual Presentation Modes on Students' Attention Styles and Enjoyment in Listening to Unfamiliar Music.(2006) Research has indicated that students typically do not enjoy or engage with unfamiliar pieces of music. This is discouraging and puzzling to music educators who whish to introduce their students to a diverse range of musical genres. This study explored the effects of two factors on students' initial reactions to an unfamiliar Shakuhachi piece. Using a 2 by 2 crossed-factor design, 438 students in grades 9-11 were assigned at random to listen to the piece in either audio-only or audiovisual form, and with or without verbal background information.

Results indicated that while the provision of information significantly ($p<0.05$) increased students' enjoyment of the music and their interest in hearing more of the same kind of music, it had no effect on their listening attention styles (e.g., focusing on the melody or idiomatic details of the piece). Conversely, use of the audiovisual presentation mode significantly impacted on one aspect of students' attention styles (focus on idiomatic details) and perceived familiarity with the piece, but had only a marginally significant effect on their enjoyment or interest.

Implications of these results for the introduction of unfamiliar music to high school students will be discussed.

BLACKMORE J., JOHNSON R., WARREN W.[20], (2006) States that the potential of new learning technologies for transforming teaching and learning, and indeed the organization of schooling. Much has also been written about teacher responses to new learning technologies-how they resist, ignore, or innovate. A number of recent reports indicate a gap between policy, practice and the capacity of organizations to provide the conditions and resources sin schools to creatively use new learning technologies. Few of these discourses draw upon theories of educational change, in particular those which relate to the dissonance between attitudes and feelings about radical change, and how it impacts on teacher work identity with respect to learning technologies. Much of the literature has focused upon the technical aspects, the hardware and software, but not the 'warm ware', so critical to sound pedagogical practice. This paper draws from the Learning in New Environments Research Group action research project, a pilot study in a large metropolitan secondary college, which is exploring the social implications of new learning technologies for changing relations between students, between teachers and students, between teachers and between family and school. The paper draws from the first round of data collection from the teachers in an ongoing action research project in a region with a high level of socio-economic and cultural diversity.

It draws on concepts of Lieberman's notion of learning networks and Wenger's notion of communities of practice, as well as past research on the reception of gender equity reform in educational organizations, which focuses upon emotional aspects of professional work identity and organizational change.

Joseph Kacharayll[25] (2006) – "Suitability of colleges for Web Bases Learning" reported that Web based learning environment is expensive to establish, government and private managements should take necessary steps to provide adequate infrastructure facilities in colleges for web based learning. A proper utilization of available human resources would help improve web based learning. In order to overcome technical limitation, training has to be given to both teachers and learners to create flexible and uninterrupted learning environment. The training of material designers should be especially focused upon. Most of the colleges have not properly utilized the available web resources in their teaching learning strategies. There is only nominal technical support and assistance from technical staff and from government and private managements at the institutional level for web based learning. The author collected sample for the survey of 152 college lecturers was obtained through random sampling.

Objectives

- To find the effect on learning competency of the students by using Multi media for teaching economics
- To find the active participation of the teachers in using multi media for teaching economics.
- To find how the teaching of economics has been efficiently improved using the multi media.
- To find the importance of computers and internet in teaching economics.

Methodology

The investigator, for the present study adopts the survey method of research. It is a procedure in which data is systematically collected from a population through some form of direct solicitation such as face to face interview, questionnaire or schedule. The survey is extensive and cross sectional dealing with the relatively large number of cases of a particular time and yielding statistics that are abstracted from particular cases. It is the method of investigation which attempts to describe and interpret what exists at present in the form of conditions, practices, process, trends, effects, attitudes, and beliefs. Using this method the investigator had gathered information measure the Effect of Multi Media Aids in teaching economics for Higher Secondary Students in Chennai.

Sample

For the present study 155 Higher Secondary Students in Chennai.

Data Collection

Primary data, required for the present research work were collected by conducting direct interviews using questionnaire. All the respondents were given sufficient information about the study. These respondents were provided with the same questionnaires. They were also informed that they have to answer in the same fashion.

Statistical Tools for Analysis

The following tools statistical tools were used for the analysis of data. t-test, one way ANOVA and correlation analysis is used for the present study.

Analysis and Interpretation

Table 1: Six wise distribution of "t" value between the boys and girls of the higher secondary economics students using multimedia resources in their schools

Dimensions	Boys N = 55		Girls N = 100		Calculated value of "t"	Level of significance at 5% level
	Mean	S.D	Mean	S.D		
Working knowledge of computers	79.42	8.17	80.42	8.68	0.71	NS
Knowledge about internet	78.15	9.51	76.88	9.80	0.91	NS
Knowledge using A.V. Aids	79.76	7.48	76.26	10.79	2.37	S
Preparation of computer based study materials	76.40	7.97	74.77	11.04	1.06	NS
Assignment and project	81.75	6.31	78.35	10.18	2.56	S
Interaction with others through web	395.47	28.53	386.5	42.77	1.56	NS

(At5% level of significance, the table value of "t" is 1.96)

It is refereed from the above table that there is a significant difference between boys and of Higher Secondary Students of economics group in there, Knowledge in using A.V. Aids and Assignment and project but there is no significant difference between Male and Female Higher Secondary students of economics group in their Working knowledge of computers, knowledge about internet, Preparation of computer based study materials, interaction with others through web.

Table – 2 : Area wise distribution of "t" value between the urban and rural higher secondary economics students using multimedia resources in their schools

Dimensions	Urban N = 55		Rural N = 100		Calculated value of "t"	Level of significance at 5% level
	Mean	S.D	Mean	S.D		
Working knowledge of computers	79.42	8.17	80.42	8.68	0.71	NS
Knowledge about internet	78.15	9.51	76.88	9.80	0.91	NS

Knowledge using A.V. Aids	79.76	7.48	76.26	10.79	2.37	S
Preparation of computer based study materials	76.40	7.97	74.77	11.04	1.06	NS
Assignment and project	81.75	6.31	78.35	10.18	2.56	S
Interaction with others through web	395.47	28.53	386.5	42.77	1.56	NS

(At 5% level of significance, the table value of "t" is 1.96)

It is referred from the above table that there is no significant difference between urban and rural Higher Secondary Students of economics group in there, Knowledge in using A.V. Aids, Assignment and project, Working knowledge of computers, Knowledge about internet, Preparation of computer based study materials, Interaction with other through web.

Table – 3: "F" value among the boys and girls of Higher Secondary economics Group Students in Using Multimedia resources

Dimensions	df= 2,152			Calculated "f" Value	Remarks at 5% Level
	Source of variation	Sum of squares	M.S.V		
Working knowledge of computers	Between With in	118.75 11110.63	59.38 73.10	0.81	NS
Knowledge about internet	Between With in	7.94 14650.81	3.97 96.39	0.04	NS
Knowledge in using A.V. Aids	Between With in	23.44 15123.38	11.72 99.50	0.12	NS
Preparation of computer study materials	Between With in	155.56 15619.63	77.78 102.76	0.76	NS
Assignment and project	Between With in	164.39 12793.88	82.19 84.17	0.98	NS
Interaction with others through web	Between With in	216.00 23034.00	108.00 1515.39	0.07	NS

(For 2,152 df. At 5% level of significance, the table value of "f" is 3.06)

It is inferred from the above table that there is no significance difference among the boys and girls of Higher Secondary economics group students in using Multimedia resources in the Higher Secondary schools of Chennai.

Table – 4: "F" value among the Rural and Urban Higher Secondary Students of economics Group in Using Multimedia source in Chennai

Dimensions	df= 2,152			Calculated "f" Value	Remarks at 5% Level
	Source of variation	Sum of squares	M.S.V		
Working knowledge of computers	Between With in	39.50 11189.88	19.75 73.62	0.27	NS
Knowledge about internet	Between With in	394.39 14264.50	197.16 93.85	2.10	NS
Knowledge in using A.V. Aids	Between With in	130.31 15016.50	65.16 98.79	0.66	NS
Preparation of computer study materials	Between With in	444.44 153330.75	222.22 100.86	2.20	NS
Assignment and project	Between With in	364.69 12593.56	182.32 82.85	2.20	NS
Interaction with others through web	Between With in	5628.00 224924.00	2814.00 11479.76	1.90	NS

(for 2,152 df.at 5% level of significance, the table value of "f" is 3.06)

It is inferred from the above table that there is no significance difference among the Rural and Urban Higher Secondary students of economics group in using Multi media resource in the Higher Secondary Schools of Chennai.

Table – 5: "F" value among the Higher Secondary Students of economics Group in Using Multimedia source in Government and Private Higher Secondary Schools in Chennai

Dimensions	**df= 2,152**			**Calculated "f" Value**	**Remarks at 5% Level**
	Source of variation	**Sum of squares**	**M.S.V**		
Working knowledge of computers	Between With in	39.50 11189.88	19.75 73.62	0.27	NS
Knowledge about internet	Between With in	394.39 14264.50	197.16 93.85	2.10	NS
Knowledge in using A.V. Aids	Between With in	130.31 15016.50	65.16 98.79	0.66	NS
Preparation of computer study materials	Between With in	444.44 153330.75	222.22 100.86	2.20	NS
Assignment and project	Between With in	364.69 12593.56	182.32 82.85	2.20	NS

Interaction with others through web	Between With in	5628.00 224924.00	2814.00 11479.76	1.90	NS

(For 2,152 df. at 5% level of significance, the table value of '' is 3.06)

It is inferred from the above table that there is no significance difference among the Government and Private Higher Secondary students of economics group in using Multimedia resource in the Higher Secondary School of Chennai

Table – 6 : The Correlation value between the Male and Female Higher Secondary Students in using multimedia resources in the Higher Secondary Schools of Chennai

Category	?X	?X²	?Y	?Y²	?XY	Calculated	Remarks
Boys	683	8595	545	5495	6775	.68	NS
Girls	1199	14757	970	9584	11740	.425	S
Total	1882	23354	1515	15079	18515	.325	S

(Table value of Correlation Co-efficient at 5% level of Significance is 0.161)

It is inferred from the above table that there is no significant relationship between the rural and high secondary economics group boys in using multimedia resources and there is a significant relationship between rural and urban high secondary economics group girls in using multimedia resources.

Findings

There a significant difference among the higher secondary commence group students of boys and girls, higher secondary commence students of government and private schools, higher secondary commence group students of rural and urban schools, in their interest towards learning commence through multimedia resources in Chennai.

There is significant difference among the higher secondary economics group students in their levels of using multimedia shows moderate knowledge except interaction with others through web and no significant difference in low of using multimedia except interaction with other through web and no significant difference in higher level knowledge of using multimedia.

There is no significant difference among the higher secondary economics group boys in their level of using multimedia shows moderate knowledge and higher level of using multimedia and there is a significant difference low of using multimedia at the area of assignment and project, interaction with others though web.

There is no significant difference among the secondary economics group girls in all the levels of using multimedia resources. There is no significant difference among the higher secondary economics group students of government school in their level of using multimedia shows moderate knowledge and there is a significant difference in low level of interaction with others though web and shows significant difference in higher level of in knowledge about internet, knowledge in using AV aids and in the preparation of computer based study materials.

There is no significant difference among the higher secondary economics group students of private school in their level of using multimedia shows moderate knowledge and higher level knowledge of using multimedia and there is a significant difference in low level of using multimedia at the area of working of computer and in interaction with others though web.

There is no significant difference among the higher secondary economics group of rural school in their level of using multimedia shows moderate knowledge and there is a significant difference in low level of preparation of computer in high level of using multimedia at the is a significant difference in high level of using multimedia at the area of working knowledge of computer and in interaction with others with through web.

There is no significant difference between boys and girls or higher secondary students of economics group in their, knowledge in using A.V aids and assignments and project but there is no significant differences between male and female higher secondary of economics group in their working knowledge of computers, knowledge about internet, preparation of computer based study materials with others thought web.

There is no significant difference between urban and rural higher secondary of economics in their, knowledge in using A.V aids, assignment and project, working knowledge of computer knowledge about internet preparation of computer based study martial interaction with others web.

There is no significant difference among the Male and female higher secondary schools of economics group in using multimedia resource in the Higher secondary schools of Chennai.

There is no significance difference among the Rural and urban higher secondary students of economics group in using Multimedia resource in the higher secondary of Chennai.

There is n no significant difference among the Government and private Higher Secondary students of economics group in using Multimedia resource in the higher schools of Chennai.

There is no significant relationship between the Rural and urban high secondary group boys in using multimedia resources and there is a significant relationship between Rural and Urban high secondary economics group girls in using multimedia resources.

The research overwhelmingly demonstrates that usages of multimedia will definitely improve the quality of teaching economics in higher secondary classes.

The research found that the students are actively involved in learning part if the multimedia is introduced in classroom teaching.

The research shows the students are highly motivate towards the subject by using multimedia teaching aids and they are attracted more and improve their understanding and memory power in various economics topics like advertising, banking, etc. While using multimedia resources.

It is concluded that there is a positive effect of using multimedia aids in the economics achievement of the students in economics in Chennai.

Conclusion

The present study aims to find out the implications of multimedia in teaching economics with special reference to higher secondary. The researcher framed objectives and hypotheses on the basis of the above context. The research was carried out in 155 samples based randomly. A questionnaire constructed by R was used to collect the relevant data. After collecting the data they were analyzed using statistical tools such as t-test, ANOVA and Correlation analysis. The result concluded that students have average implications of multimedia in teaching at Higher Secondary level.

Reference

Beavis C. (2006), popular culture, textual practice and identify and identify: literacy and the new technologies, in the midde years

Berry l. And Chapman e, (2006); Effect of Background Information and Audiovisual Presentation Modes on Students' Attention style and enjoyment listening to Unfamiliar Music.

Blackmork j., Johnson R., Warren W. (2006), A handbook of Education Technology.

Bruce B.C (2004); Diversity and critical social engagement: How changing technologies enable new modes of literacy in changing circumstances. IN D.E. Alvermann (E.d), Adolescents and illiteracies in a digital world (pp. 1-18). New York: Peter Lang publication.

Chisamore, chris (2006), Multimedia and Education today.

Coyne, Margaret Ann (2006), Emerging Literacy: Assisting Parents to scaffold the emerging literacy skills of their preschool aged children through the use of electronic story books.

Lanksherar, C and Knoble, M (2003); New literacies: changing Knowledge and classroom learning. Philadelphia: Open university press.

Lewis, C and Finders, M. (2004); implied adolescents and implied teachers; A generation gap for new times. D.E Alvermann (Ed.), Adolescents and literacies in adugital world (pp.101-113).New York: peter Lang publishing.

❐

21.

Effectiveness of Multimedia Programme in Perceiving Human Anatomy among Higher Secondary Students

Introduction

Research work is being continuously done in the field of science and also in the related teaching methods and materials. In order to keep pace with the development of science, the need for new instructional strategies was greatly felt. One such innovative teaching strategy, called multimedia programme, has been chosen and studied by the investigator in this research work. Upgrading Biology curriculum by introducing Human anatomy demands a change in the instructional strategy. The need for developing an instructional strategy for teaching Human anatomy and physiology is very important to make the teachers and students aware of the scientific principles that govern the advances being made in medicine. The functions of the internal organs of human body can be easily explained through a multimedia programme. This also saves the use of expensive chemicals and sophisticated instruments which are beyond the reach of higher secondary schools. In schools, the required equipment to explain the human anatomy is not available. In this situation, the working mechanism of internal organs can be explained by a multimedia programme, which when used as an instructional strategy will make the task of learning human anatomy easier, effective and less expensive. The present study aims to find out the effectiveness of multimedia programme in perceiving human anatomy among higher secondary students in Tindivanam. A samples of 100 higher secondary students selected randomly were studied. A questionnaire method of survey was used to find out the effectiveness of multimedia programme in perceiving human anatomy. The data were collected by using questionnaire as an instrument. Primary data were collected by conducting direct structured interview using questionnaire. All the respondents were asked the same questions in the same fashion and they were informed the purpose of study. Mean, SD, and t-test analysis was applied to test the hypotheses. The findings and observations are the result and outcome of the interpretations made during the study of analysis. The result found that majority of the higher secondary students satisfied about multimedia programme.

In view of growing importance of science education, old concepts of science teaching have therefore, rather become completely outmoded and an entirely new ethos and approach to science curriculum have come into existence. Moreover, unprecedented development of scientific research, new discoveries, and new methods of investigation, in the early twentieth century, has created a need and urge to examine and reorganize science teaching programmes at all levels in schools. Institutions are functioning in an era of rapidly emerging new technologies. Some of them, like information and communications technology, have fuelled a veritable explosion of rising expectations everywhere. When such is the pace of developmental processes, it becomes fairly imperative on the part of the students not only to possess sound knowledge and understanding of fundamental concepts, but also to understand and appreciate the ramifications of various developments in the field of science and technology, especially in the context of their future career. The situation underscores the significance of research in science education and it is time for the educationists to evolve a proper and appropriate strategy for teaching science.

At the Higher Secondary level, the science subject is divided into Physics, Chemistry, Botany, and Zoology according to Tamil Nadu State Board syllabus. Zoology deals with the life history, distribution, structure, reproduction, and importance of animals including Homosapiens, the human beings. 'Human anatomy' is one of the units of the Zoology subject. Human anatomy is the branch of anatomy devoted to the structure of the human body. In general the study of human anatomy helps the students to do their higher studies in Medicine, Physiotherapy, Nursing, Degree courses like B.Sc., Zoology, and Microbiology etc. Apart from acquiring the technical knowledge, it is necessary for human beings to know and control their own systems of their body for healthy life. Hence the investigator has selected the unit "human anatomy" to teach through multimedia programme for the higher secondary students in the present investigation.

An instructional or teaching strategy refers to a pattern of teaching act that serves to attain certain goals and to guard against others. An instructional strategy is a purposefully-conceived and determined plan of action. It also occupies a central position in formal education. Instructional strategies aim at establishing relationship between teaching inputs and learning outputs, mainly in terms of realizing the learning outcomes. Instructional strategies include teaching methods, approaches and techniques.

Methods of instruction may be teacher-centered such as Historical method, Biographical method, Lecture method, Lecture-demonstration method or pupil-centered method which includes group methods such as project method, discussion, seminar and workshop. The pupil-centered methods also include individual methods such as programmed instruction, Computer Aided Instruction, Instructional Modules and Multimedia packages.

Review of Literature

Chang, Kuo-En et al. (2008) studied **the effects of learning support in simulation-based physics learning.** The results of the study revealed that the outcome for learning about the basic characteristics of an optical lens was significantly better for simulation-based learning than for laboratory learning.

Djeassilane (2008) investigated the effect of computer aided instruction (CAI) in enhancing the academic achievement of higher secondary students in commerce. The findings of the study showed that the computer aided instruction was effective in helping the students of the experimental group to perform better in the post-test. It proved the effectiveness of the computer aided instruction in commerce developed by the investigator. And also it was found that the experimental students had more favourable attitude towards computer assisted instruction.

Garnett, Hackling and Oliver (2009) developed an interactive multimedia package to improve students' understanding of the particulate basis of chemical reaction, and their ability to interpret chemical equations and solve problems based on equations. The study showed that Interactive multimedia provided learners with access to a rich information source and appropriate activities to promote learning and understanding.

Junaidu, Sahalu (2009) studied effectiveness of multimedia in learning & teaching data structures online. This paper explores and reports on the importance of creating multimedia-rich course content and the important role that animations can play in creating a successful online learning experience. Results indicated that students consistently perform much better in questions requiring application of material taught in carefully animated algorithms. These results should carry over to other educational environments.

Liao, Yuen-kuang C., Chang, Huei-wen and Chen, Yu-wen (2009) compared the effects of computer applications (i.e., computer-assisted instruction, computer simulations, and Web-based learning) versus traditional instruction on elementary school students' achievement in Taiwan. The results suggest that computer application instruction is more effective than traditional instruction for elementary school students in Taiwan.

O'Day, Danton (2010) studied on "using animations to teach biology: past & future research on the attributes that underlie pedagogically sound animations".

Multiple technical resources (commonly referred to as multimedia) are currently used by many instructors to communicate difficult topics and concepts to their students in meaningful ways. Various sources have shown that animations are more effective than static sequential images. This study evaluated how animations can be and have been used as effective teaching and learning tools in biology and what more needs to be done to understand their true value.

Ozmen, Haluk (2010) studied on "The influence of CAI on students' conceptual understanding of chemical Bonding and attitude towards chemistry: A case for Turkey". The results of this study suggested that teaching-learning of topics in chemistry related to chemical bonding can be improved by the use of computer-assisted teaching materials.

Ponraj and Nellaiyapen (2010) investigated the effectiveness of CAI in teaching Zoology. The major finding of the study showed that the experimental group performed better than the Control group in the post-test. The results of the study revealed that experimental method of teaching is more effective than the traditional method of teaching the topic 'Nucleus' in Zoology.

Pryor, Caroline and Bitter, Gary (2010) used multimedia to teach in-service teachers and studied its impacts on learning, application, and retention. The study found that the video modeling in the module was effective in helping teachers learn, and discourse strategies were learned, applied, and retained.

Rotbain, Marbach-Ad and Stavy (2011) used a computer animation to teach high school molecular biology. The achievements of the experimental group were compared with those of a control group. Analysis of the post-test showed that the mean score of the experimental group was significantly higher than the mean score of the control group.

Venkataraman (2011) prepared software packages (CAI) for XI standard physics and studied the effectiveness of it's among selected modes of CAI in physics in relation to learners' personality. The results of the study showed that the CAI is effective with different modes. Computer Assisted Instruction shows significant difference in the achievement of different instructional objectives. Further Computer Assisted Instruction enhances the retention of the learnt content.

Vernadakis et al. (2012) examined the effect of multimedia computer-assisted instruction (MCAI), traditional instruction (TI), and combined instruction (CI) methods on learning the skill of shooting in basketball. Additionally, a comparison of the students' attitudes towards the MCAI and TI methods was made. Students took pre-, post-, and retention written test covering techniques and rules of the games. Post-test results indicated no significant differences between the groups concerning the written test. Nevertheless, the attitude test scores of the CI group were more favourable to MCAI method than the TI method. Retention test results showed that groups retained the knowledge acquisition. However, the combined method of instruction tended to be the most effective for cognitive learning.

Victor, Adeosun Olufemi (2012) investigated the relative effects of three multi-media instructional packages on Nigerian students' achievement in social studies. The purpose was to determine which of the combinations of videotape recording presentation, pictures and the chalk and talk method; the combination of audiotape recording presentation, pictures and the chalk and talk method and the combination of pictures and the chalk and talk method. The study revealed that the combination of pictures and the chalk and talk method was most effective among the packages tested in the learning of social studies.

Objectives

- To develop a Multimedia Programme for the unit of Human anatomy from XI standard Zoology subject in order to teach the higher secondary students.
- To find out the effectiveness of Multimedia Programme in teaching Human anatomy among higher secondary students.

Methodology

The methodology adopted for the study is explained in detail. The sampling technique, size of the sample, variables of the study, description of the tool used and administration of tool are elaborated.

Sample

A samples of 100 higher secondary students in selected randomly were studied in Tindivanam Town.

Data Collection

The present study aims at developing and using Multimedia programme for perceiving human anatomy for higher secondary students to enable them to understand the concepts very easily through individualized instructional technique. It is maintained that the Multimedia programme may reduce monotony in the classroom by bringing out real life situations and motivate them for self-study and provides opportunities for individual pace and ability.

The study intends to develop a multimedia programme for human anatomy for XI standard Zoology subject prescribed by Tamil Nadu State Board Syllabus and find out the effectiveness of the Multimedia programme through experimentation in perceiving human anatomy among the higher secondary students. The study provides scope for the development and use of many Multimedia programmes in the concerned discipline as well as other disciplines for the benefit of learners of different categories. Hence the multimedia programme can be used as an individualized instructional technique for the students of different categories in the science subjects as well as other subjects.

Analysis and Interpretation

Performance of control group students between the pre test and post test in human anatomy.

The Mean, Standard Deviation and Co-efficient of Variation were computed for the control group students in their performance in human anatomy between the pre test and post test.

Table 1: Distribution of Mean, Standard Deviation and Co-efficient of Variation on the performance of control group students between the pre test and post test in human anatomy

Group	N	Mean	S.D	CV
Pre test	100	42.69	13.60	31.86
Post test	100	52.46	13.28	25.31

The Co-efficient of Variation of the pre test and post test for the control group students was found to be 31.86 and 25.31, which reveals that the control group students are more consistent in their performance in human anatomy in the post test than the pre test. It reveals that the control group students have improved in their performance in human anatomy in the post test than the pre test.

To find out the significance of the difference between the control and experimental group students in their performance in human anatomy in the pre test, the 't' test was used.

Table 2: Distribution of 't' value between the control and experimental group students in their performance in human anatomy in the pre test

Group	N	Mean	S.D	't' value	Level of Significant
Control	100	42.69	13.60	0.17	p>0.05
Experimental	100	43.31	12.59		

There is no significant difference between the control and experimental group students in their performance in human anatomy in the pre test.

The obtained 't' value 0.17 is not statistically significant since it is less than the table 't' value 1.96 for 50 df at 0.05 level of significance. Hence the null hypothesis is accepted. It shows that there is no significant difference between the control and experimental group students in their performance in human anatomy in the pre test. It is therefore concluded that both control and experimental group students have the same level of performance in human anatomy in the pre test.

To find out the significance of the difference between the control and experimental group students in their performance in human anatomy in the post test, the 't' test was used.

Table 3: Distribution of 't' value between the control and experimental group students in their performance in human anatomy in the post test

Group	N	Mean	S.D	't' value	Level of Significant
Control	100	52.46	13.28	14.38	$p<0.05$
Experimental	100	92.81	5.31		

There is no significant difference between the control and experimental group students in their performance in human anatomy in the post test.

The obtained 't' value 14.38 is statistically significant since it is greater than the table 't' value 1.96 for 50 df at 0.05 level of significance. Hence the null hypothesis is rejected. It shows that there is significant difference between the control and experimental group students in their performance in human anatomy in the post test. It is therefore concluded that the experimental group students performed significantly better in human anatomy than that of control group students in the post test.

To find out the significance of the difference between the pre and post test mean scores of control group students in the performance in human anatomy, the 't' was used.

Table 4: Distribution of 't' value for the pre and post test mean scores of control group students in the performance in human anatomy

Group	N	Mean	S.D	't' value	Level of Significant
Pre test	100	42.69	13.60	2.62	$p<0.05$
Post test	100	52.46	13.28		

There is no significant difference between the pre and post test mean scores of control group students in the performance in human anatomy.

The obtained 't' value 2.62 is statistically significant since it is greater than the table 't' value 1.96 for 50 df at 0.05 level of significance. Hence the null hypothesis is rejected. It shows that there is significant difference between the pre and post test mean scores of control group students in the performance in human anatomy. It is therefore concluded that the control group students have improved in their performance in human anatomy in the post test.

Suggestions

The present study aims at developing and using Multimedia programme for perceiving human anatomy for higher secondary students to enable them to understand the concepts very easily through individualized instructional technique. It is maintained that the Multimedia programme may reduce monotony in the classroom by bringing out real life situations and motivate them for self-study and provides opportunities for individual pace and ability.

Conclusion

The study intends to develop a multimedia programme for human anatomy for XI standard Zoology subject prescribed by Tamil Nadu State Board Syllabus and find out the effectiveness of the Multimedia programme through experimentation in perceiving human anatomy among the higher secondary students. The study provides scope for the development and use of many Multimedia programmes in the concerned discipline as well as other disciplines for the benefit of learners of different categories. Hence the multimedia programme can be used as an individualized instructional technique for the students of different categories in the science subjects as well as other subjects.

The present study reveals that the experiment group students who used multimedia programme performed significantly better than that of the control group students who did not use, which implies that the multimedia programme has tremendous impact upon the performance in human anatomy than the students learning through traditional method. This proves the effectiveness of the multimedia programme in human anatomy developed by the investigator.

The present study reveals that the performance of the control and experimental group students in the post test is significantly higher than the pre test. But the performance of the experimental group students in the post test is more significantly higher than the post test performance of control group students. Thus, it proves the supremacy of the multimedia programme over traditional method.

References

Chang, Kuo-En; Chen, Yu-Lung; Lin, He-Yan; Sung, Yao-Ting (2008). E**ffects of learning support in simulation-based physics learning. Computers & Education,** 51(4): 1486-1498..

Djeassilane, N. (2008). Effect of computer aided instruction (CAI) in enhancing the academic achievement of higher secondary students in commerce. Unpublished Doctoral Dissertation, Alagappa University, Karaikudi.

Garnett, P., Hackling, M., & Oliver, R. (2009). Designing interactive multimedia materials to support concept development in beginning chemistry classes.

Junaidu, Sahalu (2009). Effectiveness of multimedia in learning & teaching data structures online. Turkish Online Journal of Distance Education-TOJDE, 9(4), Article 7. Retrieved March.

Liao, Yuen-kuang C., Chang, Huei-wen & Chen, Yu-wen (2009). Effects of Computer Applications on Elementary School Students' Achievement: A Meta-Analysis of Students in Taiwan. Computers in the Schools, 24(3-4): 43-64. Retrieved.

O'Day, Danton H. (2010). Using animations to teach biology: past & future research on the attributes that underlie pedagogically sound animations. The American Biology Teacher, 70(5):274-278. Retrieved March 20.

Ozmen, Haluk (2010). The influence of Computer-Assisted Instruction on students' conceptual understanding of chemical Bonding and Attitude toward chemistry: A case for Turkey. Computers and Education, 51(1): 423-438. Retrieved March.

Ponraj, P., & Nellaiyapen, N. O. (2010). CAI in teaching Zoology. Research and Reflections on Education, 6(2): 18-21.

Pryor, Caroline R., & Bitter, Gary G. (2010). Using multimedia to teach in-service teachers: Impacts on learning, application, and retention. Computers in Human Behavior, 24 (6): 2668-2681. Retrieved March.

Rotbain, Y., Marbach-Ad, G., & Stavy, R. (2011). Using a computer animation to teach high school molecular biology. Journal of Science Education and Technology, 17(1): 49 – 58. Retrieved March.

Venkataraman, S. (2011). Relative effectiveness among selected modes of CAI in physics in relation to learner's personality. Unpublished Doctoral Dissertation, Annamalai University. Chidambaram.

Vernadakis, N., Zetou, E., Tsitskari, E., Giannousi, M., & Kioumourtzoglou, E. (2012). Student attitude and learning outcomes of multimedia computer-assisted versus traditional instruction in basketball. Education and Information Technologies, 13(3): 167-183.

Victor, Adeosun Olufemi (2012). Relative effects of three Multi-Media Instructional Packages on Nigerian student's achievement in Social Studies. Pakistan Journal of Social Sciences, 5 (5): 415 – 420. Retrieved March.

❒

22.

Awareness on Digital Techniques Applying in Classroom Teaching for Present Generation among Teacher Educators

Introduction

Education is the foundation stone of a Nation's intellectual power which steps its power profile. Thus, it is rightly said that it depends upon the quality of its Teachers. The destiny of India is being shaped in its classrooms. In class room Teaching, Digital Technology provides the opportunity to go beyond the class room boundaries to the outside world and events. Hence the Government is very keen in implementing the scheme of Teaching through computer in Government schools. When the Government is very much interested in the computer Teaching, It is essential that the Teachers must be well aware of the potentiality of the computer Technology. Hence the Investigators were interest to know the level of the Awareness on Digital Technology of Teacher Educators. It is a survey Research. The Investigators developed the opinion scale contains 40 statements with different dimensions such as Computer in Teaching Learning, Power point Presentation and Internet. Four points scale ranges from Strongly Agree, Agree, Strongly Disagree and Disagree was used. Developed Opinionnarie was administered to 100 Teacher Educators who are working in various Colleges of Education in Perambalur and Trichy Districts. Gender, Locality and Subject they studied were taken as the variables. The collected data was using Statistical Analysis like Mean, SD and't' test which have revealed the varied results.

Modernization is generally regarded as a process of change of traditional society into a society based on technology. As Teaching has entered the Digital age over the last several years, Technology in the Classroom is an area that all Teachers and Students are Embracing. For Teachers who have taught many years before this can be a challenging one. There are many Computer lesson plans, CDs, DVDs, audio e -books and videos available that will help in the transition. Digital Technology in the Classroom involves a lot of time and focus in its infancy, but with the Computer Lesson plans mentioned, it will develop into a fun and creative learning experience for Students and new and exciting challenges for Teachers. The incorporation of Digital technology in the education sector is important to meet the challenges presented by new trends, especially with the Global Communication of Knowledge. It is essential that the Students become familiar with the concept and use of Computer Technology in order to equip them for future job market. Similarly, the teacher can achieve better quality in Teaching Methodology.

Rationale of the Study

Computer plays key role in Education. Learning through Computer is an interesting affair. Now–a-days Digital Technology in Education has become the essential part of the system. In fact Teacher must well aware of the potentiality of the Digital Technology. Government is very much interested in introducing Computer Technology in Class Room instruction in Teacher Education. Hence the Investigator was interested to know the level of Awareness on Digital techniques applying in classroom teaching for present generation among Teacher Educators.

STATEMENT OF THE PROBLEM

The important key words used in this problem were :

i) **Awareness:** Alertness, New Idea.

ii) **Digital Technology**: The Technology which is used to change the method of Class Room. Teaching with the help of Electronic machines and Computer,

iii) **Teacher Educators** Teachers who are working in the Colleges of Education.

Overview of the Study Already Done

Asan(2003) studied on "Computer Technology Awareness by Elementary School Teachers: A Case Study from Turkey" and found that many Teachers were not computer users. At the same time Wheatley, (2003) also studied on increasing computer use in early childhood Teacher Education. The study was found that Teachers lacked a functional Computer Literacy Foundation to new Technology and skills. Nickish and Reinhard (1992) in their study "Teacher Anxiety toward Computer Technology" found that Urban Teachers are used Computer often than Rural Teachers. Sengamalam @ Vanathi (2013) Studied on Awareness on e learning among M.Ed scholars under Bharathidasan University, found that the awareness of scholars whose major subject is Science was found to be superior to the scholars with Arts as major subject.

Objectives of the Study

The objectives of the study were i) to measure the level of Awareness on Digital Technology among Teacher Educators. ii) To measure the level of significant difference on the Awareness on Digital Technology among Male and Female, Rural and Urban, Science and Arts group Teacher Educators.

Method and Materials

It is the Normative Survey method. Investigator constructed a Tool Awareness on Digital Techniques applying in Classroom Teaching for present generation among Teacher Educators. That consists of 40 statements with different dimensions such as Computer in Teaching Learning, Power point Presentation and Internet, which have four point scale such a Strongly Agree, Agree, Disagree and Strongly Disagree. After the Development of the Questionnaire, the Investigator distributed it to Teacher Educators for validation. Their valuable ideas were taken care. Then the questionnaire was given to 10 Teacher Educators by Test - Retest method. The obtained r value 0.84 reveals that the tool is reliable one. Investigators randomly selected 100 Teacher Educators from various Colleges of Education in Perambalur and Trichy Districts.

Analysis

The collected data was analysed by using different statistical technique like Mean, SD and 't' test. The results are given in the following Tables

Table- 1: Significant Difference on the Mean Scores of Male and Female Teacher Educators

S.No	Dimension	Gender	Mean	SD	t test	Remarks
1.	**Total**	Male Female	64.3 63.0	0.74 0.92	**7.38**	S
2.	**CTL**	Male Female	60.54 61.62	1.19 1.41	1.48	NS
3.	**PPT**	Male Female	65.04 61.24	3.89 0.98	**6.43**	S
4.	**INT**	Male Female	71.07 69.58	1.92 3.35	**2.38**	S

CTL – Computer in Teaching Learning **PPT** – Power Point Presentation
INT Internet **NS** - Not Significant **S** - Significant

From the above Table it is noted that the 't' values are significantly difference at 5% level of the Teacher Educators for Total, PPT(Power Point Presentation) and INT(Internet). Total, PPT (Power Point Presentation) and INT (Internet) the Mean score of Male Teacher Educators are higher than the Female Teacher Educators. In CTL(Computer in Teaching Learning) there is no significant difference at 5 % level of the Teacher Educators.

Table-2: Significant Difference on the Mean Scores of Rural and Urban Teacher Educators

S.No	Dimension	Locality	Mean	SD	t test	Remarks
1.	**Total**	Rural Urban	64.7 63.07	0.837 0.823	**5.46**	S
2.	**CTL**	Rural Urban	60.74 63.18	1.61 0.989	1.69	NS
3.	**PPT**	Rural Urban	62.90 63.07	0.78 0.65	1.06	NS
4.	**INT**	Rural Urban	74.53 70.93	1.72 1.68	**3.62**	S

From the above Table, the calculated 't' values are revealing that there is no significant difference at 5% level for the dimensions CTL and PPT. But there exists significant difference at 5% level with respect to Total and INT. In the Total and INT the Mean score of the Rural Teacher Educators are higher having higher awareness on Digital Technology than the Urban Teacher Educators.

Table-3: Significant Difference on the Mean Scores of Science and Arts Teacher Educators

S.No	Dimension	Subject	Mean	SD	t test	Remarks
1.	**Total**	Science Arts	63.83 64.31	0.929 0.779	1.21	NS
2.	**CTL**	Science Arts	62.43 61.28	1.06 1.11	**4.79**	S
3.	**PPT**	Science Arts	63.02 60.34	4.22 0.934	**3.27**	S
4.	**INT**	Science Arts	71.94 73.38	1.19 1.02	6.03	S

The Mean scores and the calculated 't ' values from the above table shows that there is significant difference in all the mean score of CTL, PPT and INT at 5% level except Total. It can be understood that the level Awareness on Digital Technology among Teacher Educators are good in CTL , PPT and INT.

Results and Discussion

The salient findings of the study are :

i) All the Teacher Educators am having good Awareness on Digital Technology.

ii) The Mean score of Male Teacher Educators are higher than the Female Teacher Educators towards Awareness on Digital Technology with respect to the dimensions such as Total, PPT and INT.

iii) With regards to Locality, the Mean score of Rural Teacher Educators are higher than the Urban Teacher Educators towards Awareness on Digital Technology in Total and INT.

iv) The Mean scores of Teacher Educators with respect to Science Subject are higher in CTL, PPT and Arts Teacher Educators are higher in INT.

The result shows that Gender, Locality and Subject of Teacher Educators were not the influencing factor in determining Awareness on Digital Technology. While considering the Gender, Male Teachers are having higher Awareness on Digital Technology than the Female Teachers. This is because Male Teacher Educators may have more time to work in the Computer but the Female Teachers have the commitment to look after their family. By this way Rural Teachers are having Good Awareness on Digital Technology than the Urban Teachers. This is due to the fact that Rural Teachers may show more interest to know about the new things. As well as Science Group Teacher Educators are show more awareness than Art Group Teacher Educators. It may be due to their subject knowledge.

Recommendations for Policy Makings

The result of this study shows that the Teacher Educators are having Good awareness on Digital Technology. Hence the usage of Computer must be increased to develop their practical knowledge. They are having more involvement in using Digital Technology in their class room Teaching. Effective teaching to promote better learning, proper orientation training Programme must be provided them to develop their knowledge in Digital Technology. The Government must ensure proper training to Teacher Educators to maintain Computers and Electronic things. Educational Authorities should create, improve and sustain the Awareness of Teacher Educators about Computer Knowledge. Teacher Educators should be encouraged by Administrators to use the stand alone Computer Applications in their Teachings. Using Internet application should be given special concentration, because, it empowers and enhance creativity. Digital Technology acts as a catalyst to support change in Teacher Pedagogy.

Conclusion

The Good Awareness on Computer Technology among Primary and Middle School Teachers will show the Conducing Climate towards Educational Technology.

The Instruction through Computer has been making wonders in the Class Room Activities. Hence Teachers must have Awareness on Computer Technology to get success and enjoy their Professions.

Reference

BEST,J.W,(2003). *Research in Education,* Prentice – Hall of India (P) Ltd., New Delhi.

LOKESH KOUL.(2005). *Methodology of Educational Research*, Vikas Publishing House (P) Ltd, New Delhi.

SINGH.Y.K,(2005). *Instructional Technology in Education,* P. P. H Publishing Corporation,NewDelhi-110002.

SAREEN.N, (2005). *Information and Communication Technology*, Anmol Publication Pvt.Ltd, New Delhi-110002.

❒

23.

Hyper Diverse Teacher and Digital Skills

Introduction

Social media have risen to prominence in recent years, beginning first with sites like Classmates in the mid-1990s, followed by Friendsterin 2003. The most significant growth of social media has occurred since 2004 when Facebook.com was introduced. Today there are over 550 million Facebook users alone, along with millions more using sites such as Twitter, MySpace, Plaxo, LinkedIn and others. While early adopters of these sites were digital natives (i.e., those born and/or raised in the internet era), all age groups are now embracing these sites. Teacher Educators and Student teachers always find it easier to use the already made teaching aids for teaching practice for preparation of lessons and in their theory learning and submission of assignments .in such situation the modern technology i.e. internet is challenging them to be more innovative , explorative and modern in their teaching and learning experiences . Teaching faculty is challenged by the digital world to be in pursuit of skills development. At present there is a gap between campus pedagogy and social media usage among students and faculty. Teaching community need to be skilled digitally. This paper works to examine that chasm, and to draw some conclusions as to why it may be time to incorporate this technology into our classrooms. The researcher used the self constructed tool HYPER ADOPTION SCALE (HAS) to achieve this motive. The samples were 100 teacher educators and 200 student teachers. In methodology the statistical used were MEAN, Standard Deviation and 't' test. The findings show that the level of hyper diversification among the samples is high, and there is no significant difference among the samples based on the variables Locality, Residence, Status(teacher educators/student teachers) and Educational qualification(UG/PG)

. However there exists a significant difference in term of Browsing habit. The educational implications suggest ways to diversify the teaching community and empower them digitally.

Social media have risen to prominence in recent years, beginning first with sites like Classmates in the mid-1990s, followed by Friendsterin 2003. The most significant growth of social media has occurred since 2004 when Facebook.com was introduced. Today there are over 550 million Facebook users alone, along with millions more using sites such as Twitter, MySpace, Plaxo, LinkedIn and others. While early adopters of these sites were digital natives (i.e., those born and/or raised in the internet era), all age groups are now embracing these sites. At present there is a gap between campus pedagogy and social media usage among students and faculty. Teaching community need to be skilled digitally. This paper works to examine that chasm, and to draw some conclusions as to why it may be time to incorporate this technology into our classrooms.

Need For the Study

Social media sites such as Face book and Twitter have come to dominate internet usage in recent years. Face book alone has over 550 million users as of fall 2010, while Twitter claims over 100 million users. While academia was fairly quick to adopt online education models in the 1990s, it has thus far not yet embraced social media portals as a way to deliver course content and engage students. This may be due to uncertainties regarding student perceptions about social media, its purposes, and its applications. Teacher Educators and Student teachers always find it easier to use the already made teaching aids for teaching practice for preparation of lessons and in their theory learning and submission of assignments .in such situation the modern technology i.e. internet is challenging them to be more innovative , explorative and modern in their teaching and learning experiences . Teaching faculty is challenged by the digital world to be in pursuit of skills development. Hence the need for the study.

Background of the Study

The researcher is involved in the educational institution which is in the forefront to promote quality of pedagogy. The experience of the researcher has often been frustrating with lack of digital climate .Since the Tamil nadu Teachers Education University has created a platform for such pondering this study found its way out to reach out to the professional mob to leverage the educational system through virtualization of the academia. The HD (Hyper Diversified) Classroom is the need of the hour. Just as the digital divide vanished over time (males once dominated all computer and internet usage), it is possible that similar usage divides will also disappear. Online college courses, for example, have broad-based appeal, and even traditional campus-based courses often have high computer usage expectations. Given that social media are now part of the cultural fabric, it is necessary to explore if and how social media might find their place in academia. Therefore the researcher undertook this study.

Sample for the Study

300 Samples Comprising Teacher Educators and Student Teachers (100 teacher Educators and 200 Student Teachers)

Objectives of the Study

- To construct a tool to find out the level of hyper diversification among teacher educators and student teachers
- To realize the importance of hyper diversification and developing digital skills among teacher educators and student teachers.
- To find out whether any difference exists among teacher educators and student teachers in their hyper diversification and digital skills in terms of the following variables:
    - Locality
    - Residence
    - Status(teacher/student)
    - Educational qualification(UG/PG)
    - Browsing habit

Hypotheses of the Study

The level of hyper diversification among teacher educators and student teachers is high.

There is a significant difference among teacher educators and student teachers in their hyper diversification and digital skills in terms of the following variables:

- Locality
- Residence
- Status(teacher/student)
- Educational qualification(UG/PG)
- Browsing habit

Methodology

In order to carry out the study the researcher used the following statistical

Techniques

MEAN, STANDARD DEVIATION and 't' test

Mean

Mean was calculated by the formula

Where X = Score, N = Total Number of the scores.

Standard Deviation

Standard deviation was calculated by the following formula

Where = Mean

X = Individual score
N = Total Number of the scores

Test of significant difference ('t' test)

Since the groups were large independent samples, the 't' test was applied through the statistical package by using the following formula:

$$t = \frac{M_1 - M_2}{\sqrt{\frac{ó_1^{\,2}}{N_1} + \frac{ó_2^{\,2}}{N_2}}}$$

Where M_1 - denotes mean of group 1
M_2 - denotes mean of group 2
σ_1 - denotes standard deviation of group 1
σ_2 - denotes standard deviation of group 2
N_1 - denotes total number of respondents in group 1
N_2 - denotes total number of respondents in group 2

Hypothesis 1

The level of hyper diversification and digital skills among teacher educators and student teachers is high.

Table 1: showing the analysis of hyper diversification and digital skills among teacher Educators and student teachers.

Entire Sample	N	Mean	S.D
Hyper Diversification	300	109.1	2.79
Digital Skills	300	24.21	3.40

The above table 1 shows that the mean and standard deviation on hyper diversification of the entire sample of teacher educators and student teachers' scores are 109.1 and 2.79 respectively. As 109.1 is higher than the mid-value of 64.1 (maximum score 129), it is concluded that the teacher educators and student teachers have a high level of hyper diversification. The mean and standard deviation on digital skills of the entire sample of teacher educators and student teachers' scores are 24.21 and 3.40 respectively. As 24.21 is higher than the mid-value of15 (maximum score 30), it is concluded that the teacher educators and student teachers have a high level of hyper diversification and digital skills.

HYPOTHESIS 2(a): There is a significant difference among teacher educators and student

Teachers in their hyper diversification and digital skills in terms of Locality.

The details of the results of the't' test in the level of hyper diversification and digital skills among teacher educators and student teachers based on Locality is given in table no.2.

Table- 2: Difference in the level of hyper diversification and digital skills based on Locality

Variables	Sub variables	N	Mean	SD	' t' value	Level of Significance	Result
Locality	Urban	160	21.31	3.12	**1.13**	**0.05**	**NS**
	Rural	140	23.52	2.86			

It is evident from table no.2 that the calculated't' value 1.13 is less than the table value 1.96 at 0.05 level. This shows that there is no significant difference among teacher educators and student teachers in their hyper diversification and digital skills in terms of Locality.

Hence, there is no significant difference between the samples (teacher educators and student teachers) that live in Urban and Rural areas in their hyper diversification and digital skills.

Hypothesis 2(b): There is a significant difference among teacher educators and student teachers in their hyper diversification and digital skills in terms of Residence.

The details of the results of the 't' test in the level of hyper diversification and digital skills among teacher educators and student teachers based on Residence is given in table no.3.

Table- 3: Difference in the level of hyper diversification and digital skills based on Residence

Variables	Sub variables	**N**	**Mean**	**SD**	**' t' value**	**Level of Significance**	**Result**
Residence	Hostel	130	22.42	3.40	**1.049**	**0.05**	**NS**
	Home	170	25.63	4.60			

It is evident from table no.3 that the calculated 't' value 1.049 is less than the table value 1.96 at 0.05 levels. This shows that there is no significant difference among teacher educators and student teachers in their hyper diversification and digital skills in terms of Residence.

Hence, there is no significant difference between the samples (teacher educators and student teachers) who reside at hostel and at home in their hyper diversification and digital skills.

Hypothesis (2C): There is a significant difference among teacher educators and student teachers in their hyper diversification and digital skills in terms of Status (teacher educator/student teacher).

The details of the results of the 't' test in the level of hyper diversification and digital skills among teacher educators and student teachers based on Status((teacher educator/student teacher) is given in table no.4.

Table- 4: Difference in the level of hyper diversification and digital skills based on Status (teacher educator/student teacher)

Variables	Sub variables	N	Mean	SD	' t' value	Level of Significance	**Result**
STATUS	Teacher Educators	100	20.24	3.983	**1.61**	**0.05**	**NS**
	Student Teachers	200	22.57	3.793			

It is evident from table no.4 that the calculated 't' value 1.61 is less than the table value 1.96 at 0.05 levels. This shows that there is no significant difference among teacher educators and student teachers in their hyper diversification and digital skills in terms of Status.

Hence, there is no significant difference between the samples (teacher educators and student teachers) in Status in their hyper diversification and digital skills.

Hypothesis 2(d): There is a significant difference among teacher educators and student teachers in their hyper diversification and digital skills in terms of Educational Qualification (UG/PG).

The details of the results of the 't' test in the level of hyper diversification and digital skills among teacher educators and student teachers based on Educational Qualification(UG/PG) is given in table no.5.

Table-5: Difference in the level of hyper diversification and digital skills based on Educational Qualification (UG/PG)

Variables	**Sub Variables**	**N**	**Mean**	**SD**	**' t' value**	**Level of Significance**	**Result**
Educational Qualification	UG	100	22.35	3.902	**1.21**	0.05	NS
	PG	200	21.50	3.340			

It is evident from table no.5 that the calculated 't' value 1.21 is less than the table value 1.96 at 0.05 levels. This shows that there is no significant difference among teacher educators and student teachers in their hyper diversification and digital skills in terms of Educational Qualification(UG/PG).

Hence, there is no significant difference among teacher educators and student teachers in their hyper diversification and digital skills in terms of Educational Qualification (UG/PG).

Hypothesis 2(e): There is a significant difference among teacher educators and student teachers in their hyper diversification and digital skills in terms of Browsing habit. The details of the results of the 't' test in the level of hyper diversification and digital skills among teacher educators and student teachers based on browsing habit is given in table no.6

Table-6: Difference in the level of hyper diversification and digital skills based on Browsing Habit

Variable	Sub variables	N	Mean	SD	' t' value	Level of Significance	Result
Browsing Habit	Frequently	120	17.73	3.679	**5.820**	**0.05**	S
	Rarely	180	19.28	3.431			

It is evident from table no.6 that the calculated 't' value 5.820 is higher than the table value 1.96 at 0.05 levels. This shows that there is a significant difference among teacher educators and student teachers in their hyper diversification and digital skills in terms of Browsing habit.

Hence, there is a significant difference among teacher educators and student teachers in their hyper diversification and digital skills in terms of Browsing habit.

Hypotheses Verification

The level of hyper diversification among teacher educators and student teachers is high- **Accepted**

There is a significant difference among teacher educators and student teachers in their hyper diversification and digital skills in terms of of Locality - **Rejected**

There is a significant difference among teacher educators and student teachers in their hyper diversification and digital skills in terms of Residence - **Rejected**

There is a significant difference among teacher educators and student teachers in their hyper diversification and digital skills in terms of Status(teacher/student) - Rejected

There is a significant difference among teacher educators and student teachers in their hyper diversification and digital skills in terms of educational qualification(UG/PG) - **Rejected**

There is a significant difference among teacher educators and student teachers in their hyper diversification and digital skills in terms of Browsing habit - **Accepted**

Educational Implications

The result of the study leads to encourage Teacher Educators Student teachers to be hyper diversified and digitally skilled .

- The usage of virtual world can be enhanced in colleges to develop skills and build capacity as part of professional life.
- Therefore Teacher Educators and Student Teachers can:
- create and edit digital audios
- use Social bookmarking to share resources with and between learners
- use blogs and wikis to create online platforms for students
- Exploit digital images for classroom use
- Use video content to engage students
- Use infographics to visually stimulate students
- Use Social networking sites to connect with colleagues and grow

professionally

- Create and deliver asynchronous presentations and training sessions
- Compile a digital e-portfolio for their own development
- Have a knowledge about online security
- be able to detect plagiarized works in students assignments
- Create screen capture videos and tutorials
- Curate web content for classroom learning
- Use and provide students with task management tools to organize their work and plan their learning
- Use polling software to create a real-time survey in class
- Understand issues related to copyright and fair use of online materials
- Exploit computer games for pedagogical purposes
- Use digital assessment tools to create quizzes
- Use of collaborative tools for text construction and editing
- Find and evaluate authentic web based content
- Identify online resources that are safe for students browsing
- Use digital tools for time management purposes
- Learn about the different ways to use YouTube in your classroom
- Use note taking tools to share interesting content with your students
- Annotate web pages and highlight parts of text to share with your class
- Use of online graphic organizers and printables
- Use of online sticky notes to capture interesting idea
- Use of screen casting tools to create and share tutorials
- Exploit group text messaging tools for collaborative project work
- Conduct an effective search query with the minimum time possible
- Conduct A Research Paper Using Digital Tools
- Use file sharing tools to share docs and files with students online
- Reduce Infrastructure Costs Through Consolidation
- Virtualize the Most Demanding Workloads
- Virtualize for High Availability
- Improve Security and Reliability with Microkernelized Hypervisor
- Protect Important Data Using Live Backup
- Minimize Downtime with Quick Migration
- Delegate Virtual Machine Management
- Reduce Support Time with Integrated Management
- Save Time and Money with a More Flexible Test Environment
- Take Advantage of Broad Compatibility
- Reduce Support Time with Integrated Management
- Save Time and Money with a More Flexible Test Environment
- Take Advantage of Broad Compatibility
- Exploit Facebook,Youtube,Flickr andSocial networking Sites(SNS) for sharing eduinformation

- Use Smartphones, iphones, tablets as educational resources.
- Accomplish content delivery and student engagement by creating and maintaining a Fan Page, at no cost to anyone involved, and completely away from the limitations of course management systems such as Bloackboard, Angel and WebCT.

Bibliography

Baird, D., Fisher, M. (2005). Neomillennial user experience strategies: Utilizing social networking media to support "always on" learning styles. Journal of Educational Technology Systems. 34 (1) 5 - 32.

Bimber, B. (2000). Measuring the gender gap on the Internet. Social Sciences Quarterly, 81 (3):25-32.

Broos, A. (2005). Gender and information and communication technologies (ICT) anxiety: Male self-assurance and female hesitation. Cyber psychology & Behavior8(1):21-31.

Dennis, A.R., Kinney, S.T., & Hung, Y.T.C. (1999) Gender differences in the effects of media richness.Small Group Research . 30 (4): 405-437.

Dillon, D. (2001). E-books: The University of Texas Experience. Library Hi Tech. 19 (4) 350-62.

Gefen, D. & Straub, D. W. (1997) Gender differences in the perception and use of email: an extension to the technology acceptance model. MIS Quarterly 4: 389-400.

Horowitz, R. & Mohum, A. (1998). His and Hers: Gender Consumption & Technology. University of Virginia Press.

Jackson L.A., Ervin, K.S., Gardner, P.D. & Schmitt,N. (2001). Gender and the internet: women communicating and men searching.

Lenhart, M. (2010). Teens and Social Media, An Overview. Pew Internet and American Life Project.

Summerfield, M., Mandel, C., Kantor, P. (1999). Online books at Columbia: Early findings on use, satisfaction, and effect. Technology and Scholarly Communication. Berkley; University of California Press 282-308.

Wilska, A. (2003). Mobile use as part of young people's consumption styles.

❐

24.

Effectiveness of Blended Learning Programme in Teaching Biology at Higer Secondary School Students

Introduction

The technology is an integral part in the lives of young people who are direct beneficiaries of the educational process. This was often made argument for the need to develop learning methods that use modern technology in the formative and educational. By such methods students are responsible for their own learning, on which they themselves have control and manage it according to their interests and needs. The specialists' researches reveal that the methods which combine the traditional education with the modern technologies (*blended learning*) have increased the effectiveness. Blended Learning is a strategy which integrates the teaching learning process with different learning environments like face-to-face, online, social networking etc. Its rapid growth has been facilitated by the Internet and other emerging technologies like cloud computing, social networking etc. This paper provides a view about the effectiveness of blended learning programme in teaching biology at higher secondary school students

The recent research in science education has focused on instruction that is specific science content, specific instructional strategies and how they are related to biology learning contexts and instructional outcomes. In the present scientific and technological age, the conventional teaching methods are not sufficient to arouse interest among the students and do not meet up to the intellectual, psychological and emotional needs of the students in the new millennium. The methods of teaching biology need to be changed.

In a vast country like India, enormous work is now being done in the field of education but it is still not possible to equip each and every higher and higher secondary school with all the facilities for teaching biology in the near future. Most of the higher secondary schools, both in rural and urban area are suffering from lack of modern science laboratories. They need equally advanced gadgets to support their education. Technology enables students get a live vision of life's aspects and scientific factors. Any diagram can be explained in detail with 3d effect, it helps the student to understand the lesson clearly. Keeping in mind the investigator felt it appropriate to use blended learning for the teaching of the concepts in biology topics included in the XI standard biology syllabus (Tamil Medium).

Blended Learning

Blended learning provides platform to attract the senses of the learner for easy and happy learning. Blended learning is a programme which integrates teaching learning process with different leaning environment. Its rapid growth facilitated by the internet and other emerging technology cloud computing and social networking. "Blended learning is the thoughtful fusion of face-to-face and online learning experiences. The basic principle is that face-to-face oral communication and online written communication are optimally integrated such that the strengths of each are blended into a unique learning experience congruent with the context and intended educational purpose."

Blended learning – an instructional practice that combines teaching methods from both face-to-face instruction and online learning, gives to educational institutions new approaches and strategies for addressing the challenges they face and for taking advantage of the exciting new learning opportunities that are now available.

Blended learning does not exclude the traditional learning methods, but adds new and modern methods as: IT tools (email, web, chat, online conferences, e-learning platforms), workshops, individual project groups, practical demonstrations, etc.

Objectives of the Study

The objectives of the study as follows:

- To find out the effectiveness of blended learning programme for the teaching of biology at higher secondary level.
- To compare the effectiveness of blended learning programme in the teaching of biology with conventional method of teaching biology.

Hypotheses of the Study

The following null hypotheses have been formulated.

- There is no significant difference between the experimental group and control group in the achievement of biology at pre test level.
- There is no significant difference between the experimental group and

control group in the achievement of biology at posttest level.

- There is no significant difference between the pretest and posttest in the achievement of biology for the experimental group.
- There is no significant difference between the pretest and posttest in the achievement of biology for the control group.

Sample

The sample of the study consists of 100 students studying in XI standard under State Board syllabus at perambalur district. The sample includes both boys and girls.

Tools Used

The following tools had been used for the present study:

An achievement test in biology constructed and validated by the investigators. Blended learning programme was developed by the investigator for the teaching of the concepts in biology topics included in the XI standard biology syllabus.

The progrmme was arranged logically based on the psychological principles of learning. Experimental design was adopted. For the experimentation pretest was conducted and sample was divided into two groups. The students of the experimental group were taught with the blended learning progrmme and the control group through the conventional method. After the treatment period the posttest was administered. The collected data were subjected to statistical analysis and the results obtained were interpreted.

Testing of Hypotheses

Hypothesis 1: There is no significant difference between the experimental group and control group in the achievement of biology at pre test level.

The't' test applied to test the significance of difference between the mean achievement test scores of the experimental group and control group of pretest level.

Table -1: Mean Achievement Test Scores of the Experimental Group Compared with that of the Control Group at Pretest level

Groups	N	Mean	S.D	't' value	Level of Significance at 0.05 level
Experimental	30	20.43	2.09	0.46	Not significant
Control	30	19.63	1.87		

The table indicates that the 't' value is not significant at 0.05 level. The students of the experimental group do not differ significantly from the students of the control group in the mean achievement test scores at pre test level.

Hypothesis 2: There is no significant difference between the experimental group and control group in the achievement of biology at posttest level

Th 't' test applied to test the significance of difference between the mean achievement test scores of the experimental group and control group of posttest level.

Table -2: Mean Achievement Test Scores of the Experimental Group Compared with that of the Control Group at Posttest level

Groups	N	Mean	S.D	't' value	Level of Significance at 0.01 level
Experimental	30	36.40	3.96	15.08	significant
Control	30	20.10	5.14		

The table indicates that the 't' value is significant at 0.01 level. Hence there is there is a significant difference between the two groups. As indicated by the mean value, it can be concluded that the students of the experimental group fared better in the achievement test than the students of the control group. This shows that learning with the help of blended learning programme will increase the achievement of the students better than learning through the conventional method.

Hypothesis 3: There is no significant difference between the pretest and posttest in the achievement of biology for the experimental group.

The 't' test applied to test the significance of difference between test scores of the pretest with that of the posttest for the experimental group.

Table -3: Mean Achievement Test Scores of Pretest Compared with that of the Posttest for the Experimental Group

Groups	N	Mean	S.D	't' value	Level of Significance at 0.01 level
Experimental	30	20.43	2.07	20.52	Significant
Control	30	37.40	3.96		

Table 3 indicates that the't' value is significant at 0.01 level. Hence, it could be concluded that there is a significant difference between the mean achievement test scores of the pretest and posttest for the experimental group. The higher mean value in the posttest shows that the students fared better in the posttest than in the pretest. This shows that the blended learning programme has helped the students to score more in the posttest.

Hypothesis 4: There is no significant difference between the pretest and posttest in the achievement of biology for the control group.

The 't' test applied to test the significance of difference between the mean achievement test scores of the pretest with that of the posttest for the control group.

Table-4: Mean Achievement Test Scores of Pretest Compared with that of the Posttest for the Control Group

Groups	N	Mean	S.D	't' value	Level of Significance at 0.05 level
Experimental	30	19.76	1.87	0.034	Not significant
Control	30	20.00	5.06		

Table 4 indicates that the 't' value is not significant at 0.05 level. Hence, it could be concluded that there is no significant difference between the mean achievement test scores of the pretest and posttest for the control group.

Findings of the Study

There is no significant difference between the experimental group and control group in the achievement of biology at pretest level.

There is a significant difference between the experimental group and control group in the achievement of biology at posttest level. The students leaning with the help of blended learning programme fared better in biology than in students learning through the conventional method.

There is a significant difference between the mean achievement test scores of the pretest and posttest for the experimental group. This shows that the blended learning programme has helped the students to score more marks in the posttest.

There is a significant difference between the mean achievement test scores of the pretest and posttest for the control group. This shows that the conventional method of teaching will not help the students to score more marks in the posttest.

Conclusion

In the field of education is not possible to equip the teaching leaning in higher and higher secondary level because most of the higher secondary schools suffering from lack of modern methods of teaching, they still follow the conventional method of teaching in higher secondary level. This should be change in the modern era; they should follow the blended learning methods in their teaching learning methods because it supports the education department well in advance.

Reference

Barbour Michael, et al, (2012), *Online and Blended Learning: A Survey of Policy and Practice of K-12 Schools Around the World*, available at http://www.inacol.org/cms/wpcontent/uploads/2012/11/iNACOL_IntnlReport2011.pdf

Rogers Carl (1983), *The Interpersonal Relationship in the Facilitation of Learning*, London: Rutledge

The Oxford Group (2013), *Blended Learning—Current Use, Challenges and Best Practices*, report 2013, available at http://www.kineo.com/m/0/blended-learning-report-202013.pdf (accessed July 2013)

25.

Comparative Study of Effectiveness of Computer Assisted Instruction on Circulatory System for IX Standard Students

Introduction

This study investigated the compare effectiveness of computer-assisted instruction (CAI) and conventional teaching method in biology on senior high school students. A science class was selected in each of two randomly selected schools. The pre-test, post-test equivalent quasi experimental design was used. The students in the experimental group learned science concepts (circulatory system) through the CAI, whereas the students in the control group were taught the same concepts by the conventional approach. The conventional approach consisted of teaching, discussions and question and answer teaching methods. The students' pre-test and post-tests scores were subjected to Analysis of't' Test, ANOVA. The results indicated that students that were instructed by the experimental group performed better on the post-test than those instructed by the conventional approach. This may help teachers in organizing meaningful teaching learning experiences and adopt innovative methods and approaches in teaching. Computer assisted Instruction (CAI) is a supplementary instructional strategy ineffective teaching. In this paper, researcher elaborates use, utility and importance of CAI in teaching-Learning. To create new approaches technique and appropriate digital learning environment applying in education for present and future generation. Based on the research findings recommendations were made on the need to develop relevant CAI packages for teaching-Learning biology in secondary schools.

Education should be an individual activity to a much greater content. Not at all children should be forced to go through the same steps of learning at the same speed. The high achievers will move faster in their learning where as the under achievers will need more time. Children have their own ways of learning. Some children may learn better through the use of different learning materials them by merely listening to an inspirational talk by the teacher. The style of learning may also change according to age. They use their season in acquiring knowledge. An important feature of education is its use of physical and intellectual tools. Education must reflect the influence of technology. This new technology demands new interpretations of the instructional process and those changed with educating the next generation must engage in a continual cycle of education and revaluation in the light of technological influence at all levels.

Education Technology

Educational technology is not a simple combination of these two words. It is usually thought of even more than the sum of the following two interpretations.

1. Technology in Educatione the effectiveness of the educatioal l combination or seperately bjective - vis-a
2. Technology of Education

Technology in Education

This is based on the application of engineering principle for developing electro mechanical equipment like motion pictures, tape-recorders, teaching machines, computers, television etc. This approach of education a technology is a bye product of the 21th century. Davis (1971) thinks that the hardware approach is based on the application of physical science to the education and training system which mechanics the process of teaching gradually so that teachers would be able to deal with more students resulting in less cost and economy in finances. It is said that good teachers have always used visual ads to assist their teaching ancient great masters used illustrations and models to increase the interests of their students. Today educational technology is stressing modern audio – visual and computer equipment.

Technology of Education

It refers to the study of principles and theories, formulate to solve problems in the teaching, learning process. The main frame work of education technology is provided by Technology or Education. 'Technology in Education' provides the support to implement the broader instructional design. It primarily implies systematic approach to instructional design incorporating alternative methodologies, media and aids with reference to the objective vis-à-vis learning content. This accommodates the systems approach, programmed learning etc.

According to the encyclopedia of education (1971. vol-9 P.22) Educational Technology is the purposeful combination or separately of objects, techniques, devices, events and relationships to increase the effectiveness of the educational process.

Application of Education Technology

Educational Technology has gradually influenced and developed the teaching learning process. Since the world is moving towards Technological growth information and special place in education. The trend is to introduce technological principles in the classroom. Educational technology consists of all modern media, methods and materials, which can be used to maximizing the learning experience of student at various levels.

Historical Perspective of Individual Instruction

The classical conditioning of PAVLOV opened a new chapter in teaching and learning and the behaviour gave importance to reinforcement as a major condition for learning. Edward Thorn dike improved the reinforcement procedure with stimulus (reinforce) response reaction, SKINNER (1967) expanded this idea as operative conditioning which led to the invention of teaching machine. Both kin aesthetic and information feedback are identified to play crucial role in skill learning by GAGNE (1963) LUMSDANOE (1964) proposed a new definition to instructional technique which was later applied in programmed instruction. The five golden rules applied in this preparation of programmed learning material (PLM) and the need for defining the objectives in behavioural terms in the preparation of instructional software material are proposed as essential by DANIEL DAVIS (1965). The three phases that help the teacher to decide in the ongoing focus on pedagogy are; what to teach (objectives) whom to teach (entering behaviour) and how to flash the procedures which are similar to the CAI model. FLANDERS' (1964) recommendation for interactivity in learning are subjoined through various learning activities built in the CAI package.

Individualized Instruction

Individualized instruction is the one-to-one relationship between a student and what he learns (DUNN and DUNN 1977). Individualized instruction is one of the most active areas in the education innovations. This kind of instruction helps the learner to learn at his own pace. Modern class rooms are characterized by a high degree of heterogeneity. Individual differences are pronounced among learners in large classes and to cater to the needs of the learners in such classes individualized instruction bodies is required.

Through individualized instruction materials self learning can be enhanced. This land of self learning helps the learners to learn even more difficult contents and learning of higher categories. Through self learning the needs and levels of the learners are considerably satisfied. The individual differences are considered and hence individualized instruction certainly leads to mastery level of learning.

Individualized instruction may be provided for the following reasons (DUNN and DUNN 1977)

A gifted student, able to come with new consents or skills independently may work well ahead of his peers through the use of this method. He need not wait to learn until the teacher can work with him individually or the rest of his peers catch up with him.

An interested student may learn more about a given topic, consent or skill after most of his peers have mastered it, may spend as much time as needed reinforcing the knowledge at his desire and pace until he too is ready to move ahead.

An interested student may learn more about a given topic, consents or skill at the moment in time when he wants to, not when the teacher is able to get to the subject.

An average student who cares to something new in an interesting way may become sufficiently motivated to work on his own because of the nature of the varied multi sensory experience.

Individualized instruction materials should have certain characteristics. According to MORE (1968), an individualized instructional material should have the following features. It should as

1. Permit the learners to explore freely.
2. Inform the learner about the consequence of his action.
3. Be self – pacing that is the student can more at his own rate of learning.
4. Permit the learner to make full use of his capacity for discovering relations of various kinds.

GOLDSCHMID (1973) maintain that any form of individualized instruction should possess the following characters. It should

1. Emphasize learning
2. Ensure active students participation
3. Stress evaluation and feed back
4. Principle of individual pacing

There are different forms of individualized instruction. Some of them are

1. Learning Module
2. Multimedia Package
3. Programmed Learning Material (PLM)
4. Personalized system of instruction (PSI)
5. Audio Tutorial Instruction (ATI)
6. Learning Module

A learning module is a short unit of instruction dealing with a single unit of subject matter self contained with define objectives. Based on the specified instructional objectives, questions are given and the learner assesses his/her performance in the subject.

Multimedia Package

A multimedia package consists of a collection of soft ware's of several media dealing with a specific topic on subject area and forming an integrated whole. Based on the interest and aptitude of the students, the students can select the media through which they want to learn the subject.

Programmed Learning Material (PLM)

Skinner has pronounced Programmed Learning Material (PLM) based on the theory of operant conditioning PLM consists of planned sequence of learning activity for achieving mastery in terms of stimulus response reinforcement relationship.

Personalized System of Instruction (PSI)

The Personalized System of Instruction refers to training which is based on self pacing and master learning. In PSI, learners work in their own and they must achieve mastery of a series of written learning unit. They are assisted by teachers and professors. It is possible to apply PSI.

Audio Tutorial Instruction (ATI)

Here the instructor's remarks, directions and interpretations of learning assignments and resources are given through audio cassettes. The cassettes are prepared by the concerned subject experts keeping in mind the target for which the cassette is prepared. Even for distance education system, audio cassettes are being used for instruction.

Computer Assisted Instruction (CAI)

The most exciting innovation in educational technology is the Computer Assisted Instruction (CAI). Though it was not skill developed like other individualized instructional materials, the day is not far off when it will revolutionize the whole process of instruction. **Taneja (1999)**

A computer is programmed with linear or branching programmes. It acts like a super teaching machine catering to the needs of a number of students at the same time. The characteristic aspects of the CAI is its capacity to initiate flexible instructional with the student. In this respect it is superior to the teaching machine. The computer can do this in different ways. The computer is able to record and store all the responses of all the students. It can use the information in deciding what information is to be given to the student next. It can branch not just in terms of on answer but also in terms of a whole series of previous answers. It can also record the time taken to answer a question and the decree of correctness of the student's response. It uses the information in planning to determine which branch or format would be conductive to a learner for effective instruction.

Computer Assisted Instruction is not merely a sophisticated type of programmed instruction but a different kind of instruction but a different kind of instruction altogether. No doubt, data processing, data communication, consents of audio-visual and media theory, communication theory, system theory and learning theory are annelid in the preparation of the CAI material. In contrast to CAI, Computer Managed Instruction (CMI) analysis the relationship between various factors concerned with the learning of a pupil and suggests activities appropriate to individual students.

Different Forms of Computer Assisted Instruction

Computer Assisted Instruction can be take any one of the following modes depending on the purpose of the material, the five different modes of CAI are

- Drill and Practice
- Tutorial Mode
- Simulation Mode
- Discovery Mode
- Gaming Mode

Tutorial Mode

In this mode information is presented in small units followed by a question. The student's response is analyzed by the computer and an appropriate feedback is provided. This is similar to programmed instruction. As in programmed instruction, the information may be given in a linear fashion as in branched pathways. The greater the number of alternative paths, more adaptive the tutorial can be to individuals.

Drill and Practice Mode

The learner, provided with a number of graded examples on the concepts and principles learnt earlier. The idea is to develop proficiency and fluency through doing all the correct responses are reinforced and the incorrect responses are diagnosed and corrected. The compute continues the drill and the learners continue his practice until mastery is achieved by the learner.

Simulation Mode

In this mode, the learners are presented with scheduled down stimulated. Situations bearing correspondence with real situation. Simulations are made to avoid risk, save money and conserve time, simulation of an aero plane in flight, an experiment on titration, a nuclear reaction, collision of two bodies are good examples of the simulation models in science.

Discovery Mode

The individual approach to teaching and learning is as followed. The learner is encouraged to proceed through trial and error approach i.e., by solving a given problem, realizing where and how he/she went wrong, trying again and finally solving the complex problem.

Gaming Mode

In this mode, the learner is engaged in playing opposite. The computer or opposite another learner. The extent of learning depends upon the type of the game. Games on spelling names of places and general knowledge are some examples of the gaming mode.

Information Handling

One area where processing and information handling capacity of computer is profitably used in counseling and guiding the computer stores complete cumulative records and match them against employment needs and potentialities as required for personal and vocational guidance.

Merits of Computer Assisted Instruction

Computer Assisted Instruction has several advantages over other systems of instructions.

- Each student receives instruction at his own pace
- Each student receives immediate feedback for his response
- Each student responds continuously as he receives instruction

All units of learning are broke down into subunits and elements of learning in accordance with skinner's approach of teaching in small steps

Reinforcement of learning is achieved by personal message

Learning sessions are not manageable by designing the duration between half an hour to one hour

- Student can access the computer any place
- Students can learn in their own styles and ways
- Students can test their own learning at any point of time to an end

Lesson from the theories of learning are taken into account at stage instructional design

Teacher's time is saved from the routine job of giving activity and employed in innovative instruction design and student guidance

Objectives of the Study

- To understand about computer system and its working
- To understand the educational application of computer
- To develop scientific attitude among school students
- To provide a broad – based biological knowledge, stimulate a deep interest in the natural world
- To develop a CAI package for self instruction on the unit circulatory system in science for IX standard students

- To enable the pupils to utilize effectively the instructional material in learning biology
- To verify whether there is any difference in learning level between
- Boys and Girls
- Rural and Urban School
- Government, Government Aided and Unaided Schools
- Hypothesis

There is no significant difference between the pretest and posttest scores of government school pupils' following the Computer Assisted Instruction.

There is no significant difference between the pretest and posttest scores of Aided School Pupils' following the Computer Assisted Instruction.

There is no significant difference between the pretest and posttest scores of Unaided School Pupil following the Computer Assisted Instruction.

There is no significant difference between the pretest and posttest mean scores of the experimental group following Computer Assisted Instruction.

There is no significant difference in post test performance of Computer Assisted Instruction between the different types of school pupil.

There is no significant difference between the post test performance of Urban and Rural school pupil following Computer Assisted Instruction.

There is no significant difference between the post test performance of Boys and Girls following Computer Assisted Instruction.

Scope of the Study

The students can get more and adequate knowledge through self instruction material.

It helps the students to develop self study habits, since individual study can be brought out with the help of self instruction material.

The study is expected to help the students at all levels, since computer plays a vital role in all the aspects of life especially in the field of education.

The present study is experimental study to compose the effectiveness of CAI and on "Circulatory System" for IX standard students.

In future instruction materials will act as a source of the knowledge for the teacher and students.

It will help the teacher in the teaching learning process, as it can draw the attention of the students by teaching learning computer.

Studies Conducted on CAI in India

In India at present several efforts are being taken up to develop the software for CAI, for individual instruction several studies also have been conducted to identify the effectiveness of CAI and Handout over the achievement of the students. SHARMA and GEORGE (1979) developed a CAI package of mathematics. Their objectives were to study the effectiveness of the CAI for school children and the findings revealed that the CAI packages produced significant result over the achievement of the children. BADRINATH (1986) conducted a study on developing and validating CAI package for reflection of light at the VIII standard level. He found that experience in CAI program appeared to be an effective method than the conventional method.

NACHIMUTHU (1988) has studied the development of CAI program on "Leaves". He expressed in his thesis about the difficulties in programming a lesson. He also suggested that teaching will be more effective if the researcher himself programmed the lesson than using readymade diskettes. Because when the research programme, he can give all the points to be taught, as in conventional method and so the learners also will score marks up to the researchers' expectation.

PALANIAPPAN (1989) made a study on computers in education. He found that after introducing computers is schools for teaching, the attitude of teachers as well as students have changed. Many dull students scoreless through CAI, than the conventional method.

HEMALATHA (1989) studied on orientation of CAI. She concluded that the computers are commonly used in three main response sensitive strategies in CAI and suggested some levels of comparative involvement in decision making feature. They are drill and practice, tutorial and dialogue.

KARPAGA KUMARAVEL. R (1990) in his study on the effectiveness of computer assisted instruction video assisted instruction and conventional instruction in English language learning found that the achievement of video assisted instruction group in better than computer assisted instruction and conventional instructional group.

P. JEYAMANI (1991) pointed out that learning with computers offers a very powerful tool for educators and all efforts must be made to learners the potential of computers in education. This educational technology could therefore have a more on comparing role to play in the developing world. Thus the stimulation model of teaching through computer assisted instruction can readily be used for all types of teaching.

SARVANAN (1991) developed and validated a CAI package on X – rays for XI standard students. His findings revealed that the CAI packages were effective for individualized instruction.

PURUSHOTHAMAN and STELLA (1991) studied the effectiveness of CAI learning testing and guidance. The study reported that for low achievers self-testing and guidance through computer was found to be more effective.

BENEDICTO (1992) developed and validated a CAI packages on pollution for XI standard Biology students. The major findings of his study was learning the unit through CAI was faster for both slow and fast learners when compared with traditional teaching. He also reported the software developed ensures uniformity of achievement among Biology students.

MATHIVANAN (1994) attempted to develop and validate a CAI package on organisms an environment for IX standard pupils. His report revealed that the CAI package produced more significant effect on the achievement of the pupils of knowledge, comprehension, application and analysis level.

Dr. P. ANNARAJA and Smt. NIRMALA SUNDARARAJ (2005) made a study on power point presentation in teaching zoology pre post design was used in this that, they found that the power point presentation is effective in teaching zoology for higher secondary students.

JAYAKRUSHA CHOUDHARY (2005) conducted a study on effect of Computer Assisted Learning using method of enquiry in teaching physics in secondary school. Main objectives of this study was to test the efficiency of computer aided learning using method of inquiry in teaching physics at the secondary level on achievement and concept attainment. He found that CAI experimental method is to be more effective than conventional method of teaching.

G. SUBRAMANIAN (2006) pointed out major findings were computer assisted instruction significantly improves the performance of students, learning accountancy at higher secondary level. The combination of the colour, text, music and animation of the CAI package was well received by the students and the positive effect of same is perceptible from their achievement scores.

A computer factorial program on the laws and consents encountered in introductory physics courses among high school students was studied by EAUGHN AND KUHN (1979) these programmer were written with the weaker students in mind. But the researchers found that even stronger students used them presumably to check whether or not they really understood a particular phenomenon. This success was attributed to the fact that the programs were written so that each student's incorrect answer was dealt with in the novelty of using the computer encouraged students usage much more than the prospect of working from a study guide.

In another study, the efforts of CAI and reinforcement schedules on physics achievement towards physics of high school were measured by BANNET (1986). Seventy one high school students were taken as sample. The result of this study supported that students who received CAI would achieve significantly higher physics test scores. .

PASCUAL (1993) conducted a twofold study. He applied linguistics approach and empirical study designed to measure the degree of motivation in students learning English using CAI material and Non CAI material. He found that students belonging to CAI material showed more motivation than their counterparts.

SIEGLE (2000) the purpose of this study was to investigate whether exposure to multimedia and presentation software on laptop computers influenced student achievement in a secondary level anatomy and physiology science course. The study demonstrated that students learned more when they had access to laptop computers, were exposed to multimedia software, and created projects with presentation software.

VENDLINSKI et al (2002) conducted a quasi-experimental study with 134 first-year high school chemistry students using the Interactive Multimedia Exercises computer based learning and assessment tool to solve qualitative chemistry problems. Results of this study show a strong and significant correlation between computer aided measures of student understanding and the teacher's manual evaluation of student understanding using her own rubric.

SUSAN et al (2003) in his study examined 165 teachers' beliefs about student centered learning as they implemented Alien Rescue, a computer based programme for middle school science that was designed to create a Student Centered Learning Environment (SCLE) in the class room. Discusses the goal of student activity, the role of the teacher, assessment, and student interaction.

RABIA TABASSUM (2004) conducted a study on effect of Computer Assisted Instruction CAI on the Secondary School Students Achievement in Science. In his study analysis of data revealed that the class IX standard students taught through computer assisted instruction as supplementary strategy performed significantly better. The CAI was found equally effective for both male and female students.

WINTERS et al (2005) in this study 62 high school biology students, paired heterogeneously based on prior knowledge, learned about genetic using Gen Scope, a Computer Based Learning Environment. The results of this naturalistic study could potentially be used to inform educational practice by highlighting scaffolds that may foster self-regulated learning in a CBLE mediated science inquiry context.

HARSKAMP et al (2005) conducted a study on solving Physics Problems with the help of Computer Assisted Instruction" In this study the main goal of most Physics text books is to develop declarative and procedural knowledge exercises provide pupils with opportunities to apply this knowledge. The computer group taking part in the experiment did achieve higher results in solving problems.

CEPNI et al (2006) pointed out that the study on effects of Computer Assisted Instruction Material related to photosynthesis topic on student cognitive development misconceptions and attitudes. This study result showed that using CAIM in teaching photo synthesis topic was very effective for students to reach comprehension and application levels of cognitive domain.

MAHAMOOD FARHADIAN (2007) in his research, he studied the co-operative learning, Computer Assisted Instruction and combination of these two methods called Co-operative Computer Assisted Instruction (CCAI). In CCAI method with the use of computer and attractive software, there would be appropriate grounds in instruction and educational achievement of mathematics for students. This method was examined for small group of student in a workshop. He had investigated some hypotheses on reduce of the students negative beliefs about mathematics, the speed of learning mathematics and its independence from time scheduling. Findings of the study, the difference between pretest and posttest scores were meaningfully significant.

Methodology

Educational software development and validation is a major research and development activity in the field of education. The major area in educational software is occupied by the instructional software development. The nature and the impact of computer and learning were led to its acquiring more significance. In the latest concept of improvement in the instructional software produced and the role played by educational technologists in the consents and process of software development. The CAI package depends on the electronic device. Further there is need for the subject export, technical expert. Individualized instruction is the one-to-one relationship between learners and the subject to be learnt.

Selection of Area

The investigator has selected six schools in Udumalpet at Tiruppur District which come under the Tamil Nadu State Board of Education. The sample selected for study consists of boys and girls from rural and urban schools.

Selection of the Sample

Sample selection is an important aspect of the research study, violation of a proper sampling method may yield based information of research and therefore maximum care is necessary for solution of sample.

English medium students of standard were selected from different types study the investigator selected three hundred students. Hundred and fifty boys and hundred and fifty girls of ninth standard from two government schools, two governments aided schools and two unaided schools have been selected.

Considering the non-feasibility of formulating randomized groups in a school setting, it was decided to have purposive sampling as the method of sampling for this experiment. Hundred and fifty students of Class IX in each of the three type of schools were taken as CAI experimental group and hundred and fifty students of

Hundred and fifty students of Class IX in different types of rural schools and hundred and fifty students of Class IX in different types of urban schools were taken as the experimental group. The same schools are brought under the categories, group of different variables are follow. Purposive sampling procedure is applied for selecting the sampling and so that it is free from any prejudice. The following table presents the details of the samples selected for the study.

Sampling Technique Pupils orzied and e samples selected for the study. e from any pre-judice.

For the present study purposive sampling method is used. The purposive sampling is selected by some arbitrary method because it is known to be representative of the total population. It is appropriate in a study which lays special emphasis on the control of certain specific variables.

Design of the Study

The design selected for the study is the pretest and posttest of two groups.

1. Administrating a pretest measuring the dependent variable at initial stage for elimination of novelty factor.
2. Applying the treatment to the subject, to measure treatment effect.
3. Administering a posttest again for measuring the impact of the dependent variable.

Differences attributed to application of the experimental treatment are then determined by comparing pretest and posttest scores.

Development of Instructional Materials

The subject is to be converted into CAI package was "Circulatory System" in biology for IX standard students. The content frame work of the syllabus was adapted from the prescribed text by the Tamil Nadu State Board Text Book for IX standard. The teaching points were collected from the text books and other reference books mentioned and sequence according to the designed learning level of students in the local school. The content prescribed was corrected into a reading material in simple language according to their vocabulary level.

The teaching frames were structured on the learning materials following the norms and theories set for the preparation of CAI package. The teaching points were structured in small dosage called "Frame". Frames were arranged in proper sequence. In each frame information was presented with simple illustration or examples.

Objectives Starting Phase

Bloom's Taxonomy was used for objective formation specific behavioral objective was formulated as performance objectives on completion of learning the unit "Circulatory System" the student should be able to identify. Content analysis was done. Care was taken to link the content by appropriate sequencing strategy.

1. Define "Blood"
2. State the composition of blood
3. Name the types of blood
4. List the properties of blood
5. Distinguish RBC, WBC and Platelet
6. Describe the functions of blood and
7. Define "Blood Group"

Description of the Tool Used

a) Computer Assisted Instruction Package: The instructional soft ware package developed to help the learners through a prescribed form of self instruction the subject are to be converted into frame. In this study in biology CAI package was Circulatory System for IX standard students. This CAI package contains various stimuli such as showing pictures and animation. This CAI was an instructional effective material individualized.

b) Performa Sheet: The investigator herself has developed a Performa sheet to collect necessary information regarding the individuals back ground such as the name, age, sex, name and address of the school, locality, type of school, system of school,

c) Science Achievement Test In this present study the investigator was prepared the achievement test question paper based on the IX standard State Board Syllabus. The question has been given to IX students of the selected school situated in and around Coimbatore. In consists of 40 questions and each objective has been provided 4 multiple choice from which the individual is asked to mark the response which he/she feels to be right in their point of view.

d) Scoring Key: The answer scripts for the conducted achievement test were collected and scored based on the scoring key. The score the test it was decided to give one mark as weight age for each correct answer. Thus a maximum of 40 marks who give correct response for all the items.

JURY OPINION

The copies of achievement test were submitted to a group of five subject experts who are teachers in schools and colleges for their valuable suggestion. Based on their ideas, the structure of questions was modified, options of some questions were changed and the number of question was also increased. They were asked to examine whether the items fully covered the content of "Circulating System" presented for IX standard by Tamil Nadu Text-book society. Items which were choose or similar or deviant was dropped as recommended by experts. They items reflected the entire context. Thus the context validity of the test was established based on expert judgments. As a result the test tool for the final study was prepared with forty multiple choice questions.

Pilot Study

Pilot study is a vital factor is any research. The pilot study administered to 50 student of IX standard level.

Administration of Tool

The study was conducted and materials were distributed to the students after taking prior permission from the head master of the selected schools. The investigator personally visited each school and collected the data. The purpose and intention of the study were briefly explained. The subjects had been repeatedly assured that they could freely express their opinions without and reservation since the purpose was purely educational research. The co-operation extended by the respondents/students was encouraging remarkable.

Methods of Experimentation

Each sample was pre-tested with criteria referenced test to measure the entry level. Before the experiment or treatment the students were pre-tested using the test. The test was helpful in accessing subject knowledge of the students prior to treatment. The same test was administered again after treatment effects. The individual instruction analysis was carried by employing 't' test for difference between the CAI groups.

Data Collection

As presented pre test, post test was planned to achieve the objective of the study. The sample was selected for conducting the experiment. For conducting the experiment the investigator selected six Higher Secondary School, The investigator selected Higher Secondary School hence it would be easy to provide the treatment in the school to the sample.

Statistical Techniques Used in the Study

Appropriate statistical techniques were used which included the mean, standard deviation, t-test and ANOVA.

ANALYSIS AND INTERPRETATION OF THE DATA

Computation of Statistics

The first section deals with background information of the selected sample based on age, gender, type of school, educational status of parents, and socio-economic status of the family. In second section the scores of pre test and post test were calculated and the statistical techniques like mean, standard deviation, t-test and ANOVA were used for analyzing and interpreting.

Descriptive analysis for Background information of the selected sample

Differential Analysis

The collected data were consolidated, tabulated and analysed statistically by using the following tests.

1. Test of Significance ('t' Test and ANOVA)
2. Mean and Standard Deviation

(1) Test of significance: 't' Test and ANOVA

't' Test is used to find out the significant level of difference between two groups of population. The values are calculated with the help of the mean scores and standard deviation.

(2) Mean and Standard Deviation

Mean and standard deviation were done using the results of the study to make simple comparisons wherever necessary.

Analysis of 'T' Test Scores of Government Schools Pupil Following the Computer Assisted Instruction

Source	N	Mean	Standard Deviation	't' value
Pre test Score	50	14.300	3.2467	34.799 **
Post test Score	50	32.22	3.3030	

** Significant at 1% level.

There is no significant difference between the pretest and posttest scores of Government schools pupil following the Computer Assisted Instruction was rejected.

Analysis of 'T' Test Scores of Aided Schools Pupil Following the Computer Assisted Instruction

Source	N	Mean	Standard Deviation	't' value
Pre test Score	50	15.44	4.6342	22.206 **
Post test Score	50	29.76	4.3451	

** Significant at one percent level.

There is no significant difference between the pretest and posttest scores of Aided Schools Pupil following the Computer Assisted Instruction was rejected.

Analysis of 'T' Test Scores of Unaided Schools Pupil Following the Computer Assisted Instruction

Source	N	Mean	Standard Deviation	't' value
Pre test Score	50	13.16	3.6048	33.969 **
Post test Score	50	28.98	3.1975	

** Significant at 1% level.

There is no significant difference between the pretest and posttest scores of Unaided Schools Pupil following the Computer Assisted Instruction was rejected.

Significance of Difference between Pre and Post Tests Scores of Computer Assisted Instruction Group

Test	N	Mean	Standard Deviation	't' value
Pre test	150	14.30	3.9591	47.644 **
Post test	150	30.32	3.8831	

** Significant at 1% level.

There is no significant difference between the pretest and posttest mean scores of the experimental group following CAI was rejected.

Comparison of Posttest Performance of Computer Assisted Instruction Group between the Different Types of Schools

Type of the School	N	Mean	Standard Deviation	'F' value
Government School	50	32.22	3.3030	12.824 **
Aided School	50	29.76	4.6451	
Unaided School	50	30.32	3.1975	

** Significant at 1% level.

ANOVA test was applied and the calculated ANOVA value is 12.824, which is found to be significant at 0.01% level. There is no significant difference in posttest performance of Computer Assisted Instruction between the different types of schools pupil was rejected.

Comparison of the Post Test Performance of the Experimental Group Following the CAI with Reference to Locality

Area	N	Mean	Standard Deviation	't' value
Urban	75	32.00	3.2715	5.862 **
Rural	75	28.64	3.7331	

** Significant at 1% level.

There is no significance difference between posttest performance of Urban and Rural Schools Pupil following the Computer Assisted Instruction was rejected.

Comparison of the Posttest Performance of the Experimental Group following the CAI with Reference to Gender

Gender	N	Mean	Standard Deviation	't' value
Boys	75	29.6667	4.0415	2.084 **
Girls	75	30.9733	3.6279	

** Significant at 5% level.

There is no significance difference between the posttest performance of Boys and Girls following Computer Assisted Instruction was rejected.

Summary of the Study

The study is an attempt to find out, a comparative study of effectiveness of Computer Assisted Instruction and Handout Instruction on circulatory system for IX standard students.

A sample of 300 pupils studying in IX standard from six different schools in Udumalpet Taluk, Coimbatore District was selected. 150 formed of the 300 students experimental group following Computer Assisted Instruction. The experimental method was adopted in the study. Achievement test question paper was employed as a tool, at this time the treatment is administered on a small group of the target population. Pretest and post test are administered prior to starting and after the completion of the treatment respectively. The test scores were taken to assess the effectiveness of self learning through the Computer Assisted Instruction among students.

Findings of Study

1. The comparison of scores of pretest and post test of Government Schools Pupil following the Computer Assisted Instruction shows significant difference. The mean posttest scores is 32.22 for the Government Schools Pupil which is greater than pretest scores 14.30. This shows the Computer Assisted Instruction significantly influenced learning of pupil.

2. The mean posttest scores is 29.79 for the Aided Schools Pupil which is greater than pretest scores 15.44. This shows the CAI significantly influenced the learning of Aided Schools Pupil.

3. The mean posttest scores is 28.98 for unaided schools pupil which is higher than mean pretest scores 13.16. This shows the CAI significantly influenced the learning of unaided schools pupil.

4. The comparison of the scores of pretest and posttest of overall sample in target group following Computer Assisted instruction shows significant difference. This mean posttest scores is 30.32 for samples which is greater than the mean pretest scores 14.32. This shows CAI significantly influenced learning of all selected samples following CAI.

5. In this study it was found that same Government Schools has also showing better performance, while they received experimental treatment through CAI when compared to unaided schools and aided schools respectively in post test score.

6. The comparison of the posttest scores of urban and rural area in the CAI experimental group shows significant difference, the mean value of this CAI experimental group is 32.00 and 28.64 respectively.

7. Gender wise comparison in the CAI experimental group proved the significant. The calculated 't' value is 2.084. The mean scores of girls are 30.97, which is greater than the mean scores of boys 29.66 in the posttest performances.

Recommendation

Computer assisted instruction should be implemented in more number of the schools.

The Government should allot more funds to provide adequate number of computer materials for the schools.

It is recommended that Government may give concession for purchase of computer.

College students who are studying computer science may be asked to do projects in the development of necessary software for high school syllabus. This can solve the problem of non availability of software.

Special training shall be given to the teachers through in-service training programme to inculcate knowledge about different instructional strategies.

Educational institutions should have adequate instructional materials.

Training shall be given to the teachers to prepare and handle instrumental materials.

Instruction materials of learning provide scope for self instructional activities. Here the role of the teacher is limited and maximum activities are prescribed to the learners.

Teacher can improve their competence by attending in service training camps and also by writing research articles in the field of educational technology.

The students can learn effectively when they learn on their own. Self learning develops critical thinking in handling of study materials on one's own and enhances communication skills and self reliance.

The teachers must motivate the pupils to make more instructional package for self learning.

Suggestions for Further Research

A Research study would be incomplete if it doesn't provide necessary guidelines as well as potential research topics for further exploration. The following suggestions are made for further research in this area.

A similar study can be carried out in different types of school in different parts of Tamil Nadu.

In the present study researcher didn't take students from Tamil medium high schools students from such schools can be taken for further study.

Conclusion

The density of the country is destined in the classroom. Yes, it is true. The education has a wider meaning now-a-days. The education in the present trend does not mean the mere text book learning. It aims at giving complete life to the pupils. It is more important for the learners to know how to learn rather than what to learn.

From the results of the study, the investigator has ideas of Computer Assisted Instruction provided greater learning opportunities for children both theoretical and practical. Its use in bringing new kinds of experiences for children in school is really interesting and meaningful. The investigator therefore desires that the more number of educational institutions should come forward to make the learning best out of all available instruction materials for learning. So, this amount is just the beginning… not the end.

References

Aggarwal J.G (1995), Essential of Educational Technology; Teaching Leaning Innovations in Education New Delhi.

Bloom, Benjamin S (1956), Taxonomy of Educational Objective Hand books. The cognitive domain. Logmas Publication, New York.

Chauhan S.S (1983), Innovations in Teaching Learning Process, New Delhi.

Coulson S.E (1962), Programmed Learning and Computer based instruction.

David Hawkeridge (1990), New information in Technology and Education, Croomhelm.

David Layton (1992), Innovations in Science and Technology Education, Edition III, UNESCO.

Ellington, Henry (1985), producing teaching materials. A Hand book for Teachers and Trainers, London.

Forcier (2000) The Computer as a Productivity Tool in Education, Prentice Hall of India.Glass G.V (1970), Statistical method in Education and Psychology, Prentice Hall, Englewood Cliffs.

S.P.Gupta (1985), Statistic methods Sultan Chand & Sons Pub. New Delhi. Pp930.

Henry, Ellington, Percival, Fred and Race, Phil (2003), Hand book of Educational Technology, New Delhi. Hemalatha Parasnis, An Orientation to Computer Instruction Experiments in Education. July 1989.

John Best. W (1963), Research in Education Prentice Hall of India Private Limited, New Delhi.

Jaganath Mohanty, Modern Trends in Educational (2003).

Kothari C.R (1993), Research Methodology Methods and Techniques.

Krishnamoorthy. R (1995) Computer Programming, JJ Publishers, Madurai.

Kulkarni S.S (1986), Introduction to Educational Technology, New Delhi. Oxford, IBH Pub. Co.,

Mangal S.K (2000), Reversed Edition Foundation of Education Technology.

Murthy S.K (1995), Educational Technology Parkash Brothers, Jallandhar.

Narayana L.M, A text book of Chordates, Saras Publication, Nagercoil.

Palaniappan, V.P (1990), Effectiveness of Computer Assisted Instruction in Learning Triangles, Media and Technology for Human Resource Development.

Pillay, Subramania G (1995), Readings in Educational Technology, Nirmal Publication, Madurai.

Rajaraman, V (1985), Fundamentals of Computer, New Delhi, Prentice Hall of India Pvt. Ltd.,

Rao B, Anand and Ravishankar. S (1989), Reading in Educational Technology. Himalaya Publishing House, Bombay.

Romesh Verma, Suresh Sharma (1998), Modern Trends in Teaching Technology, Anmol Publications Pvt. Ltd., New Delhi.

Sadha and Singh (1982) Methodology of Educational Research, Prentice Hall of India.

Sampath and Pannerselvam (1994), Introduction to Educational Technology, Sterling Publishers, New Delhi.

Satyanarayana (1985), Research Methodology, Methods and Techniques, Atlantic Pub.

Vachan Sing (2005), Practical Approach Educational Technology, Akansha Publishing House, New Delhi.

S.Venkataian (2000), Encylopedio of Contemporary Education Series Science Education, Anmol Pub.

M.S.Yadav (2000), Modern method of teaching sciences, Anmol Publisher, Delhi.

S.M.Zaidi (2004), Modern method of teaching Science, Anmol Publisher, New Delhi.

Kiboss, et al Journal of Educational Multimedia Hypermedia, Vol. 15/4, Pp.397-410, October 2006.

G.Subramanian, Journal of Educational Research & Extension, Vol.43/1, Pp.43, Jan-March 2006.

Cepni et al Computers and Education, Vol. 46/2 Pp 192-205, Feb 2006.

Harskamp, International Journal of Science Education, Vol.27/4, P.451-469, March 2005.

Roger (2005), Journal of Educational Computing Research, V/33/2, Pp.189-217.

Jayakrishna Choudhury, School Science, June 2005, Pp 99.

Sharon et al (2005), Journal of Computers In Mathematics and Science Teaching,V/24,No.2, Pp.149-156.

Ndirangu et al, Journal of Science, Education and Technology, V/13, No.2, Pp.207-213, June 2004.

Chang. C.Y, Journal of Computer Assisted Learning, Vol.20/1, Pp. 4-10, Feb 2004.

Susan (2003), Education Technology Research and Development, Vol.51/2, Pp. 57-76.

B.H. Helen Joy and L.SS. Manickam (2002), Perspectives in Education, Vol. 18/4, Pp 235.

❑❑❑